Osho defies categorization, reflecting everything from the individual quest for meaning to the most urgent social and political issues facing society today. His books are not written but are transcribed from recordings of extemporaneous talks given over a period of thirty-five years. Osho has been described by the *Sunday Times* in London as one of the '1000 Makers of the 20th Century' and by *Sunday Mid-Day* in India as one of the ten people—along with Gandhi, Nehru and Buddha—who have changed the destiny of India.

Osho has a stated aim of helping to create the conditions for the birth of a new kind of human being, characterized as 'Zorba the Buddha'—one whose feet are firmly on the ground, yet whose hands can touch the stars. Running like a thread through all aspects of Osho is a vision that encompasses both the timeless wisdom of the East and the highest potential of Western science and technology.

He is synonymous with a revolutionary contribution to the science of inner transformation and an approach to meditation which specifically addresses the accelerated pace of contemporary life. The unique Osho Active Meditations™ are designed to allow the release of accumulated stress in the body and mind so that it is easier to be still and experience the thought-free state of meditation.

OTHER BOOKS BY OSHO IN PENGUIN

- *The Book of Man*
- *The Book of Woman*
- *Yoga: The Science of Living*
- *The Essence of Yoga*
- *Little Book of Relationships*
- *Little Book of Osho*
- *Osho: New Man for the New Millennium*
- *The Inner Journey: Spontaneous Talks Given by Osho to Disciples and Friends at a Meditation Camp in Ajol, Gujarat, in India*
- *Life's Mysteries: An Introduction to the Teaching of Osho*

OSHO

Yoga: The Path to Liberation

PENGUIN BOOKS

PENGUIN BOOKS

Published by the Penguin Group

Penguin Books India Pvt Ltd, 11 Community Centre, Panchsheel Park, New Delhi 110 017, India

Penguin Group (USA) Inc., 375 Hudson Street, New York, New York 10014, USA

Penguin Group (Canada), 90 Eglinton Avenue East, Suite 700, Toronto, Ontario, M4P 2Y3, Canada (a division of Pearson Penguin Canada Inc.)

Penguin Books Ltd, 80 Strand, London WC2R 0RL, England

Penguin Ireland, 25 St Stephen's Green, Dublin 2, Ireland (a division of Penguin Books Ltd)

Penguin Group (Australia), 250 Camberwell Road, Camberwell, Victoria 3124, Australia (a division of Pearson Australia Group Pty Ltd)

Penguin Group (NZ), cnr Airborne and Rosedale Roads, Albany, Auckland 1310, New Zealand (a division of Pearson New Zealand Ltd)

Penguin Group (South Africa) (Pty) Ltd, 24 Sturdee Avenue, Rosebank, Johannesburg 2196, South Africa

Penguin Books Ltd, Registered Offices: 80 Strand, London WC2R 0RL, England

Published by Penguin Books India 2005

Originally published as *Yoga: The Alpha and the Omega Vol. 9*

First publication Copyright © 1978 Osho International Foundation
Copyright © all revisions 1953–2005 Osho International Foundation
OSHO is a registered trademark of Osho International Foundation, used under licence

ISBN-13: 978-1-44000-288-5 ISBN-10: 0-14400-028-8

Typeset in Sabon by Mantra Virtual Services, New Delhi
Printed at Pauls Press, New Delhi

Contents

Contents

Preface

Every few thousand years an individual appears who irrevocably changes the world around them in ways that are never immediately apparent, except to the most perceptive.

Osho is one such individual: his spoken words will resonate for centuries to come.

All those words have been recorded and transcribed into books like this one, written words that can carry a transforming message to the reader.

For Osho, all change is individual. There is no 'society' to change—it can only happen to each one of us, one at a time.

So, no matter what the subject matter of the book, the thread that runs through all Osho's words is like a love song that we can suddenly, mysteriously, hear at just the right moment. And strangely, no matter what the words seem to be referring to, they are really only referring to us.

And this is no ordinary love song, but more of an invitation to open our hearts to hear something beyond the words, beyond the heart . . . a silence beyond all understanding . . . where we all belong.

*

1

Mastery over the Five Elements

*The power of contacting the state of
consciousness which is outside the mental body
and therefore inconceivable
is called* mahavideha.
*Through this power
the covering of the light is destroyed.*

Performing samyama *on their gross, constant,
subtle, all-pervading, and functional state
brings mastery over the* panchabhutas—*the five
elements.*

From this follows the attainment of anima,
*perfection of the body, and
the removal of the elements' power to obstruct
the body.*

*Beauty, grace, strength, and adamantine
hardness constitute the perfect body.*

THE YOGA SYSTEM of Patanjali is not a philosophical system. It
is empirical; it is a tool to work with—but still it has a
philosophy. It is just to give an intellectual understanding of

where you are moving, what you are seeking. The philosophy is arbitrary, utilitarian, just to give a comprehensive picture of the territory you are going to discover—but the philosophy has to be understood.

The first thing about the philosophy of Patanjali: he divides human personality into five seeds, five bodies. He says you don't have one body, you have several layers of bodies, and there are five layers.

The first body he calls *annamay kosh*—the food body, the earth body, which is made of earth and is constantly to be nourished by food. Food comes from earth. If you stop taking food, your *annamay kosh* will wither away. So one has to be very alert to what one is eating because that makes you and it will affect you in millions of ways. Sooner or later your food is not just food—it becomes your blood, your bones, your very marrow. It circulates in your being and goes on affecting you. So the purity of food creates a pure *annamay kosh*—the pure food body.

And if the first body is pure and light, not heavy, then it is easy to enter into the second body; otherwise it will be difficult, you will be loaded. Have you noticed when you have eaten too much, and heavy foods? Immediately you start feeling a sort of sleep, a sort of lethargy. You would like to go to sleep; awareness immediately starts disappearing. When the first body is loaded it is difficult to create great awareness. Hence fasting became so important in all the religions. But fasting is a science and one should not fool around with it.

Just the other night one sanyasin came and she told me that she has been fasting and now her whole body, her whole being, is disturbed—tremendously disturbed. The stomach is not functioning well, and when the stomach is not functioning well, everything is weakened, the vitality is lost, and you cannot be alive. You become more and more insensitive and dead.

But fasting is important. It should be done very carefully, and only when one has understood the functioning of the *annamay kosh*. And it should be done under proper guidance, of one who has moved through all the phases of his *annamay kosh*. Not only that, one who has gone beyond it and who can look at the *annamay kosh* as a witness. Otherwise fasting can be dangerous . . . then, just the right amount of food and the right quality of food has to be practised; fasting is not needed.

But this is important because this is your first body and, more or less, people cling to their first body; they never move to the second. Millions of people are not even aware that they have a second body, a deeper body, hidden behind the first sheath. The first covering is very gross.

The second body Patanjali calls *pranamay kosh*—energy body, electric body. It consists of electric fields. That is what acupuncture is all about. This second body is more subtle than the first, and people who start moving from the first body to the second become fields of energy, tremendously attractive, magnetic, hypnotic. If you go near them, you will feel vitalized, charged.

If you go near a man who lives only in his food body, you will be depleted—he will suck you. Many times you come across people and you feel that they suck you. After they have left, you feel depleted, dissipated, as if somebody has exploited your energy. The first body is a sucker, and the first body is very gross. So if you live too much with first body-oriented people, you will always feel burdened, tense, bored, sleepy, with no energy, always at the point of the lowest rung of your energy; you will not have any amount of energy which can be used for higher growth.

The *annamay kosh*-oriented person lives for food. He eats and eats and eats, and that is his whole life. He remains, in a way, childish. The first thing that the child does in the world is to suck air, and then to suck milk. The first thing the child has to do in the world is to help the food body, and if a person remains addicted to food, he remains childish; his growth suffers.

The second body, *pranamay kosh*, gives you a new freedom, gives you more space. The second body is bigger than the first; it is not confined to your physical body. It is inside the physical body and it is also outside the physical body; it surrounds you like a subtle climate, an aura of energy. In Russia they have now discovered that photographs can be taken of this energy body. They call it 'bioplasma', but it exactly means *prana*—the energy, élan vital, or what Taoists call *chi*. It can be photographed now; it has become almost scientific.

Another great discovery that has been made in Russia is that when you suffer some illness, the energy body feels it six months before it happens to the physical body. If you are going to have tuberculosis, or cancer, or any illness, your energy body starts showing indications of it six months before it actually happens. No examination, no testing of the physical body shows anything, but the electric body starts showing it. First it appears in the *pranamay kosh*, and then it enters into the *annamay kosh*.

So now they say that it has become possible to treat a person before he has fallen ill. Once it becomes so, then there is no need for humanity to fall ill. Before you become ill, your photographs by Kirlian methods will show that some illness is going to happen to your physical body—and it can be prevented in the *pranamay kosh*.

That is why yoga insists on the purity of breathing. The

pranamay kosh is made of a subtle energy that travels inside you through breathing. If you breathe rightly, your *pranamay kosh* remains healthy and whole and alive. Such a person never feels tired; such a person is always available to do anything. Such a person is always responsive, always ready to respond to the moment, ready to take the challenge. He is always ready. You will never find him unprepared for any moment. Not that he plans for the future, no—but he has so much energy that whatsoever happens he is ready to respond. He has overflowing energy. T'ai-chi works on *pranamay kosh*. *Pranayam* works on *pranamay kosh*.

If you know how to breathe naturally, you will grow into your second body—and the second body is stronger than the first, it lives longer than the first.

When somebody dies, for almost three days you can see his bioplasma. Sometimes that is mistaken for his ghost. The physical body dies, but the energy body continues to move. Those who have experimented deeply about death say that for three days it is very difficult for the person who has died to believe that he has died, because the same form— and more vital, healthy and beautiful than ever—surrounds him. Depending on how big a bioplasma you have, it can continue for thirteen days or even more.

In India we burn everyone's body except the body of one who has attained *samadhi*—we don't burn his body, for a certain reason. Once you burn the body, the bioplasma starts moving away from the earth. You can feel it for a few days, but then it disappears into the cosmos. But if the physical body is left, then the bioplasma can cling to it. And a man who has attained *samadhi*, who has become enlightened, if his bioplasma can remain somewhere around his *samadhi*, many people will be benefited by it. That is how many people come to see their gurus' forms.

In Aurobindo ashram, Aurobindo's body is put in a *samadhi*, not destroyed or burned. Many people have felt as if they have seen Aurobindo around it. Or sometimes they have heard the same footsteps, the way Aurobindo used to walk, and sometimes he is there just standing before them. This is not Aurobindo. This is the bioplasma. Aurobindo is gone, but the bioplasma, the *pranamay kosh*, can persist for centuries. If the person has been really in tune with his *pranamay kosh*, it can persist. It can have its own existence.

Natural breathing has to be understood. Observe small children—they breathe naturally. That is why small children are so full of energy; their parents are tired, but they are not tired.

Three children were talking amongst themselves.

The first child said, 'I am so full of energy that I wear out my shoes within seven days.'

Another said, 'That is nothing. I am so full of energy I wear out my clothes within three days.'

The third said, 'That too is nothing. I am so full of energy I wear out my parents within one hour.'

In the US they have done an experiment where a very powerful man, with an athletic body and tremendous energy, was told to follow a small child and imitate him. Whatsoever the child was going to do, this athlete was to do, for eight hours. The child enjoyed this very much and started doing many things. Within four hours the athlete was flat on the floor, unable to keep up with the child's jumping, jogging, shouting, and yelling. The child was perfectly full of energy after four hours; the athlete was completely tired. The athlete said, 'He will kill me. Eight hours! Finished! I cannot do anything more.' He was a great boxer, but boxing is a different thing. You cannot compete with a child.

From where does the energy come? It comes from *pranamay kosh*. A child breathes naturally, and of course breathes more *prana* in, more *chi* in, and accumulates it in his belly. The belly is the accumulating place, the reservoir. Observe a child; that is the right way to breathe. When a child breathes, his chest is completely unaffected. His belly goes up and down. He breathes as if from the belly. All children have a little belly; that belly is there because of their breathing and the reservoir of energy.

That is the right way to breathe; remember not to use your chest too much. Sometimes it can be used; in emergency situations, say, you are running to save your life, then the chest can be used. It is an emergency device; then you can use shallow, fast breathing, and run. But ordinarily the chest should not be used. And one thing to be remembered: the chest is meant only for emergency situations because it is difficult in an emergency situation to breathe naturally. If you breathe naturally, you remain so calm and quiet that you cannot run, you cannot fight; you are so calm and collected that you are Buddha-like. But in an emergency, say, the house is on fire, if you breathe naturally you will not be able to save anything. Or if a tiger jumps upon you in a forest and you go on breathing naturally you will not be bothered. You will say, 'Okay, let him do whatsoever he wants.' You will not be able to protect yourself.

So nature has given an emergency device—the chest. When a tiger attacks you, you have to drop natural breathing and you have to breathe from the chest. Then you will have more capacity to run, to fight, to burn energy fast. And in an emergency situation there are only two alternatives—flight or fight. Both need a very shallow but intense energy, a very disturbed, tense state.

Now if you continuously breathe from the chest, you will have tensions in your mind. If you continuously breathe from the chest, you will always be afraid because chest-breathing is meant only for fearful situations. And if you have made it a habit then you will be continuously afraid, tense, always in flight. The enemy is not there, but you will imagine the enemy is there; that is how paranoia is created.

In the West also a few people have come across this phenomenon, such as Alexander Lowen and other people who have been working on bio-energy. That is *prana*. They have come to feel that people who are afraid, their chest is tense and they are taking very shallow breaths. If their breathing can be made deeper, to go and touch the belly, the *hara* centre, then their fear disappears. Their musculature can be relaxed, as it is done in Rolfing. Ida Rolf has invented one of the most beautiful methods to change the inner structure of the body because if you have been breathing wrongly for many years, you have developed a musculature, and that musculature will be in the way and will not allow you to rightly breathe or deeply breathe. And even if you remember for a few seconds and breathe deeply, again when you are engaged in your work you will go back to shallow chest-breathing. The musculature has to be changed. Once the musculature is changed, the fear and the tension disappear. Rolfing is tremendously helpful in working on *pranamay kosh*, the second bioplasmic body, bio-energy body, *chi* body, or whatsoever you want to call it.

Watch a child—*that* is natural breathing—and breathe that way. Let your belly come up when you inhale, let your belly go down when you exhale. And let it be in such a rhythm it becomes almost a song in your energy, a dance—with rhythm, with harmony—and you will feel so relaxed, so alive, so vital that you cannot imagine that such vitality is possible.

Then is the third body, *manomay kosh*—the mental body. The third is bigger, subtler, and higher than the second. Animals have the second body but not the third body. Animals are so vital. See a lion walking—what beauty, what grace, what grandeur! See a deer running—what weightlessness, what energy, what a great energy phenomenon! Man has always felt jealous, but man's energy is moving higher.

The third body is more spacious than the second. And if you don't grow it, you will remain almost just a possibility of man but not a real man. The word 'man' comes from *man, manomay*. The English word also comes from the Sanskrit root *man*. The Hindi word for man is *manushya*; that too comes from the same root *man*, the mind. It is the mind that makes you man, but more or less you don't have it; what you have in its place is just a conditioned mechanism. You live by imitation—then you don't have a mind. When you start living on your own, when you start answering your life's problems on your own, when you become responsible, you start growing in *manomay kosh*. Then the mind-body grows.

Ordinarily, if you are a Hindu or a Mohammedan or a Christian you have a borrowed mind; it is not your mind. Maybe Christ attained a great explosion of *manomay kosh,* but since then people have been simply repeating it. That repetition will not become a growth in you. That repetition will be a hindrance. Don't repeat; rather, try to understand. Become more and more alive, authentic, responsive. Even if there is a possibility to go astray, go astray—because there is no way to grow if you are so afraid of committing errors. Errors are good; mistakes have to be committed. Never commit the same mistake again, but never be afraid of committing mistakes. People who become afraid of committing mistakes never grow. They go on sitting in their place, afraid to move. They are not alive.

The mind grows when you encounter situations on your own. You bring your own energy to solve them. Don't go asking for advice forever. Take the reins of your life in your own hands; that is what I mean when I say do your thing. You will be in trouble—it is safer to follow others, it is convenient to follow the society, the routine, the tradition, the scripture. It is very easy because everybody is following—you have just to become a dead part of the herd, you have just to move with the crowd wherever it is going; it is none of your responsibility. But your mental body, your *manomay kosh*, will suffer tremendously, terribly; it will not grow. You will not have your own mind, and you will miss something very, very beautiful and something which functions as a bridge for higher growth.

So always remember, whatsoever I say to you, you can take it in two ways. You can simply take it on my authority: 'Osho says so, it must be true'—then you will suffer; you will not grow. Whatsoever I say, listen to it, try to understand it, implement it in your life, see how it works, and then come to your own conclusions. They may be the same, they may not be. They can never be exactly the same because you have a different personality, a unique being. Whatsoever I am saying is my own. It is bound to be in deep ways rooted in me. You may come to similar conclusions, but they cannot be exactly the same. So my conclusions should not be made your conclusions. You should try to understand me, you should try to learn, but you should not collect knowledge from me, you should not collect conclusions from me. Then your mind-body will grow.

But people take shortcuts. They say, 'If you have known,

then that is fine. What is the need for us to try and experiment? We will believe in you.' A believer has no *manomay kosh*. He has a false *manomay kosh* which has not come out of his own being but has been forced from without.

Then higher and bigger than *manomay kosh* is *vigyanamay kosh*—it is the intuitive body. It is very, very spacious. There is no reason in it; it goes beyond reason and has become very, very subtle. It is an intuitive grasp. It is a *seeing* directly into the nature of things. It is not trying to think about it.

That cypress tree in the courtyard: you just look at it. You don't think about it; there is no 'about' in intuition. You simply become available, receptive, and reality reveals to you its nature. You don't project. You are not searching for any argument, for any conclusion, nothing whatsoever. You are simply waiting, and reality reveals. The intuitive body takes you to very far out horizons.

But there is still one more body—the fifth body, *anandmay kosh,* the bliss body. It is really far out! It is made of pure bliss. Even intuition is transcended.

These five seeds are just seeds, remember. Beyond these five is *your* reality. These are just seeds surrounding you: the first is very gross—you are almost confined in a six-foot body—the second is bigger than it, the third still bigger, the fourth even bigger, the fifth is very big; but still these are seeds. All are limited. If all the seeds are dropped and you stand nude in your reality, then you are infinite. That is what yoga says: *aham brahmasmi*—'I am godly'. You are the very Brahman. Now you are ultimate reality itself; now all barriers are dropped.

Try to understand this. The barriers are there surrounding you in circles. The first barrier is very, very hard. To get out of it is very difficult. People remain confined to their physical bodies and they think their physical life is all that there is to life.

Don't settle: the physical body is just a step to the energy body. The energy body is again just a step for the mind body, which again, is just a step for the intuitive body. That too is a step for the bliss body. And from the bliss body you take the jump—now there are no more steps—you take the jump into the abyss of your being that is infinity, eternity.

These are five seeds. Corresponding to these five seeds, yoga has another doctrine about five *mahabhutas*, five great elements. Your body is made of food, earth; the earth is the first element. It has nothing to do with this earth, remember. The element simply says wherever there is matter it is earth; the material is the earth, the gross is the earth. In you it is the body; outside you it is the body of all. The stars are made of earth. Everything that exists is made of earth. The first shell is of earth. Five *mahabhutas* means five great elements: earth, fire, water, air, ether.

Earth corresponds to your first body, *annamay kosh*, the food body. Fire corresponds to your second body, energy body, bioplasma, *chi*, *pranamay kosh*; it has the quality of fire. Third is water. It corresponds to the third body, *manomay kosh*, the mental body; it has the quality of water. Observe the mind, how it goes on like a flux, always moving, river-like. The fourth is air, almost invisible; you cannot see it but it is there. You can only feel it. That corresponds to the intuitive body, *vigyanamay kosh*. And then there *is akash*, ether; you cannot even feel it. It has become even more subtle than air. You can simply believe it, trust it that it is there. It is pure space; that is bliss.

But you are purer than pure space, subtler than pure space. Your reality is almost as if it is not. That is why

Buddha says '*anatta*'—no-self. Your self is like a no-self; your being is almost like a non-being. Why non-being? Because it has gone so far away from all gross elements. It is pure is-ness. Nothing can be said about it, no description will be adequate for it.

These are five *mahabhutas*, five great elements, corresponding to five *koshs*, bodies, within you.

Then the third doctrine—I would like you to understand all these because they will be helpful in understanding the sutras that we will be discussing now. There are seven chakras. The word *chakra* does not really mean centre; the word *centre* cannot explain it or describe it or translate it rightly because when we say 'the centre', it seems something static. And chakra means something dynamic. The word *chakra* means 'the wheel', the moving wheel. So chakra is a dynamic centre in your being, almost like a whirlpool, a whirlwind, the centre of the cyclone. It is dynamic; it creates an energy field around it.

Seven chakras . . . the first is a bridge and the last is also a bridge. Sex is a bridge, a bridge between you and the grossest—the *prakriti*, nature. *Sahasrar*, the seventh chakra is also a bridge, a bridge between you and the abyss—the ultimate. These two are bridges. The remaining five centres correspond to five elements and five bodies.

This is the framework of Patanjali's system. Remember it is arbitrary. It has to be used as a tool, not discussed as a dogma. It is not a doctrine in any theology. It is just a utilitarian map. You go to some territory, to some strange country, unknown, and you take a map with you. The map does not really represent the territory; how can the map represent the territory? The map is so small, the territory is so big. On the map cities are just points. How can those points correspond to big cities? On the map roads are just lines. How can roads be just lines? Mountains are just marked, rivers are just marked—and small ones are left out, only big ones are marked. This is a map; it is not a doctrine.

There are not only five bodies; there are many bodies because between two bodies there is another to join it, and so on and so forth. You are like an onion, layers upon layers, but these five will do. These are the main bodies, the chief ones. So don't be too worried about it. Buddhists say there are seven bodies, and Jains say there are nine bodies. Nothing wrong and there is no contradiction because these are just maps. If you are studying the whole world's map, then even big cities disappear, even big rivers disappear. If you are studying a map of a nation, then many new things appear which were not on the world map. And if you are studying the map of a province, then many more things appear. Similarly, if you are studying the map of a district, or of one city, or even of one house, then of course things go on appearing.

Jains say nine. Buddha says seven. Patanjali says five. There are schools which say only three. And they all are true because they are not discussing any argument; they are just giving you a few tools to work with.

And I think five is almost perfect because more than five is too much, less than five is too few. Patanjali is a very balanced thinker.

Now a few things about these chakras: The first chakra, the first dynamic centre, is sex—*muladhar*. It joins you with nature, it joins you with the past, it joins you with the future. You were born out of two persons' sexual play. Your parents' sexual play became the cause of your birth. You are related to your parents through the sex centre and to your parents' parents and so on. To the whole past you are related through the sex centre. The thread runs through the sex centre and if you give birth to some child, you will be related to the future.

Jesus insisted many times, 'If you don't hate your mother and your father, you cannot come and follow me.' It is almost unbelievable that a man like Jesus would use such hard words—he is compassion incarnate, he is love. Why did he say 'hate your mother and your father if you want to follow me'? The meaning is: drop out of the sexual context. What he said symbolically is go beyond the sex centre, then immediately you are no more related with the past, no more related with the future.

It is sex that makes you part of time. Once you go beyond sex, you become part of eternity, not of time. Then suddenly only the present exists. You are the present but if you see yourself through the sex centre, you are the past also because your eyes will have the colour of your mother and your father, and your body will have atoms and cells from millions of generations. Your whole structure, biostructure, is part of a long continuum. You are part of a big chain.

In India they say your debt to your parents cannot be fulfilled unless you give birth to children. If you want that your debt should be fulfilled with the past, you have to create future. If you really want to repay, there is no other way. Your mother loved you, your father loved you—what can you do now they are gone? You can become a mother, a father of children and repay it to nature—to the same reservoir from where your parents came, you came, and your children will come.

Sex is the great chain. It is the whole chain of the world, *samsar*, and it is the link with others. Have you noticed it? The moment you feel sexual you start thinking of the other; when you are not feeling sexual you never think of the other. A person who is beyond sex is beyond others. He may live

in the society, but he is not in the society. He may be walking
in the crowd, but he walks alone. And a man who is sexual,
he may be sitting on the top of Everest, alone, but he will
think of the other. He may be sent to the moon to meditate,
but he will meditate about the other.

Sex is the bridge with the others. Once sex disappears,
the chain is broken. For the first time, you become an
individual. That is why people may be too much obsessed
with sex, but they are never happy with it because it is double-
edged. It links you with others; it does not allow you to be
individual. It does not allow you to be yourself. It forces
you into patterns, into slaveries, bondages. But if you don't
know how to transcend it, that is the only way to use your
energy—it becomes a safety valve.

People who live at the first centre, *muladhar*, live only
for a very foolish reason. They go on creating energy and
then they are too much burdened with it. Then they go on
throwing it—they eat, they work, they sleep, they do many
things to create energy. Then they say, 'What to do with it?
It is very heavy.' Then they throw it. Seems a very vicious
circle! When they throw it they again feel empty. They fill
themselves with new fuel, with new food, with new work,
and again when the energy is there they say they are 'feeling
too full'. Somewhere it has to be released. And sex becomes
just a release: a vicious circle of accumulating and throwing
energy. It is absurd.

Unless you know that there are higher centres within
you which can take that energy and use it in a creative way,
you will remain confined to the sexual vicious circle. That
is why all the religions insist on some sort of sexual control.
It can become repressive, it can become dangerous. If new
centres are not opening and you go on damming energy,
condemning, forcing, repressing, then you are on a volcano.

Any day you will explode; you will become neurotic. You are going to be mad. Then it is better to relieve it. But there are centres which can absorb the energy and greater being and greater possibilities can be revealed to you.

Remember, we have been saying that the second centre, near the sex centre, is the *hara*, the centre of death. That is why people are afraid to move beyond sex because the moment the energy moves beyond sex it touches the *hara* centre and one becomes afraid. That is why people are even afraid to move deep in love because when you move deep in love the sex centre creates such ripples that the ripples enter into the *hara* centre and fear arises.

So many people come to me and they say, 'Why do we feel so afraid of the other sex?'—men or women—'Why do we feel so afraid?' It is not the fear of the other sex; it is the fear of sex itself. Because if you go deep in sex then the centre becomes more dynamic, creates bigger energy fields and those energy fields start overlapping with the *hara* centre. Have you observed that in a sexual orgasm something starts moving just below your navel, throbbing? That throb is the overlapping of the sex centre with the *hara*. That is why people become afraid of sex. Particularly, people become afraid of deep intimacy, of orgasm itself.

But that second centre has to be entered, penetrated, opened. That is what Jesus means when he says that unless you are ready to die you cannot be reborn.

Just two or three days earlier, at Easter, somebody had asked a question: 'Today is Easter. Osho, have you something to say?' I have only one thing to say, that each day is Easter, because Easter is the day of Jesus' resurrection—his crucifixion and resurrection, his death and his being reborn. Each day is Easter if you are ready to move into the *hara* centre. You will be crucified first—the cross is there within your *hara* centre. You are already carrying it; you just have to move to it and you have to die through it, and then there is resurrection.

Once you die in the *hara* centre, death disappears; for the first time you become aware of a new world, a new dimension. Then you can see the centre higher than the *hara*; that is the navel centre. And the navel centre becomes the resurrection, because the navel centre is the most energy-conserving centre. It is the very reservoir of energy.

And once you know that you have moved from the sex centre to the *hara*, now you know that there is a possibility of moving inwards. You have opened one door. Now you cannot rest unless you have opened all the doors. Now you cannot remain on the porch; you have entered the palace. Then you can open another door and yet another door . . .

Just in the middle is the centre of the heart. The heart centre divides the lower and the higher. First, the sex centre, then the *hara*, then the navel, and then comes the heart centre. Three centres are below it, three centres are above it: The heart is exactly in the middle.

You must have seen Solomon's seal. In Judaism, particularly in Cabalistic thinking, Solomon's seal is one of the most important symbols. Solomon's seal is the symbol of the heart centre. Sex moves downwards, so sex is like a triangle pointed downwards. *Sahasrar* moves upwards, so *sahasrar* is a triangle pointed upwards. And the heart is just in the middle, where the sex triangle comes to meet the *sahasrar* triangle. Both triangles meet, merge into each other, and it becomes a six-pointed star, that is the seal of Solomon. The heart is the seal of Solomon.

Once you have opened the heart, then you are available for the highest possibilities. Below the heart you remain man; beyond the heart you have become superman.

After the heart centre there is the throat centre, then there is the third-eye centre, and then *sahasrar*.

The heart is feeling love. The heart is absorbing love, becoming love. The throat is expression, communication, sharing, giving love to others. And if you give love to others, then the third-eye centre starts functioning. Once you start giving, you go higher and higher. A person who goes on taking goes lower and lower and lower, whereas a person who goes on giving goes higher and higher and higher. A miser is the worst possibility a man can fall into, and a sharer is the greatest possibility to which a man can become available.

Five bodies, five *mahabhutas*, and five centres, plus two bridges; this is the framework, the map. Behind this framework is the whole effort of the Yogin, of bringing *samyama* to every nook and corner, so one becomes enlightened, full of light.

Now, the sutras:

> *The power of contacting the state of consciousness*
> *which is outside the mental body,* manomay sharir,
> *and therefore inconceivable*
> *is called* mahavideha.
> *Through this power*
> *the covering of the light is destroyed.*

Once you are beyond the mind-body, for the first time you become aware that you are not the mind but the witness. Below the mind you remain identified with it. Once you know that thoughts, mental images, and ideas are just objects, floating clouds in your consciousness, you are separate from them immediately.

The power of contacting the state of consciousness which is outside the mental body and therefore inconceivable is called mahavideha. You become beyond body. *Mahavideha* means one who is beyond body, one who is no longer confined to any body, one who knows that he is not the body, gross or subtle, one who knows that he is infinite, with no boundaries. *Mahavideha* means one who has come to feel that he has no boundaries. And all boundaries are confinements, imprisonments; and he can break them, drop them, and can become one with the infinite sky.

This moment of realizing oneself as the infinite is the moment . . . *Through this power the covering of the light is destroyed.* Then the covering that has been hiding your light is dropped. You are like a light which is being hidden under covers and covers, and by and by each and every cover has to be taken away; then more light will shine through.

Once *manomay kosh*, the mental body, is dropped, you become meditation; you become a no-mind. All our effort here is how to go beyond the *manomay kosh*—how to become aware that I am not the thinking process.

Performing samyama *on their gross, constant, subtle, all-pervading, and functional state* brings mastery over the panchabhutas—*the five elements.*

This is one of the most potential sutras of Patanjali, and very significant for future science. One day or the other, science is going to discover the meaning of this sutra.

Science is already on the path towards it. This sutra says that all the elements in the world, the *panchabhutas*—earth, water, fire, air, ether—they come out of nothing, and they go again into nothingness to rest. Everything comes out of nothing and when tired goes back and rests into nothingness.

Now science, particularly physics, agrees with it: that matter has come out of nothing. The deeper they have studied matter, the more they have discovered that there is nothing material. The deeper they go, matter becomes more and more elusive and finally it slips out of their fingers. Nothing remains, just emptiness, just pure space. Out of pure space everything is born. Looks very illogical . . . but life is illogical. The whole of modern science has become illogical because if you persist on your logic you cannot move into reality. If you move into reality you have to drop the logic. And of course when there is a choice between logic and reality, how can you choose the logic? You have to drop the logic.

Just fifty years ago scientists came to realize that quanta, electric particles, behave in a very ridiculous way, behave like a Zen master—unbelievable, absurd—and sometimes they look like waves and sometimes they look like particles. Now before that it was a tacit understanding that something can be *either* a particle or a wave. One and the same thing cannot be both together, simultaneously. A particle and a wave? It means something can be a point and a line together, at the same time. Impossible! Euclid will not agree! Aristotle will simply state that you have gone mad. A point is a point, and a line is many points in a row, so how can one point be a line but at the same time remain a point? Looks absurd . . . and Euclid and Aristotle prevailed.

Just fifty years earlier, their whole edifice collapsed because scientists came to know that the quantum, the electric particle, behaves in both ways simultaneously.

Logicians raised arguments, and they said, 'This is not possible.' Physicists said, 'What can we do? It is not a question of possibility or impossibility. It is so! We cannot do anything. If the quantum is not going to follow Aristotle, what can we do? And if the quantum behaves in a non-Euclidean way and does not follow the geometry of Euclid, what can we do? It is behaving that way and we have to listen to the behaviour of the real and the reality.'

This is one of the very critical moments in the history of human consciousness. Until then it had always been believed that something can come only out of something. It is simple and natural, obviously so. How can something come out of nothing? Then matter disappeared, and the scientists have to conclude that everything is born out of nothing, and everything again disappears into nothing. Now they are talking about black holes. Black holes are holes of tremendous nothingness. I have to call it 'tremendous nothingness' because that nothingness is not just absence. It is full of energy, but the energy is of nothingness. There is nothing to find, but there is energy.

Now they say black holes are in existence. They are parallel to stars—stars are positive, and parallel to each star there is a black hole. The star is; the black hole is not. And each star when burned, exhausted, becomes a black hole. And each black hole, when rested, becomes a star.

Matter and no-matter go on changing. Matter becomes no-matter; no-matter becomes matter. Life becomes death; death becomes life. Love becomes hate; hate becomes love. Polarities continuously change.

This sutra says *performing* samyama *on their gross, constant, subtle, all-pervading, and functional state brings mastery over the* panchabhutas—*the five elements*. Patanjali is saying that if you have come to understand your true nature of witnessing, and then if you concentrate—you bring *samyama* on any matter—you can make it appear or disappear. You can help things to materialize because they come out of nothingness. And you can help things to dematerialize.

For physicists, it remains to be seen whether that is possible or not. It is accepted that matter changes and becomes no-matter, and no-matter changes and becomes matter. They have come to feel many absurd things these past fifty years. It is one of the most potential ages ever, where so many things have exploded that it has become almost impossible to confine them in a system. How does one make a system? It was very easy just fifty years earlier to create a self-contained system—it is now impossible. The reality has poked its nose from everywhere and destroyed all doctrinaires, systems, dogmas. The reality has proved to be too much.

Scientists say it is happening. Patanjali says it can be made to happen. If it is happening, then why can it not be made to happen? Just observe—you heat water; at 100°C it becomes vapour. It has always been happening, even before fire was discovered. The sunrays were evaporating water from the seas and rivers, clouds were forming and water was coming back again into the rivers, again evaporating. Then man discovered fire, and then he started heating water, evaporating it.

Whatsoever is happening, ways and means can be found to make it happen. If it is already happening then it is not against reality, then you have just to know how to make it happen. If matter becomes no-matter, and no-matter becomes matter, if things change polarities, things disappear into nothingness and things appear out of nothingness—if this is already happening—then Patanjali says ways and means can be found through which it can be made to happen. And this, he says, is the way: if you have come to recognize your being beyond the five seeds, you become capable of materializing things or dematerializing things.

It still remains for the scientific workers to find out whether it is possible or not, but it seems plausible. There seems to be no logical problem in it.

> *From this follows the attainment of* anima,
> *Perfection of the body, and*
> *the removal of the elements' power to obstruct*
> *the body.*

And then come the eight *siddhis*, the eight powers of yogis. The first is *anima*, and then there is *laghima*, *garima*, etc. The eight powers of the yogi are that they can make their body disappear, or they can make their body so small that it becomes almost invisible, or they can make their bodies as big as they want. It is under their control to make the body small, big, or disappear completely, or to appear in many places simultaneously.

Seems impossible, but things that seem impossible by and by become possible. It was impossible for man to fly . . . the Wright brothers were thought to be mad, insane. When they invented their first airplane, they were afraid to tell people for fear that they will be caught and hospitalized. The first flight was done completely unknown to anybody; it was just the two brothers. And they invented their first airplane hiding in a basement, so that nobody came to know of what they were doing. Everybody had believed that they had gone completely mad—who had ever flown? Their first air flight was of sixty seconds—only a minute—but it changed the whole of history tremendously, the whole of humanity. It became possible. Nobody had ever thought that the atom could be split. It was split, and now man can never be the same again.

Many things have happened which were always thought to be impossible. We have reached the moon; it was the symbol of impossibility. In all the languages of the world there are expressions like 'Don't long for the moon'. That means don't long for the impossible. Now we have to change those expressions. And now that we have reached the moon, nothing debars the path. Now everything has become available; it is only a question of time.

Einstein has said that if we can invent a vehicle which moves at the speed of light, then a person can go on travelling and he will never age. If, at the age of thirty, a man leaves on a spaceship that moves at the speed of light, and returns after thirty years, he would still be thirty when he returns. His friends and brothers will be thirty years older; a few of them will already be dead, but that man will remain thirty years old . . . Einstein says time and its effect disappear when one is moving at the speed of light. A man can go on a great space journey and can come back after five hundred years. All the people he knew would be gone, nobody would recognize him and he would not recognize anybody, but he would remain the same age as he was when he started out. You are aging because of the speed of the earth. If the earth's speed were to be equal to the speed of light, then you would not age at all.

Patanjali says that if you have moved beyond all the five bodies, you have gone beyond all five elements. Now you are in a state from where you can control anything you wish. Just by the idea that you want to become small, you will become small; if you want to become big, you will become big; if you want to disappear, you can disappear.

It is not necessary that yogis should do it. Buddhas have never been known to do it. Patanjali himself has not been known to do it. Patanjali is merely revealing all the possibilities.

In fact, why would a man who has attained his uttermost being think to become small? For what? He cannot be so foolish. For what would he like to become like an elephant? What is the point in it? And why should he want to disappear? He cannot be interested in amusing people or their curiosities. He is not a magician. He is not interested in people applauding him. In fact, the moment a person reaches the highest peak of his being, all desires disappear. *Siddhis* appear when desires disappear. This is the dilemma: powers come when you don't want to use them. They come only when the person who always wanted to have them has disappeared.

So Patanjali is not saying that yogis will do such things. They have never been known to do such things. And the few people who try to do them are not yogis. And the few people who do them, in fact cannot do them; they are only tricksters.

Satya Sai Baba-types go on materializing Swiss-made watches. These are all tricks, and nobody should be enchanted by these tricks. Whatsoever Satya Sai Baba has been doing can be done by thousands of magicians all over the world very easily, but you never go to magicians and touch their feet because you know that they are doing tricks. But if somebody who is thought to be religious is doing the same trick then you think it is a miracle.

This part of Patanjali's *Yoga Sutras* is to make you aware that these things become possible but they are never actualized because the person who would want it, who would have always liked to go on an ego trip through these powers, is there no more. Miraculous powers happen to you when you are not interested in them. This is the economy of existence. If you desire, you remain impotent. If you don't desire, you become infinitely potent. This I call the law of banking: if you don't have money, no bank is going to give you any; if you have money, every bank is ready to give you more. When you don't need, all is available; when you are needy, nothing is available.

> *Beauty, grace, strength, and adamantine hardness constitute the perfect body.*

Patanjali is not talking about *this* body. This body can be beautiful, but can never be perfectly beautiful. The second body can be more beautiful than this, the third even more, because they are moving closer to the centre. The beauty is of the centre. The farther away it has to travel, the more limited it becomes. The fourth body is even more beautiful. The fifth is 99 per cent perfect.

But your being—the real you—is beauty, grace, strength, and adamantine hardness. It is adamantine hardness, and at the same time, the softness of a lotus. It is beautiful but not fragile—it is strong. It is strong, but not just hard—all opposites meet in it . . . as if a lotus flower is made of diamonds or a diamond is made of lotus flowers; because man and woman meet there and transcend, because sun and moon meet there and transcend.

The old term for yoga is *hatha*. This word *hatha* is very, very significant. *Ha* means sun, *tha* means moon; *hatha* means the meeting of sun and moon. The union of sun and moon is yoga—*unio mystica*.

In the human body, according to the *hatha* yogis, there are three channels of energy. The first is known as *pingala*, the right channel, connected with the left brain—the sun channel. The second channel, *ida*, is the left channel, connected with the right brain—the moon channel. Then there is the third channel, the middle channel, *sushumna*, the central, the balanced—it is made of sun and moon together.

Ordinarily your energy moves either by the *pingala* or by *ida*. Yogis' energy starts moving through the *sushumna*. When the energy moves just between the right and left, it is called *kundalini*. These channels exist corresponding to your backbone. Once the energy moves in the middle channel, you become balanced. Then a person is neither a man nor a woman, neither hard nor soft, nor both man and woman, hard and soft. All the polarities disappear in *sushumna*; and *sahasrar* is the peak of *sushumna*.

If you live on the lowest point of your being, that is *muladhar*, the sex centre, then either you move by *ida* or you move by *pingala*—the sun channel or the moon channel—and you remain divided. And you go on seeking the other, you go on asking for the other—you feel incomplete in yourself, you have to depend on the other.

Once your own energies meet inside and there happens a great orgasm, a cosmic orgasm—when the *ida* and *pingala* dissolve into *sushumna*—then one is thrilled, eternally thrilled. Then one is ecstatic, continuously ecstatic; that ecstasy knows no end. Then one never comes down, then one never comes low; one remains high. That point of highness becomes one's innermost core, one's very being.

Remember again, I would like to say to you: this is the framework. We are not talking about actual things. There are foolish people who have even tried to dissect the human body to see where *ida* and *pingala* and *sushumna* are, and they have found them nowhere. These are just indicators; they are symbolic.

There are foolish people who have tried to dissect the

body and to find where the centres are. One doctor has even written a book to prove which centre is exactly which complex in the body according to physiologists. These are all foolish attempts.

Yoga is not in *that* way scientific. It is allegorical. It is a great allegory. It is showing something and if you go inside you will find it, but there is no way to find it by dissecting a body. By post-mortem you will not find these things. These are live phenomena. And these words are simply indicative—don't be confined to them, and don't make a fixed obsession and doctrine out of them. Remain fluid. Take the hint, and go on the journey . . .

One more word—*urdhvaretas*. It means the upward journey of energy. Right now you exist at the sex centre, and from that centre the energy goes on falling downward. *Urdhvaretas* means your energy starts moving upward. It is a very delicate phenomenon, and one has to be very alert to work with it. If you are not alert then there is every possibility you will become a perverted being. It is dangerous; that is why yogis call it 'serpent power'. It is like a snake—you are playing with a snake. If you don't know what to do, there is danger—you are playing with poison.

And many people have become perverted because they tried to repress their sex energy in order to become *urdhvaretas*, to go upward. They never went upward. They even became more perverted than normal people.

I was reading an anecdote:
'Yes,' said Abe to his friend Issy. 'I am afraid my son has turned out to be a great disappointment. You know how we struggled to give him an education that we never had. I sent him to the finest business school in the country, and now what happens? He rolls up at my dress factory at

10 a.m.; at 11 a.m. he dawdles over tea; at noon he is off for lunch; he is not back till 2 p.m.; and from 2 p.m. to 4 p.m. he fools around with the models. What rubbish he has turned out to be.'

'Abe,' replied Issy. 'What troubles you have got are nothing; mine are a thousand times worse. You know how we struggled to give my son an education that we never had. I sent him to the best business school in the country, and now what happens? He rolls up at my factory at 10 a.m.; at 11 a.m. he dawdles over tea; at noon he is off for lunch; he is not back till 2 p.m.; and from 2 p.m. to 4 p.m. he fools around with the models. What rubbish he has turned out to be!'

'But, Issy, since when is that a thousand times worse than me? It is the same story what you have told me.'

'Abe, you forget one thing: I am in the men's clothing.'

Get it? If you don't know what to do with sex energy, and you start fooling with it, either your energy will become masturbatory or homosexual or there are a thousand and one other perversions. Then it is better to leave it as it is.

That is why a master is needed—one who knows where you are, where you are going, and what is going to happen next; one who can see your future and one who can see whether the right channelling is happening or not. Otherwise the whole world is in a mess of sexual perversion.

Never repress. It is better to be normal and natural than to be perverted. But just to be normal is not enough, much more is possible: transform. Repression is not the way of *urdhvaretas*—transformation is. And that can be done only if you purify your body, you purify your mind; you throw all rubbish that you have gathered in the body and the mind.

Only with a pure, light, weightlessness will you be able to help the energy to move upwards.

Ordinarily it is like a coiled snake; that is why we call it *kundalini*, or *kundali*. *Kundali* means 'coiled up'. When it raises its head and moves upwards, tremendous is the experience. Whenever it passes a higher centre, you will have higher and higher experiences. On each centre many things will be revealed to you; you are a great book. But the energy has to pass through the centres; only then can those centres reveal you their beauties, their visions, their poetries, their songs, their dances. And each centre has a higher orgasm than the lower one.

Sexual orgasm is the lowest. Higher is the orgasm of the *hara*. Then higher than that is the orgasm of the *nabhi*, the navel. Higher than that is the orgasm of the heart—love. Then higher than that is the orgasm of the throat—creativity, sharing. Then higher than that is that of the third eye, the vision of life as it really is, without any projections—the clarity to see unclouded. And highest is that of the *sahasrar*, the seventh centre.

This is the map. If you want, you can move upwards, become *urdhvaretas*. But never try to become *urdhvaretas* for *siddhis*, powers—they are all foolish. Try to become *urdhvaretas* to know who you are, not for power but peace. Let peace be thy goal, never power.

This chapter is called *Vibhuti Pada*. *Vibhuti* means 'power'. Patanjali included this chapter so that his disciples and those who will ever be following him are made alert that many powers happen on the way but you are not to get entangled with them. Once you become entangled with power, once you are on a power trip, you are in trouble. You will be tied down to that spot—and your flight will be stopped. And one has to go on flying and flying until the very end, when the abyss opens and you are absorbed back into the cosmic soul.

Let peace be thy goal.

2

Choice Is Hell

You tell me to float, but my body is so heavy
with a dead-weight mind that I feel I will drown
if I float. So I keep swimming in panic.

FLOATING IS A totally new way of life. You are accustomed
to fight; you are accustomed to swim upstream. The ego
feels nourished if you fight with something. If you don't
fight, the ego simply evaporates. It is very essential for the
existence of the ego to continue fighting. This way or that,
in worldly matters or in spiritual matters—but go on
fighting! Fight with others or fight with yourself, but
continue the fight. The people you call worldly are fighting
with others, and the people you call spiritual are fighting
with themselves. But the basic thing remains the same.

The real vision arises only when you stop fighting. Then
you start disappearing because without fight the ego cannot
exist for a single moment. It is just like a bicycle—it needs
constant pedalling. If you stop pedalling, it has to fall; it
cannot continue for long, just a little while because of the
past momentum. But your cooperation is needed to keep
the ego alive, and the cooperation is through fight, resistance.

When I ask you to float, I mean that you are such a tiny
part of the cosmos that it is absolutely absurd to fight with

it. With whom are you fighting? All fight is basically against existence, because it surrounds you. If you are trying to go upstream, you are trying to go against existence. If it is flowing downwards to the ocean, go with it.

Once you start floating with the river, you will have a totally different quality arising in you. Something of the beyond will descend. You will not be there; you will become just emptiness—tremendous emptiness, receptivity. When you fight you shrink, when you fight you become small, when you fight you become hard. When you don't fight— you surrender, you open, like a lotus opening its petals— then you receive. Unafraid you start moving, moving with life, moving with the river.

The question is: 'You tell me to float, but I am afraid if I float I will drown.' It is good if you drown because only the ego can be drowned, not you. When you are fighting, the ego is fighting with your innermost core. You will drown, but by that drowning, for the first time you will be able to float. Choose and you choose the ego. Don't choose, let life choose for you, and you become egoless. Choose and you always choose hell. Choice is hell. Don't choose. Let this prayer of Jesus resound in your hearts: 'Thy kingdom come, Thy will be done'—let Him do for you.

Drop yourself, drown yourself; disappear from that plane of being. And then suddenly you are no longer human; you are superhuman. Your whole life will become a life of beatitude.

Let me tell you an anecdote:

One unfortunate soul arrived at the doors of hell and was interviewed by old Nick himself. 'Which group would you like to join?' he asked with a leer.

'What do you mean, "group"?' asked the new arrival.

'You see,' said the Devil. 'We have all sorts of torments here, and we allow people to choose their own. We believe in democracy, and we are not dictatorial. It is for you to choose. It is for eternity, remember, so you must choose carefully. I will take you on a tour.'

So the Devil took him through hell. One group were wallowing in slime and being perpetually eaten by maggots, another group were constantly being prodded with red-hot tridents, another group were being stretched on racks, etc., and the new arrival was feeling very despondent.

Then the Devil led him to one group in which all the inhabitants were standing up to their waists in a particularly evil-smelling cesspit and drinking cups of tea.

'This does not look too bad,' he thought to himself. 'I will choose this group,' he said to the Devil.

'Are you sure?' asked Satan. 'Remember, you can't change your mind, and it is forever and ever and ever.'

'No, I am quite sure—this will do me,' said the newly damned.

'Very well,' said the Devil. 'In you go.'

And just as the wretched soul jumped into the pit, a whistle blew and a voice called out: 'All right, everybody! Tea break is over—stand on your heads!'

If you choose you choose hell. Choice is hell. That is how you have created your hell all around you—by choosing. When you choose you don't allow existence to choose for you.

Krishnamurti goes on insisting on choicelessness. That is just one end of the whole story—the other end is if you *are* choiceless, existence chooses for you. The moment you are choiceless, life continues. You will not be there; life will continue. And you are nothing but a hell. Once you don't stand between you and existence, it chooses for you. Existence has been always choosing for you. There is a proverb which says 'Man proposes and God disposes'. The reality is just the opposite: God proposes and man goes on disposing.

Once you have felt that beatitude of non-choosing and floating, you will never choose again. Because whenever you choose you choose hell, and whatsoever you choose you choose hell.

So I would like you to drown—drown with my blessings.

When Jesus says that those who cling to themselves will lose themselves, and those who are ready to lose will gain, he means exactly the same thing. When Sufis say 'Die before your death, and then you will become deathless', they mean the same.

The death of the ego happens only through surrender. People come to me and they ask, 'How do we not be egoistic?' But you cannot do anything to be non-egoistic. Whatsoever you will do will make you egoistic again. You can try to discipline the ego, but you cannot be non-egoistic because whatsoever you do enhances the ego. You may try to be humble, but if it is *your* humbleness—practiced, disciplined by you—then deep down in your humbleness the ego will remain crowned, and it will go on saying, 'Look. How humble I am!'

I have heard about one man who went to see Adler, the great psychologist who coined the words 'inferiority complex'. The man was psychoanalyzed. After a few months and much effort, Adler told him, 'Now you are cured.'

The man said, 'Yes, I also feel that I am cured. Now I am the one who has the most beautiful inferiority complex in the world . . . the best inferiority complex in the world.'

Inferiority complex . . . and the most beautiful and the best? It is possible. It happens every day. You can become egoistic about the inferiority complex. You can feel a superiority complex about an inferiority complex. Man is so ridiculous.

Go to religious people and see their faces. They show all signs of humbleness, but you will have to go a little deeper, deeper than their skin, to know them. Deep down the ego is very happy, feeling that 'Nobody is more humble than me'. If you say to a religious man, 'I have found a man who is more humble than you', he will be hurt. He will feel insulted—it is impossible, nobody can be more humble than him. But that is the whole effort of the ego—nobody has a better house than me, nobody has a better car than me, nobody has a better face than me, nobody has better knowledge than me. In that comparison and feeling better, is the ego.

You cannot do anything to change it. You can simply see the point that nothing is needed on your part. And once you drop it—or rather it will be better to say: once in your deep understanding it drops—you are open to life. Then life starts flowing through you, like a cool breeze in an open room. You are like a windowless room: all doors closed, no ray of light enters you, no new breeze passes through you. You are caved in within yourself, closed. And of course, if you start feeling suffocated, it is natural.

But I know it is difficult to allow yourself to drown. It takes time. A few glimpses will be needed. Sometimes float, don't swim, and just feel the river taking you over. Sometimes just sit in the garden, don't choose. Don't say what is beautiful, what is ugly; don't divide. Just be there, present to everything. Sometimes move in the marketplace, not saying, not condemning, not appreciating. In many ways learn how just to be, without any evaluation. Because the moment you evaluate you have chosen. The moment you say something is good, you are saying, 'I would like to have it.' The moment you say something is bad, you say, 'I don't want it; I would not like to have it.' The moment you say some woman is beautiful, you have desired. The moment you say some woman is ugly, you have already felt repulsion. You are already caught in the duality of good and bad, ugly and beautiful; and the choice has entered you.

Subtle are the ways of the ego. One has to be very alert.

And once you know—once even for a single moment the ego is not there, you are not creating it—suddenly all doors open, and from everywhere, from all directions, life rushes towards you. That rush is very fragile. If you are not alert you will not be able to see it, you will not be able to feel it. Existence's touch is very delicate. Great sensitivity is needed to feel it.

Just the other day I was reading a small poem by Huub Oosterhuis:

God does not send us his word
like a great torrent of water
raging in tempest and flood
sweeping us blindly along

but like a glimpse of the sun
or a green branch in the winter,
rain falling softly on earth:
this is how God comes to us.

'. . . rain falling softly on earth: this is how God comes to us.'

In deep surrender, sensitivity, awareness, suddenly you are full of something which you had never known before. It had always been there, but you were too gross to know it. It had always been there, but you were too much occupied in fighting, in the ways of the ego, that you couldn't look back and feel it. It was always there, but you were not present. It was always waiting for you, but you had forgotten how to come back home. Dropping the ego is the way back home.

So drown yourself. That is the whole art I am teaching you here. If I am teaching anything, I am teaching you death, because I know, only through death is resurrection.

> *This morning you spoke of the need to be responsible, to not lean on others, to be alone.*
>
> *I see I have been taking sanyas as an excuse to avoid these things—asking you all the time what to do, calling on your presence when I am sad and lonely, imagining you are with me, filling all the emptiness.*
>
> *I feel irresponsible and confused again about what sanyas is.*

You will always feel confused if you lean on somebody else because then the understanding will not be yours, and understanding cannot be borrowed. So you can befool yourself a little while. Again and again the reality will erupt and you will feel confused. So the only way to avoid confusion is not rationalization; the only way to avoid confusion is to stand on your own feet—to be alert, to be aware. Don't postpone awareness. Whenever you start leaning on somebody, you are avoiding awareness—but you have been taught and conditioned to lean on people from the very beginning. The parents, the peers, the society, the educationists, the politicians, they all go on trying to condition you in such a way that you always depend on others. Then you can be manipulated, you can be dominated. Then you can be exploited and oppressed, you can be reduced to being a slave. You lose your freedom.

This conditioning is there. When you come to me you come with that conditioning, of course; there is no other way. And immediately your mind starts functioning from your conditioning: you start leaning on me. But I am not going to allow you that. I will push you repeatedly—throw you repeatedly to yourself—because I would like you to stand on your own understanding. Then it will be something of the permanent, and you will never be confused.

Confusion comes in when I say something to you and you start believing in it—but it is not your vision, it is not your perception. Say, tomorrow something happens and you are in a difficulty. The difficulty arises because you have learned by rote—you have memorized me. Now you will try to respond through this *borrowed* understanding. Life changes every moment. My understanding of this moment will not be of any help to you the next moment. My understanding of this moment cannot be made a permanent reference. And if you take it verbally, intellectually, mentally, and you carry it with you, you will keep being confused, because life will always sabotage your so-called understanding.

Life trusts only *real* understanding. Real means your own, authentic, that which arises from you.

I am not here to give you knowledge. I am not here to

give you theories. That is what has been done for centuries and man has remained as ignorant as ever. I am here to make you alert to the fact that hidden behind you, within you, is a source of light. Tap that source. Let that light burn bright within you, and then you have something alive. Then whatsoever problems come in life, you will not tackle them from your past knowledge—you will tackle them in the present. You will face them with your present understanding.

Whatsoever I say will always become past—the moment I have said, the moment you have heard—it has already gone into the past. And life goes on changing; it is a constant movement. It knows no stopping, it knows no rest. You will keep feeling confused.

And with me also there is a problem. The next moment you will ask the same question, and I will never answer the same again. This is because I respond. I don't answer—I don't remember my old answers—I respond. Your question is there, I am here: I respond again. And if you go on collecting my answers: not only confused, you will become mad because you will not find any harmony in them, any consistency in them. They are inconsistent. What can I do? Life *is* inconsistent. If I am to be true to life, I have to remain inconsistent in my statements. If I want to be true to my statements, then I betray life. And I would like to remain true to life. I can betray my past, but I cannot betray the present. I can go against my statements, but I cannot go against the present life, this moment.

So confusion will arise. Some day I will say something, and I will say something else some other day. If you compare, if you try to make a consistent whole out of my statements, you are going to be in trouble . . . in deep trouble. Don't do that. Just listen to me. And don't learn my answer; learn my response. Don't be bothered with what I say. See the way I say it, see the way I respond to a situation, to a question. The answer is not important, but my live response is.

And if you can learn the live response, you become responsible. My meaning of the word 'responsibility' is totally different from the dictionary meaning. In the dictionary, 'responsibility' seems something like a duty, a commitment, as if you are responsible to somebody else. The word is almost dirty. The mother goes on saying to the child, 'You are responsible to me, remember.' The father goes on saying to the son, 'You are responsible to me, remember.' The society goes on saying to the individuals, 'You are responsible to us, to the society, remember.' And your so-called images of God, they also go on telling people, 'You are responsible to us . . . to me.'

When I use the word 'responsibility' I mean your aliveness, responding aliveness. You are not responsible to anybody else except your own being, this moment. You are responsible to be responsible—to respond with an open heart, with vulnerability, not with closed fists but with open hands, not hiding and holding something, opening yourself completely, in deep trust with life, not trying to be clever and cunning. Then you float with life moment to moment . . . your response will change because life is changing.

Sometimes it is hot and you cannot sit outside in the sun and you would need a shelter. Sometimes it is too cold and you cannot sit under the shelter and you would like to sit in the sun. But nobody is going to say to you that you look very inconsistent: 'The other day you were sitting in the shelter, and now you are sitting in the sun? Be consistent! Choose! If you want to sit in the sun then sit consistently in the sun.' You will laugh at this absurdity, but this is what people have expected of you in life.

Everything is changing around you. Don't get fixed ideas, otherwise you will be confused. And don't listen to what others say. Listen to your own heart.

I have heard:

What mankind had feared for generations finally happened: a nuclear reaction ran out of control and the entire globe exploded, killing every living thing in it.

Naturally, at the Pearly Gates there was terrible confusion, what with so many souls arriving at the same time, so St. Peter decided to try and sort out the grades by putting up various notices behind which the appropriate souls could form queues.

One sign read: 'Bosses Only', and another read: 'Men Who Were Under Their Wives' Thumbs'. Behind the 'Bosses Only' sign was one solitary soul, whereas under the other sign was a queue stretching right to the Milky Way.

St. Peter, curious, said to the solitary soul, 'How is it that you are the only one here?'

'I don't know—my wife told me to stand here,' was the reply.

Sometimes it is the wife, sometimes it is the husband, sometimes it is the father, sometimes the mother, sometimes the guru—somebody is telling you to stand here, and you don't know why. Make sure why you are standing there.

Listen—it is a little complex. Even if you decide to follow somebody, listen to your heart, whether you want to follow. I am not saying don't follow anybody, because if your heart says follow, then what will you do? But listen to the heart, feel your own feeling first because ultimately you are responsible to your heart. Everything else is secondary; you are primary. You are the centre of your world.

If you choose to follow me or if you choose to be initiated by me, if you choose to surrender to me, feel first your own feeling. Otherwise you will keep being confused, and you will keep thinking, 'What am I doing here?' You will start thinking, 'Why have I taken sanyas? Why?' Don't take it because somebody else is telling you to. Feel it. Then the confusion will never arise.

Confusion is a wrong functioning. If you function from *your* centre, confusion never arises. If you function from somebody else's centre, the confusion is bound to arise continuously—and people are functioning from others' understandings, from advisers, experts. They are living through them. People have completely left their lives in others' hands.

Feel it, wait for the feeling to arise. Be patient, don't be in a hurry. And if you have felt your feeling well, then you will have a deep root, and that root will make you strong, and that root will not allow any confusion to settle around you.

✳

What is a problem?

Now you create a problem for me. The question is as if somebody comes and asks, 'What is yellowness?' or 'What is this colour yellow?' There are yellow flowers, there are yellow old leaves, there is the yellow gold sun and a thousand and one things which are yellow; but have you ever seen yellowness? Yellow things you may have seen, but yellowness one never comes across, cannot come across.

There are problems and problems, but you never know what *the* problem is; that question is abstract. There is nothing like 'the problem'. There are problems because a problem is a conflict within you. When you have two minds within you, then the problem arises. You don't know where to go, whether this way or that; then the problem arises. The problem is a question of your duality: you feel you must do this, and you also feel you must do that, and the problem arises. But if you are one, there is no problem. You simply move. Whenever you ask an abstract question, like 'what is a problem?' or 'what is yellowness?' or 'what is love?', it becomes difficult.

St. Augustine has said, 'I know what time is, but when people ask me "What is time?" suddenly I lose all track.' Everybody knows what time is, but if somebody asks what it exactly is, you will be in difficulty. You can show what *the* time is, but what is time? Just pure abstract!

But I understand why this problem has arisen. There are a few people who are so confused that they cannot even decide what the problem is. They are so confused, standing on a crossroad, that, far from deciding what the solution is, they have not even decided what the problem is. There are many like that . . . because you have lost contact with your feeling, your existential heart. So not only the solution, but also the problem has to be supplied by somebody else. You are asking me that I should tell you what your problem is. Not only for the solution do you depend on me, you depend on me for the problem as well. But this is how it has been done in the past.

When people come to me I can immediately see whether their problem is theirs or whether they have borrowed it. If a Christian comes he brings a problem which no Hindu can ever bring. When a Jew comes he brings a problem no Christian can ever bring. When a Jain comes he brings a totally different problem which no Jew can ever bring. What happens? These problems cannot be life problems because life problems cannot be Jewish, Hindu, Christian, Jain. Life problems are simply life problems. These problems are theological; they have been taught. They have even been taught the problems—what to ask.

Very cunning people have been exploiting humanity. First they teach you what to ask, and then they give you the answer. If you ask the right question, they will supply the right answer. And both are bogus because the question has been taught by them and then you ask it. And they teach you only questions which they can answer. So the game goes on very well, perfectly well.

If you go to a Jain monk and you have not been taught by Jains what questions to ask, you will create trouble. You will cause embarrassment there because you will ask questions to which the tradition—their tradition—does not supply the solutions. If you ask a Jain why God created the world, he will be puzzled because in his theology there is no God. In his theology there has never been anything created. The world has existed forever and forever and forever. Creation has never been there. So if you ask why God created the world, your question is totally absurd for a Jain because there is no God and there is no creation; the world has simply continued. The word 'creation' does not exist in Jain language because creation implies the existence of a creator; and there is no creator, so how can there be creation? The world is, but it is not a creation. It is eternal, uncreated; it has always remained there.

Never ask a theological question, because that is borrowed. Find out existential questions, find out where your difficulty is, find out where your shoe pinches; find out your own problems.

Your problem may not be another's, so the other may not agree that this is a problem. Problems are individual;

they are not a universal phenomenon. My problem is my problem; your problem is your problem. They are as different as your thumbprints, and they have to be so.

I see that people are asking borrowed problems—they don't have your signature on them and thus they are futile; not worth even asking, not worth answering. Your problem should have your signature on it. It should come out of your life, out of the struggle, challenge, response, out of your own confrontation.

I have heard:

So finally the marriage broker induced Cohen to meet this girl. After all she was supposed to be beautiful, talented, educated, young, and with pots of money.

Cohen met her, liked her, and married her.

A day later he finds the marriage broker and rages: 'Some dirty trick you played on me, eh? She admits herself that she has slept with half the men in Pune.'

'So? After all, how big is Pune?' said the agent.

Your problem is not the agent's problem. Your problem is yours, nobody else's. Remember that if a problem is individual, it can be solved — because it is true. If you have borrowed it from tradition, society, or somebody else, it can never be answered because it was not your problem in the first place. It is as if you have acquired a disease from someone.

Just the other night I was reading that in a famous physician's waiting office there is a notice especially for ladies, 'Please don't talk about your diseases and symptoms to other ladies'—don't exchange symptoms because that confuses the doctor! Ladies waiting for the doctor are bound to talk, and bound to be impressed by others' symptoms.

And certainly that confuses the doctor because he cannot know what is what.

There are people who get diseases through advertisements of medicines in the newspapers. I have heard about one man who rang up his doctor in the middle of the night. Of course, the doctor was angry at having his sleep broken in the middle of the night.

He answered the phone and said, 'What is the matter?' The man started describing his disease. The doctor said, 'Cut it short, I have also read this article in the news magazine.'

People learn their diseases from magazines. Just watch your mind. It is so imitative that it can be impressed by others' problems, and you can get so suggestible that you start thinking this is your problem. Then there is no way to solve it, because in the first place it is not a problem to you.

This is my observation: if a problem is real it can be solved. My definition of a problem is that it can be solved. If it cannot be solved then it is not a problem. A disease is a disease if it can be cured. All diseases are curable—at least theoretically curable—but if you don't have the disease, then it can't be cured. Then nobody can help, it is just in your mind; no medicine can be of any help to you.

So the first thing to understand about a problem is that it should be existential—not theological, speculative, or philosophical. It should be psychological rather than being philosophical, and it should come out of the confrontation with life.

90 per cent of problems arise because you are caught in dead thoughts, and you cling to those thoughts. When a situation arises which doesn't fit with your thought, the problem arises—and you want to try changing the situation rather than changing the thought. If you come across a

situation which doesn't fit with your ideology, you struggle hard to change the situation rather than change the ideology. Then the problem arises.

Always be ready to change your mind, because life cannot be changed just because of your ideologies. We have learned ways of how to look at life, how to interpret life. We become fixated in certain routines.

Let me tell you an anecdote:

A mousy little man used to be very frightened of his boss. One day he told a fellow worker that he was sick.

His friend said, 'Why don't you go home?'

'Oh, I couldn't do that!'

'Why not? Don't be silly, he will never know. He is not even here today.'

Finally the man was convinced and went home.

When he got there, he looked in the window—and there was his boss, kissing and hugging his wife. So he ran all the way back to the office.

'A fine friend you are!' he said to his pal. 'I nearly got caught.'

It was his old pattern of thought. The situation was totally different. He could have caught the boss, but just the old idea that the boss has always been catching him prevented him from doing so.

Watch life and don't be addicted to your mind. 90 per cent of your problems will disappear simply without any bother. 10 per cent of your problems will remain—they are existential and they are needed to be there because you have to grow through them. If they are dropped, you will not grow. The conflict is needed, the pain is needed, the suffering is needed, because that will make you crystallized—that will make you more aware. And if you can transcend it, you will have earned the bliss that comes after one has transcended a problem.

It is just like mountaineering. You are going uphill, you are tired, perspiring, breathing is difficult, and it seems impossible to reach the top; and then, when you finally reach the top and you lie down under the sky, you rest and are relaxed, you are happy that you decided to climb. But only after a hard climb. You can reach that summit by a helicopter, but then you have not earned it. A man who reaches the summit by the helicopter and the man who climbs using his feet reach different peaks. They never reach the same peak. Your means changes your end. The man who has reached by helicopter will enjoy it a little; he will say, 'Yes, it is beautiful.' But his enjoyment will be like a man who is completely stuffed with food and then a delicious plate comes before him; he says, 'Good', he can smell it a little, but he is so stuffed he has no appetite. And just by his side there is another man who is hungry.

To reach the top one needs to have the appetite, and that appetite grows while you are climbing. You become hungrier, you become increasingly tired . . . and when you reach the top you rest. You have earned it.

In life, you cannot get anything unearned. And if you try to be clever with life, you will miss many opportunities.

So drop those problems which are not yours. Drop those problems which you have learned from others. Drop those problems which arise because of your fixed ideologies. Be fluid, move. Die each moment, let it go to the past, and be born again, so you don't carry any ideology, any fixed attitude towards life, and you are always open and available, responding. Then only those problems which are needed will remain, which are part of your growth.

I see there are people who are living just routine lives—they are not living true lives, just making empty gestures. Their problems are also empty, meaningless. Somebody comes and asks, 'Is there truth?' The problem is empty. How are you concerned with truth? You have not even known yourself yet. Start from the beginning, begin from the beginning. You have not even known the knower. You have not even known what this awareness is within you. And you are asking about truth? You are asking about the absolute awareness, the ultimate awareness, and you have not even known the awareness which has already been given to you as a gift. You have not learned about the flower that is in your hand, and you ask about ultimate flowering? It is foolishness.

Forget all about truth. Right now, enter into your being and see what existence has given you. And if you can learn it, more doors will be opened for you. The more you learn, the more mysteries open. Truth is the ultimate mystery—when you have learned everything else and nothing remains to be learned, when you have passed through all the turmoil, anxieties, anguishes of life, only then can you know truth. Truth is the last gift; you have to earn it.

Don't ask questions which are irrelevant to you. And don't live a routine life of empty gestures. People go to church—an empty gesture. They never wanted to go there; then why are they going? They go because everybody else is going, because it is a social formality, because people think good of you if you go to the church, because it gives you certain respectability. These people would not have gone to Jesus, but they go to church. Church is respectable; Jesus was never. To go to Jesus was difficult; to go to Jesus was to put your respectability at stake.

You are here . . . and you have had to put your

respectability at stake because you are not going to gain any respectability by coming to me. You may lose, but you cannot gain. It cannot be formal because who bothers to stake so much for a formal thing? It can only be of the heart.

People pray—it has to be done; an empty gesture. No love in their heart, no gratitude in their heart, and they go on praying. Then useless problems arise.

Do only that for which you have a feeling.

I have heard:

A former railway worker, aged eighty, had his home by the railway line. He was retired. He used to count the wagons on every goods train that passed. There was no need; it was just an old habit. One Sunday at a family picnic, his son noticed that he was ignoring a passing train and asked, 'Why are you not counting the wagons?'

Answered the old man, 'I don't work on Sundays.'

Watch your life: make it truer, authentic, real. Don't move through empty gestures, otherwise your questions will be empty. They will look like problems, but they will not be real problems.

What is the difference between a real problem and a pseudo-problem? A pseudo-problem is that which can be solved, yet nothing is really solved. And a real problem is that which, even if it is not solved, the very effort to solve it solves much. In the very effort you become more alert, more knowing, more understanding. You come to know much about yourself that was never known before.

A problem is an opportunity to face yourself, to go on a pilgrimage inside your being. A problem is a door; use it to enter into your own being.

So this is my answer: a problem is an opportunity to grow. A problem is a gift of existence, a challenge from the divine. Face it. Find out ways to transcend it, how to go above it, and you will be tremendously benefited.

✷

You say, 'Do not make the same mistake twice.'
How can I keep from doing that unless I bring
the mind in—to evaluate, compare, and judge?
And then I have to say 'no'.

When I ask you not to make a mistake twice, I am not asking you to evaluate, to judge, or to compare. I am asking you to see. When you are making a mistake, see it so totally that you see that it is a mistake. In that very seeing it is dropped; you will never be able to repeat it.

For example, if you put your hand in the fire and it is burned, next time when you will be near fire, will you do an Aristotelian syllogism—that this too is a fire, all fires burn, and therefore I should not put my hand in it? Are you going to compare with the past experience? Are you going to evaluate? If you are doing that, then you cannot avoid committing the mistake again because then the mind will say, 'Maybe this fire is different. And who knows, the fire may have changed its way of life. It may not behave the same this time. Maybe it was angry that time, and this time it is not angry.'

The mind that evaluates, judges, or compares, is already showing that it has not understood the point. Otherwise what is the need of evaluation or comparison? If you have seen a fact, the very fact is enough. You will avoid the fire.

So when you are passing through experiences, remain alert, don't be deaf and blind. I am not asking you to look back. I am asking you to just look right now, wherever you are, and if it is a mistake, it will be dropped on its own accord. Knowing a mistake as a mistake, it drops. If it is not dropping on its own, it simply shows that you have not yet totally known that it is a mistake. Somewhere or the other the illusion continues that it is not.

People come and say to me, 'We know anger is bad, we know it is poisonous, and we know it is destructive to ourselves, but what do we do? We go on being angry.' What are they saying? They are saying that they have heard people say that anger is bad; they have read in the scriptures that anger is poisonous; but they have not known these things themselves, otherwise they would have had stopped being angry a long time ago.

Socrates has said, 'Knowledge is virtue'; a great dictum. He says, 'To know is to be.' Once you have known this is a wall and not a door, you are not going to knock your head against it repeatedly. Once you have known it is a wall, you search for the door. Once you have found the door, you always pass through the door. It is not a question of repeatedly thinking about the past experiences, comparing, deciding, and concluding.

I have heard:

A deaf priest was hearing confessions, when a man came into the box, dropped onto his knees and said, 'Oh, Father, I have done a terrible thing. I have murdered my mother.'

'What?' said the old priest, cupping his hand to his ear.

'I have murdered my mother!' said the penitent, rather louder.

'What is that? Speak up.' ordered the man of God.

'I have murdered my mother!!!' roared the poor, distraught sinner.

'Ah,' said the priest. 'How many times?'
A deaf person is a deaf person; a blind person is a blind person. If you don't listen to experience, if you are deaf to your experience, then you will go on repeating the same, again and again. In fact, to say that you are repeating is not right. You are doing it again, as a new thing, because the last time you missed—it is not a repetition.

This is my understanding: no mistake is ever repeated once you have understood it as a mistake. If you repeat it, it simply shows you are doing it afresh, because the past has not entered in your consciousness yet. You are doing it for the first time again; it is not a repetition. If you have understood it, then it cannot be repeated. Understanding is alchemical; it transforms you.

So I am not telling you to become very clever and calculating, always thinking what is good and what is bad and what to do and what not to do, what is moral, what is immoral—I am not saying that. I am simply saying to you: from wherever you are passing, pass with full alertness, so nothing that is wrong is repeated again.

This is the beauty of awareness: that which is right is enhanced through it; that which is wrong is destroyed through it. Awareness functions as life energy to good and as death energy to bad. Awareness functions as a blessing to good and as a curse to bad. If you ask me my definition of sin, this is my definition: that which can be done with full awareness is not sin; that which cannot be done with full awareness is sin. Or that which can only be done in unawareness is sin, and that which can only be done in awareness is virtue. So forget about sin and virtue. Remember awareness and unawareness.

Evolution is between awareness and unawareness. Become more aware and less unaware. Bring your energy to be more aflame with awareness—that is all.

✽

Can't you take anything seriously?

I take one thing very seriously—jokes. You must have seen it: I never laugh when I tell a joke. I really take it seriously. Besides jokes, there is nothing serious in the world.

✽

If Mulla Nasruddin came here, would you put him in one of the groups? Or would you tell him to run a group of his own? If so, what kind of group would it be?

I have done it before. It didn't work. Mulla Nasruddin is a leader of leaders. He cannot be put in a group as a participant; his ego won't allow it. I had asked him and he said, 'Okay, you can make me a leader.' I gave him an opportunity, a three-day group; all the fools and all the wise people gathered to participate, because Mulla Nasruddin has appeal for both. Those who are fools, they think he is a fool. Those who are wise, they think he is a wise man. He is tricky, or maybe he is just a borderline case—he stands on both sides. He can be interpreted as a foolish man, but he can also be interpreted as one of the wisest ever.

He stood before the group and he said, 'Do you know what I am going to teach you?'

Of course, everybody said, 'How can we know? We don't know.'

He said, 'If you don't even know that much I am not going to teach, because you are not worth it.'

He left. The next day I persuaded him again. He again went there and asked the participants, 'Do you know what I am going to teach?'

Now they had learned a little, so they said, 'Yes, we know.'

He said, 'Then what is the point? If you know, you know.' And he left.

I persuaded him the third day again. He stood there and asked, 'Do you know what I am going to teach?'

Now the people had learned a little more; they said, 'Yes. Half of us know and half of us don't know.'

He said, 'Perfectly good. So those who know, tell those who don't know. What is the point of my being here?'

Mulla Nasruddin is a very, very old Sufi device. Whether this man ever existed or not is not certain. There are many countries who claim him. Iran claims him—they have a tomb in Iran of Mulla Nasruddin. Russia also claims him. There are other countries who also claim him. Almost the whole Middle East claims that he belonged to them. And there are many places where they say: 'Here his body is buried.'

He may or may not have existed, but his impact has been tremendous. Whatsoever he has done, or whatsoever is depicted as done by him is very, very meaningful. Even in the anecdote in which he asks 'do you know what I am going to teach you?', everybody said 'no' but nobody was silent. 'No' comes easily; to be an atheist is very easy. But it is difficult if you have a 'no' attitude; then it is difficult to teach you. The next day everybody said 'yes' because they were too greedy—to listen to what he wants to say. Their 'yes' was out of greed, and greed can never be satisfied. And Mulla said, 'If you know already, then what is the point?' The third day they tried to prove more cunning and clever.

They were trying to fix Mulla in his place, but you cannot fix him. He is almost like mercury; he slips out of your hands.

First they said 'no', but nobody was silent; then they said 'yes', but nobody was silent; then they said 'yes' and 'no' both, but still nobody was silent.

He came back to me and said, 'These people cannot be taught because only people who are silent can be taught.'

Silence is important for the disciple. If you come here already knowing, you cannot be taught. If you come here with a 'no' attitude, the atheistic attitude, with doubt and scepticism, you cannot be taught. Or if you say that a little I know and a little I don't know, then too you cannot be taught. You are being clever. These three attitudes – of those who say 'no', of those who say 'yes', and of those who are trying to travel on both the boats, trying to eat the cake and have it as well – belong to the three types of persons in the world who are incapable of understanding.

Only one who is silent, and answers with silence and an open heart, can be taught. This is the meaning of this anecdote.

Read Mulla Nasruddin as much as you can and try to understand him. He can be a great blessing to you because he teaches through humour. Each of his anecdotes is pregnant with tremendous meaning, but you will have to uncover it. That is why I say that there are people who think him a fool. They simply read an anecdote, laugh, and are finished. They think it is just a joke. It is not. No joke is just a joke. If you are wise you will look into it and see exactly what is happening. And once you catch the glimpse of its inside meaning, you will be tremendously happy. You will become aware of a new dimension.

Mulla Nasruddin is now read in the Western countries also, but people are missing the point—they think these are just jokes. They are not. They are a device to teach you the sacred-most through humour. And it can be taught only through humour—because only humour can relax you. And godliness can be known only in deep relaxation. When you laugh, you disappear as an ego. When the laughter is really authentic, like a belly laugh—when your whole body throbs with this orgasmic energy, when the laughter spreads over all of your being, when you are simply lost in it—you are entirely open.

Serious people have never reached godliness. They cannot, because God won't take that risk—they will bore Him to death.

A small child was brought to the church for the first time. He looked at people's faces—long, sad, serious. The whole thing looked as if somebody had died. Back home the mother asked, 'How did you feel?'

He said, 'I must say the truth. I felt as God must have been feeling bored there.'

The mother said, 'What do you mean?'

He said, 'God must be bored, seeing those long faces. And, Mom, do those same people come every Sunday?'

'Hmm—of course, the same people. There are a few who have been coming there for forty or fifty years.'

The boy became very, very sad. He said, 'Think of God. The same serious people every Sunday, the same faces. He must be bored to death.'

You reach godliness through laughter . . . I teach you laughter. You reach to godliness through dancing and singing, in joy, in jubilation and celebration. Learn laughter.

And while you are laughing, observe what is happening inside you; otherwise you will miss the whole beauty of it. While you are laughing see how the ego is suddenly not there. See how the mind has stopped for a single moment. For a split moment the mind is not there—there is no thought. When you laugh deeply there is no thought.

Laughter is meditative . . . and medicinal. For the physical body it is medicinal; for the spiritual it is 'meditational.'

I would like Mulla Nasruddin to start a group, but it seems difficult. He is a difficult man!

✳

> *Thy divine music touched a deeper core in my being. When I came here for the first time I was fully prepared for sanyas. Whether my sanyas was your benediction or my satyagraha is not clear to me. You say, 'come, follow me', but how do I follow you, when I do not know you? Sometimes I feel your fragrance and sometimes it is lost.*

When I say 'come, follow me', I am not asking you to come and follow my knowledge. When I say 'come, follow me', I am asking you to come and follow me in the sense of my 'non-knowledge.' When I say 'come, follow me', I am asking you to come towards the unknown; I am inviting you to come to the unknowable. When I say 'come, follow me', I am not saying come, follow *me*—because I am not. I am inviting you into a tremendous emptiness.

Once you enter this emptiness, you will neither find me nor you. You will find something totally different—that is what people have called 'God'.

And I know sometimes you will be able to feel my fragrance and sometimes it will be lost, because there are moods when you will be close to me and there are moods when you will be far, far away. When you are close you will have the fragrance; when you are far away you will miss it. So try to feel those moods when you feel close to me, and remain and relax in those moods longer.

It is not a question of physical space between me and you. It is a question of spiritual space. If while laughing you feel close to me, and the fragrance suddenly fills your nostrils and your being, then learn to laugh more. If you feel the fragrance is felt only when you are here just looking at me, with no stirring of thoughts, then learn to drop thoughts more and more. Whatsoever you are feeling, become more available to that certain mood, and my fragrance will become your fragrance—because it is neither mine nor yours; it belongs to existence.

✳

Five months of drinking from the source made me feel even thirstier. There must be something strange about your water. In meditation, this sentence came to me:

A small sweet-water lake,
hidden in the black forest,
is the source of the ocean.
Osho, you are sweet and salty,
and in the moment very salty.
I feel sad because of leaving.
I want to come back to this source,
drinking until I am so full that I will fall into
the source.

It is true, it is so. The more you will drink me, the thirstier you will become, because I am not going to make you content. I am going to make you even more discontent, because if you become contented with me, then you will never reach truth.

I am here to create more thirst. I am here to make you hungrier. So one day you are just thirst, just hunger, pure hunger. In that moment you explode and disappear and truth is found. If you become contented with me, I will be your enemy, not your friend—because then you will cling to me and my answers.

I am, at the most, a door. Pass through me. Don't cling to me—the journey starts with me, it doesn't end with me.

I know you must be feeling sad, but become alert to your sadness and don't get identified with it. It is there, hanging around you, but it is not you. Use that opportunity also to become more aware, more of a witness. And if you can become a witness to your sadness, the sadness will disappear. If you can become aware of your sadness and you can help it to disappear through awareness, wherever you go I will be coming with you.

There may not be any need to come back to the source because in your witnessing you will remain close to me wherever you are. You will be close to the source.

The source is not something outside you. And when you really listen to me, it is not listening to somebody who is outside you. It is listening to somebody who is inside you. It is listening to your own inner voice.

When you fall in love with me, in fact what has happened is that you have fallen in love with yourself for the first time.

3

About Your Wilder Being

Performing samyama *on their power of
cognition, real nature, egoism, all-
pervasiveness, and functions brings mastery
over the sense organs.*

*From this follows instantaneous cognition
without the use of the body,
and complete mastery over* pradhana, *the
material world.*

*Only after the awareness of the distinction
between* satva *and* purusha *does
supremacy and knowledge arise
over all states of existence.*

PATANJALI'S SKILL IN expressing the inexpressible is superb.
Nobody has ever been able to surpass him. He has mapped
the inner world of consciousness as accurately as possible;
he has almost done the impossible.

I have heard a story about Ramakrishna:
    One day he said to his disciples, 'I will tell you everything
today and will not keep anything secret.'

He described clearly the centres and the corresponding experiences up to the heart and throat, and then pointing to the spot between the eyebrows he said, 'The supreme self is directly known and the individual experiences *samadhi* when the mind comes here. There remains then but a thin transparent screen separating the supreme self and the individual self. The *sadhak* then experiences . . .'

Saying this, the moment he started to describe in detail the realization of supreme self, he was plunged in *samadhi* and became unconscious. When the *samadhi* came to an end and he came back, he tried again to describe it and was again in *samadhi*; he became unconscious again.

After repeated attempts Ramakrishna broke into tears, started crying, and told his disciples that it is impossible to speak about it.

But Ramakrishna had tried, had tried in many ways, from different directions, and this always happened throughout his life. Whenever he would go beyond the third-eye centre and nearer *sahasrar*, he would be caught hold of by something internal so deep that the very remembrance of it, the very effort to describe it, caused him to lapse into *samadhi*. For hours he would remain unconscious. This is natural, because the bliss of *sahasrar* is so great that one is almost overpowered by it. The bliss is so oceanic that one is possessed by it and taken over. One is no longer oneself, once one transcends the third eye.

Ramakrishna tried and failed; he could not describe it. Many others have not even tried. Lao Tzu for his whole life resisted saying anything about the world of Tao because of this. Nothing can be said about it, and the moment you try to say it, you are plunged into an inner whirlwind, a whirlpool. You are lost, drowned. You are bathed in such beauty and beatitude that you cannot utter a single word.

But Patanjali has done the impossible. He has described as exactly as possible each step, each chakra—its functioning and how to transcend it, up to *sahasrar*. And even beyond, he has indicated that on each chakra, on each wheel of energy, certain integration happens.

Let me tell you: at the sex centre, the first centre—the most primitive but the most natural, the one that is available to all—the integration happens between the outer and the inner. Of course, it is momentary. A woman meeting a man or a man meeting a woman come for a single moment, a split moment, where the outer and inner meet and mingle and merge into each other. That is the beauty of sex, the orgasm, that two energies, the complementary energies, meet and become one whole. But it is going to be momentary because the meeting is through the grossest element, the body. The body can touch surfaces but it cannot really enter into the other. It is like ice cubes. If you put two ice cubes together, they can touch each other, but only if they melt and become water can they meet and mingle with each other. Then they go to the very centre. And if the water evaporates, then the meeting becomes very, very deep. Then there is no I, no thou, no inner, no outer.

The first centre, the sex centre, gives you certain integration. That is why there is so much hankering for sex. It is natural. It is in itself beneficial and good. But if you stop there then you have stopped at the porch of a palace. The porch is good, it leads you into the palace, but it is not a place to make your abode, it is not a place to stop forever . . . and the bliss that is waiting for you on higher integrations of other centres will be missed. And in comparison to that bliss and happiness and joy, the beauty of sex is nothing, the pleasure of sex is nothing. It simply gives you a momentary glimpse.

The second chakra is the *hara*. At the *hara*, life and death meet. If you reach the second centre, you reach a higher orgasm of integration; life meeting death, sun meeting moon. And the meeting is inner now, so the meeting can be more permanent, more stable, because you are not dependent on anybody else. Now you are meeting your own inner woman or your own inner man.

The third centre is the navel. There the positive and the negative meet—the positive electricity and the negative electricity. Their meeting is even higher than life and death because the electric energy, the *prana*, the bioplasma or bio-energy, is deeper than life and death. It exists before life, it exists after death. Life and death exist because of bio-energy. This meeting of bio-energy at the navel, *nabhi*, gives you an even higher experience of being one . . . integrated . . . a unity.

Then, is the heart: at the heart centre the lower and the higher meet. At the heart centre: the *prakriti* and *purusha*, the sexual and the spiritual, the worldly and the other-worldly, all meet—or you can call it the meeting of heaven and earth. It is still higher because for the first time something of the beyond dawns—you can see the sun rising at the horizon. You are still rooted in the earth, but your branches are spreading into the sky. You have become a meeting. That is why the heart centre gives us the highest and the most refined experience—the experience of love. The experience of love is the meeting of earth and heaven; so love is in a way earthly and in another way heavenly.

If Jesus defined God as love, the reason is that in human consciousness love seems to be the higher glimpse.

Ordinarily people never go beyond the heart centre. Even to reach the heart centre seems difficult, almost impossible.

People remain at the sex centre. If they are trained deeply in yoga, karate, aikido, and T'ai chi, they reach the second centre, the *hara*. If they are trained in a deep mechanism of breathing, *prana*, then they reach the navel centre. And if they are trained how to look beyond earth, how to see beyond the body and how to look so deeply and so sensitively that you are no longer confined to the gross—and the subtle can penetrate its first rays into you—only then can the heart centre be reached.

All paths of devotion—bhakti yoga—work on the heart centre. Tantra starts from the sex centre, Tao starts from the *hara* centre. Yoga starts from the navel centre. Bhakti yoga, paths of devotion and love, Sufis and others, they start from the heart centre.

Higher than the heart is the throat centre. Integration happens again, even more superior, more subtle. This centre is the centre of receiving and giving. When the child is born he receives from the throat centre. First, life enters into him from the throat centre—he sucks air, breathes; then he sucks milk from his mother. The child functions from the throat centre, but it is half functioning and soon the child forgets about it. He just receives, he cannot give yet; his love is passive. And if you are asking for love, then you remain juvenile, you remain childish. Unless you mature—that is, you can give love—you have not yet become a grown-up. Everybody asks for love, demands love, and almost nobody gives. That is the misery all over the world. And all people who demand, think and believe that they are giving.

I have looked into thousands of people—all hungry for love, thirsty for love, but nobody in any way trying to give. And they all believe that they are giving but they are not receiving. Once you give, you receive naturally. It has never happened otherwise. The moment you give, love rushes in you. It has nothing to do with people; it has something to do with the cosmic energy of existence.

The throat centre is the meeting of receiving and giving. You receive from it and you give from it. If you look into Freudian psychology, you will have a parallel. Freud says the first stage of the child is oral, the second stage is anal, and the third stage is genital. The whole Freudian psychology ends with the third. Of course, it is a very poor psychology, very rudimentary, fragmentary, and concerned with the very lowest functioning of human beings. Oral—yes, the child uses the throat centre, just to receive. And once he has started receiving, his being moves to the anal.

Have you noticed that a few people cling to the oral, even up to their death? These are the people who smoke; smokers are oral people. They still go on . . . the smoke, the cigarette, the cigar, give them a feeling as if something hot like mother's milk is passing through the throat centre; they remain confined to the oral, and they cannot give. Chain-smokers are almost always not givers of love. They demand, but they will not give.

People who smoke too much are always interested in women's breasts—they are bound to be, because a cigarette is a substitute for the nipple. I am not saying that people who are not smokers are not interested in women's breasts. Those who smoke, they are interested; those who don't smoke, they are also interested—they may be chewing pan or gum or something else, or they may be simply interested in pornography—or they may just be obsessed by the breast continuously. In their mind, in their dreams, in their imagination and fantasies, breasts go on floating all around them. These are oral people, stuck in that first stage.

When Jesus says you have to be a child again, he means you have to come back to the throat centre, but with a new energy to give. All creative people are givers. They may sing a song for you or dance a dance or write a poem or paint a picture or tell you a story. For all these the throat centre is again used as a centre to give. The meeting happens at the throat, of receiving and giving. The capacity to receive and to give is one of the greatest integrations.

There are people who are only capable of receiving. They will remain miserable because you never become rich by receiving. You become rich by giving. In fact, you possess only that which you can give. If you cannot give it, you simply believe that you possess it. You don't possess it; you are not a master. If you cannot give your money, then you are not the master of it. Then the money is the master. If you can give it, then certainly you are the master. This will look like a paradox, but let me repeat it: you are the possessor only of that which you give. The moment you give, in that very moment you have become a possessor, enriched; giving enriches you.

Miserly people are the most miserable and poor people in the world—poorer than the poor. They cannot give: they are stuck. They go on hoarding. Their hoarding becomes a burden on their being—it does not free them. In fact, if you have something, you will become freer. But look at the misers. They have much, but they are burdened; they are not free. Even beggars are freer than they. What has happened to them? They have used their throat centre just to receive. They have not used their throat centre to give, and they have not even moved to the second Freudian centre, anal. These people are always constipated; hoarders, misers, always suffer from constipation. Remember, I am not saying that all people who have constipation are misers . . . there may be other reasons. But misers are certainly constipated.

Freud says that there is something common to gold and

excreta. Both look yellow, and people who are constipated are too attracted to gold. Otherwise gold has no existential value—some psychological value, but no existential value. You cannot eat it, you cannot drink it. What can you do with it? Even a glass of water is more valuable existentially. But why has gold become so valuable? Why are people so obsessed with gold? They have not moved from the oral to the anal. They are constipated in their inner being. Now their whole life will reflect their constipation: they will become hoarders of gold. Gold is symbolic. The yellowness gives them some idea.

Have you watched small children? It is difficult to persuade them to go to the toilet; they have to be almost forced to go to the toilet. And even then they insist, 'Nothing is happening. Can I come out?' They are learning the first lessons of miserliness—how to hold. How to hold, how not to give even that which is useless, even that which is harmful if you keep it within you. Even the poison—it is difficult for them to leave it, to renounce it.

I have heard about two Buddhist *bhikhus*. One of them was a miser and he used to collect money and keep it, and the other used to laugh at this foolish attitude. Whatsoever came his way, he would use it, never hoard it. One night they came across a river. It was evening, the sun was setting, and it was dangerous to stay there. They had to cross the river. On the other side was a town; this side was simply wilderness.

The miser said, 'Now you don't have any money, so we cannot pay the ferryman. What do you say now about it? You are against hoarding. Now if I don't have any money we both will die. You see the point? Money *is* needed.'

The man who believed in renunciation laughed, but he didn't say anything. Then the miser paid the ferryman, who took them across the river.

The miser said, 'Now remember, next time don't start arguing with me. You see? Money helps. Without money we would have been dead. A whole night on the other shore would have been difficult to survive—there are wild animals there.'

The other *bhikhu* laughed and said, 'But we have come across the river because you could renounce it. It is not because of hoarding that we have survived. If you had insisted on hoarding it and did not pay the ferryman, we would have died. It is because you could renounce—because you could leave it, you could give it—that is why we have survived.'

The argument must be still continuing. But remember, I am not against money. I am all for it—but use it! Possess it, own it; but your ownership arises only the moment you have become capable of giving it. At the throat centre this new synthesis happens. You can accept and you can give.

There are people who change from one extreme to another. First they were incapable of giving, they could only receive; then they change, they go to the other extreme—now they can give but they cannot receive. That too is lopsidedness. A real person is capable of accepting gifts and giving them. In India you will find many sanyasins, many so-called mahatmas, who will not touch money. If you give them any, they will shrink back, as if you have produced a snake or something poisonous. Their shrinking back shows that now they have moved to the other extreme: now they have become incapable of receiving. Again their throat centre is half-functioning and a centre never really functions unless it functions fully—unless the wheel moves the full way, goes on moving and creates energy fields.

Then, is the third-eye centre: At the third-eye centre the right and left meet, *pingala* and *ida* meet, and become *sushumna*. The two hemispheres of the brain meet at the third eye, just between the two external eyes. One eye represents the right, another eye represents the left, and the third eye is just in the middle. This meeting of the left and right brains at the third eye is a very high synthesis. People have been capable of describing up to this point. That is why Ramakrishna could describe up to the third eye. And when he started to talk about the final, the ultimate, synthesis that happens at *sahasrar*, he repeatedly fell into silence, into *samadhi*. He was drowned in it; it was too much. It was flood-like; he was taken over to the ocean. He could not keep himself conscious or alert.

The ultimate synthesis happens at *sahasrar*, the crown chakra. Because of this *sahasrar*, all over the world, kings, emperors, monarchs, and queens use the crown. It has become formal, but basically it was accepted because unless your *sahasrar* is functioning, how can you be a monarch or a king? How can you rule people if you have not even become a ruler of yourself? In the symbol of the crown is hidden a secret. The secret is that only people who have reached the crown centre, the ultimate synthesis of their being, should be kings or queens, nobody else. Only they are capable of ruling others, because they have come to rule themselves. They have become masters of themselves; now they can be helpful to others.

Really, when you achieve *sahasrar*, a crown flowers within you, a lotus with a thousand petals opens. No crown can be compared with it, but it became just a symbol, and the symbol has existed all over the world. That simply shows that everywhere people became alert and aware in one way or other of the ultimate synthesis in the *sahasrar*. Jews use the skullcap—it is exactly on the *sahasrar*. Hindus allow a bunch of hair that they call *choti*, the peak, to grow exactly on the spot where the *sahasrar* is, or has to be. There are a few Christian societies which shave just that part of the head. When a master blesses a disciple, he puts his hand on the *sahasrar*. And if the disciple is really receptive, surrendered, he will suddenly feel an upsurge of energy, running from the sex centre to the *sahasrar*.

Sometimes when I touch your head and you suddenly become sexual, don't be afraid, don't shrink back, because that is how it should be. The energy is at the sex centre. It starts uncoiling itself. You become afraid, you shrink, you repress it—you wonder what is happening. Becoming sexual at the feet of your master seems a little awkward and embarrassing. It is not. Allow it, let it be, and soon you will see it has passed the first centre and the second and, if you are surrendered, within a second the energy is moving at the *sahasrar* and you will have a feeling of a new opening within you. That is why a disciple is supposed to bow his head down—so that the master can touch the head.

The last synthesis is of object and subject, the outer and inner, again. In a sexual orgasm outer and inner meet, but only momentarily. In *sahasrar* they meet permanently. That is why I say one has to travel from sex to *samadhi*. In sex 99 per cent is sex, 1 per cent is *sahasrar*; in *sahasrar* 99 per cent is *sahasrar*, 1 per cent is sex. Both are joined, they are bridged, by deep currents of energy. So if you have enjoyed sex, don't make your abode there. Sex is just a glimpse of *sahasrar*. *Sahasrar* is going to deliver a thousand-fold, a million-fold, of that bliss to you.

The outer and the inner meet, 'I' and 'thou' meet, man

and woman meet, yin and yang meet; and the meeting is absolute. Then there is no parting, there is no divorce.

This is called yoga. Yoga means the meeting of the two into one. In Christianity mystics have called it *unio mystica*. That is the exact translation of yoga—*unio mystica*: the mysterious union. At the *sahasrar* the alpha and the omega meet, the beginning and the end. The beginning is in the sex centre, sex is your alpha; *samadhi* is your omega. And unless alpha and omega meet, unless you have attained this supreme union, you will remain miserable, because that is your destiny. You will remain unfulfilled. You can be fulfilled only at this highest peak of synthesis.

Now, the sutras:

> *Performing* samyama *on their power of cognition,*
> *real nature, egoism, all pervasiveness, and functions*
> *brings mastery over the sense organs.*

The first thing to be understood is that you have senses but you have lost sensitivity. Your senses are dull, almost dead. They are there hanging with you, but energy is not flowing in them; they are not live limbs of your being. Something has deadened within you, has become cold, blocked. It has happened to the whole of humanity because of thousands of years of repression. Thousands of years of conditioning and ideologies which are against the body have crippled you.

So the first thing to be done is: your senses should become really alive and sensitive. Only then can they be mastered. You see but you don't see deeply. You see only the surface of things. You touch but your touch has no warmth; nothing flows in and out from your touch. You hear—the birds go on singing and you hear and you say, 'yes, I am hearing', and you are not wrong—you are hearing—but it never reaches the very core of your being. It does not go dancing within you; it doesn't help a flowering, an unfolding, within you.

These senses have to be rejuvenated again. Yoga is not against the body, remember. Yoga says go beyond the body, but it is not against the body. Yoga says use the body, don't be used by it; but it is not against the body. Yoga says the body is your temple. You are in the body, and the body is so beautiful an organism, so complex and so subtle, so mysterious, and so many dimensions open through it. And those are the only doors and windows through which you will reach existence. So don't deaden them; make them more alive. Let them vibrate, pulsate, and, as Stanley Keleman puts it, 'let them "stream"'. That is exactly the right word: let them flow like a stream, rushing. If your hand is rushing like a stream of energy, you will feel a tingling sensation, you will feel something inside the hand is flowing and wants to make contact, wants to be connected.

When you love a man or a woman and you take his or her hand in your hand, if your hand is not streaming, this love is not going to be of any use. If your hand is not jumping and throbbing with energy and pouring energy into your woman or into your man, then this love is almost dead from the very beginning. Then sooner or later you will be finished. It will take a little time to recognize because your mind is also dull; otherwise you would not enter into it, because it is already dead. For what are you entering? You take time to recognize things because your sensitivity, brilliance and intelligence is so clouded and confused.

Only a streaming love can become a source of blissfulness, of joy, of delight. But for that you will need senses streaming.

Sometimes you have that glimpse; everybody had it when he or she was a child. Watch a child running after a butterfly. He is streaming, as if any moment he can jump out of his body. Watch a child when he is looking at a rose. See his eyes—the brilliance, the light that comes to his eyes. He is streaming. His eyes are almost dancing on the petals of the flower. This is the way to be: river-like. And only then is it possible to master these senses.

In fact, people have had a very wrong attitude. They think that if you want to master your senses you have to make them almost dead. But then what is the point of mastering them? You can kill, and you are the master. You can sit on the corpse. But what is the point of being a master of a corpse? It looked easier: first kill them, and then you can master them. If the body feels too strong or fast, make it weak, and then you start feeling that you are the master—but you have killed the body. Remember, *life* has to be mastered, not dead things. They will not be of any use.

But this has been found to be a shortcut, so all the religions of the world have been using it. Destroy your body by and by. Disconnect yourself from the body. Don't be in contact, remove yourself away, become indifferent. When your body is like a dead tree, no longer does it have leaves, no longer does it flower, no longer do birds come to rest on it. It is just a dead stump. Of course you can master it, but now what are you going to gain from this mastery?

This is the problem; that is why people don't understand what Patanjali means.

Your eyes see, your ears hear, your nose smells, your tongue tastes, your hands make contact—that is their power of cognition.

But they have to be powerful. Otherwise you will not

be able to even feel what power is. These senses have to be so full of power, so high with power, that you can perform *samyama*, you can meditate upon them.

Right now when you look at a flower, the flower is there, but have you ever felt your eyes? You see the flower, but have you felt the power of your eyes? It should be there because you are using your eyes to see the flower. And of course eyes are more beautiful than any flower because all flowers have to come through the eyes. It is through the eyes that you have become aware of the world of flowers, but have you ever felt the power of the eyes? They are almost dull, dead. They have become passive, just like windows, receptive. They don't go to their object.

Power means being active. Power means your eyes going and almost touching the flowers, your ears going and almost touching the songs of the birds, your hands going with the total energy in you, focussed there and touching your beloved. Or you are lying down on the grass, and your whole body, full of power, meeting in contact with the grass, having a dialogue with the grass. Or you are swimming in the river and whispering with the river and listening to the whispers of the river—connected, in communion. But power is needed.

So the first thing I would like you to do is—when you see, really see; become the eyes. Forget everything. Let your whole energy flow through the eyes. And your eyes will be cleaned, bathed in an inner shower, and you will be able to see that these trees are no longer the same; the greenery is no longer the same. It has become greener, as if dust has disappeared from it. The dust was not on the trees, it was on your eyes. And you will see for the first time and you will hear for the first time. Then you will be able to see what the real nature of your senses is. It is divine. Your body embodies the divine. It is the divine who has looked through your eyes.

Jesus went on saying to his disciples, 'If you have ears, listen. If you have eyes, see.' They were not all blind, and they were not all deaf. What did he mean? He meant that you have almost become deaf and blind. You see and yet you don't see. You hear yet you don't hear. It is not a *power*, it is not energy, it is not vital.

I remember Meister Eckhart's famous saying. He is the only one in the whole of Christianity who comes very close to Zen masters. The day he realized and became enlightened, his friends and disciples and brothers asked, 'What have you seen?' He laughed. He said, 'I have not seen the divine. It has seen itself through me. The divine has seen itself through me. These eyes are the divine's. And what a game, what a play. It has seen itself through me.'

When you really feel the nature of your senses, you will feel it is divine. It is existence who has moved through your hand. It is existence's hand. All hands are its. It is existence who has loved through you. All love affairs belong to existence. How can it be otherwise? Hindus call it *leela*—a play. It is existence who is calling you through the cuckoo, and it is existence who is listening through you. It is alone spread all over.

The word 'egoism' has to be understood because in Sanskrit we have three words for the ego and in English there is only one word. That creates difficulty. The Sanskrit word in the sutra is *asmita*, so let me first explain it to you.

There are three words: *ahankar, asmita, atma*. All mean 'I'. *Ahankar* can be translated as the 'ego'—the very gross, too much emphasis on 'I'. For *asmita* there is no word in English. *Asmita* means am-ness. I am; in ego the emphasis is on 'I'; in *asmita* the emphasis is on 'am'. Am-ness is purer than ego. Ego is still there, but in a very different form. In *atma*, even am-ness has disappeared. In the ego, 'I am'; in *asmita* only 'am'; in *atma* even that has disappeared. In *atma* there is pure being, neither I nor am-ness.

In this sutra *asmita* is used, am-ness. Remember, the ego is of the mind; senses have no ego. They have a certain am-ness but no ego. The ego is of the mind. Your eyes don't have any ego; your hands don't have any ego. They have a certain am-ness. That is why if your skin has to be replaced and somebody else's skin is planted on you, your body will reject it, because the body knows 'it is not mine'. So your skin has to be replaced from some other part of your own body. If it is not your own skin, the body will reject it. The body has no 'I' but it has an am-ness.

If you need blood, anybody's blood won't do. The body will not accept all sorts of blood, but only a particular blood. It has its own am-ness. That will be accepted; some other blood will be rejected. The body has its own feel of its being—*very* unconscious, *very* subtle and pure, but it is there.

Your eyes are yours, just like your thumbprints. Everything yours is yours. Now physiologists say that everybody's heart is different, of a different shape. In the books of physiology the picture that you will find is not a real picture. It is just an average. It is just imagined. Each person's heart has a different shape. Even each person's kidney has a different shape. These parts all have their signatures; everybody is so unique. That is the am-ness.

You will never be here again, you have never been before, so move cautiously and alertly and happily. Just think of the glory of your being. Just think that you are so superb and unique. Existence has vested much in you—never imitate, because that will be a betrayal. Be yourself. Let that be your religion. All else is politics. Don't be a Hindu, don't be a Mohammedan, don't be a Christian. Be religious, but there is only one religion, and that is just being yourself, authentically yourself.

Meditation brings mastery; nothing else brings mastery except meditation. If you meditate on your eye, first you will see the rose; by and by you will be able to see the eye that is seeing. Then you have become a master of the eye. Once you have seen the seeing eye, you have become a master. Now you can use all its energies; and they are all-pervasive. Your eyes are not as limited as you think them to be. They can see many more things which you have not seen. They can penetrate many more mysteries that you have not even dreamt about. But you are not master of your eyes, and you have used them in a very haphazard way, not knowing what you are doing.

And with objects too much in contact, you have forgotten the subjectivity of your eyes. It happens if you keep company with someone—by and by you become influenced by them. You have been in contact with objects too much and you have forgotten the inner quality of your senses. You see things, but you never see your seeing. You hear the songs, but you never hear the subtle vibration that goes on within you, the sound of your being.

Let me tell you an anecdote:

An extremely confident tramp had enormous nerve. He had just completed a very large meal in a swanky restaurant when he announced to the manager, 'My good man, I have really enjoyed your food, but unfortunately I cannot afford to pay for any of it at all. I have not a penny to my name.'

'Now don't get angry,' he continued. 'I am by profession a beggar, as you may see. I happen to be an extremely talented beggar too. I can go out and within one hour get the money I owe you for this meal. Naturally though, you cannot trust me to come back, and this I fully understand. You would be most welcome to accompany me, but can a man like you, a well-known restaurant owner, afford to be seen with a man of my calibre? No. So I have, sir, the perfect solution to our little problem. I will wait here and you go out and beg until you have the cost of this meal.'

If you keep company with a beggar, you will become a beggar. He will suggest in a thousand and one ways for you to become like him.

We have kept company with objects so long that we have forgotten our subjectivity. We have remained focussed outwardly so long on things that we have forgotten that we are persons. This long association with objects has completely destroyed your image of yourself. You have to come back home.

In yoga, when you start seeing your seeing eye, you come across a subtle energy. They call it *tanmatra*. When you can see your eye seeing, just hidden behind the eyes you see a tremendous energy—that is *tanmatra*, the energy of the eye. Behind the ear you see tremendous energy accumulated—*tanmatra* of the ear. Behind your genital organs you see tremendous energy accumulated—*tanmatra* of sexuality. And so on and so forth. Everywhere, behind your senses there is a pool of energy, unused. Once you know it, you can pour that energy into your eyes, and then you will see visions which only sometimes poets or painters see. Then you will hear sounds which only sometimes musicians hear. And then you will touch things, which only sometimes in rare moments lovers know how to touch.

You will become alive, streaming.

Ordinarily you have been taught to repress your senses,

not to know them. It is very foolish, but very convenient.

I have heard:

After a rural wedding, the bride and the groom climbed into the wagon and set out for their farm home. About a mile down the road, the horse stumbled. 'That is one!' shouted the groom.

They continued on and the horse stumbled again. 'That is two!' shouted the groom.

As they neared the farm, the horse stumbled again. 'That is three!' shouted the groom and, seizing a gun from behind the seat, put a bullet through the horse's brain.

The bride sat aghast. Then, in no uncertain terms, she told her new husband what she thought of his action. He sat quietly until she subsided, then pointed at her and shouted, 'That is one!'

The couple lived happily for sixty years.

But that happiness cannot be real happiness. It is easy to repress at the point of a gun, but then what sort of love will there be between these two people? The gun will always stand in between, and the wife will always be afraid that at any moment he is going to say 'Now this is two! Now this is three!' and finished!

That is what you have done with your senses, with your body—you have repressed it. But you were helpless. I don't say that you are responsible for repressing it. You were brought up in such a way that nobody allowed your senses freedom. In the name of love, only repression continues. The mothers, the fathers, the society, they go on repressing. By and by they teach you a trick, and the trick is not to accept yourself, but to deny. Everything has to be channelled into conformity. Your wilderness has to be thrown into the dark part of your soul and a small corner has to be clean, like a drawing room, where you can see people, meet people, and live and forget all about your wilder being: your real existence. Your fathers and your mothers are not responsible either, because they were brought up in the same way.

So nobody is responsible. But once you know it, and you don't do anything, *then* you become responsible. Being near me, I am going to make you very, very responsible, because you will know it, and then if you don't do anything, then you cannot throw the responsibility on anybody else. Then you are going to be responsible!

Now you know about how you have destroyed your senses, and you also know how to revive them. Do something. Throw the gun, the repressive mind, completely. Unblock yourself. Start flowing again, start connecting again with your being, start connecting with your senses again. You are like a disconnected telephone line. Everything looks perfectly okay, the telephone is there but the line is disconnected. Your eyes are there, your hands are there, your ears are there, but the line is disconnected. Reconnect it. If it can be disconnected, it can be reconnected. Others have disconnected it because they were also taught in the same way, but you can reconnect it.

All my meditations are to give you a streaming energy. That is why I call them dynamic methods. Old meditations were just to sit silently, not to do anything. I give you active methods because when you are streaming with energy you can sit silently, that will do, but right now first you have to become alive.

> *From this follows instantaneous cognition*
> *without the use of the body,*
> *and complete mastery over* pradhana, prakriti, *the*
> *material world.*

If you can see *tanmatras*, the subtle energies of your senses, you will become capable of using your cognition without the grosser instruments. If you know that behind the eye there is an accumulated pool of energy, you can close your eyes and use that energy directly. Then you will be able to see without opening your eyes. That is what telepathy, clairvoyance, clairaudience is.

In Russia there is a woman who has been investigated scientifically, who stands twenty feet away from any object and starts pulling it, just by energy. She makes movements with her hands, twenty feet away, as you have seen a hypnotist making passes; she simply draws, gestures. Within fifteen minutes, things start moving towards her. She has not touched them. Much investigation has been done to find what happens. And that woman loses at least half a pound of weight in a half-hour experiment. Certainly, she is losing some sort of energy.

This is what yoga calls *tanmatra*. Ordinarily you use the energy through the hand, when you pick something up: a stone, a rock. You carry it; you use the same energy through the hand. But if you know the energy directly, you can drop the use of the hand. The energy can move the object directly. The same way, telepathy: you can hear or read people's thoughts or can see faraway scenes. Once you know the *tanmatra*, the subtle energy that is being used by your eyes, the eyes can be discarded. Once you know that it is not really the sense that is functioning but the energy, you are freed of the sense.

I have heard a story:

So this guy called Cohen & Goldberg, wholesalers.

'Put me through to Mr Cohen, please.'

'I am afraid Mr Cohen has gone out, sir,' said the switchboard girl.

'Then get me Mr Goldberg.'

'I am afraid Mr Goldberg is tied up at present, sir.'

'Okay, I will call back later.'

Ten minutes later: 'Mr Goldberg, please.'

'I am afraid Mr Goldberg is still tied up, sir.'

'I will call back.'

Half an hour later: 'Get me Mr Goldberg.'

'I am terribly sorry, sir, but Mr Goldberg is still tied up.'

'I will call back.'

Another half an hour later: 'Goldberg!'

'I have dreadful news for you, sir. Mr Goldberg is still tied up.'

'But look, this is ridiculous. How can you run a business like that? One partner is out all morning and the other is tied up for hours on end. What is going on there?'

'Well, you see, sir, whenever Mr Cohen goes out he ties up Mr Goldberg.'

This is what is happening inside you as well. Whenever you go out, through the eyes, through the hands, through your genital organs, through your ears—whenever you go out, a certain type of bondage and tying is created continuously. By and by you become tight with the particular sense—eyes, ears—because that is where you repeatedly go out from. By and by you forget the energy that is going out.

This getting into bondage with senses is the whole world, the *samsar*. How to untie yourself from the senses? And once you are tied up with the senses, you start thinking in terms of them. You forget yourself.

Another story:

A disciple wanted very much to renounce the world and

follow his guru, but he said that his wife and family loved him too much and he was unable to leave his home.

The guru came up with a plan. The man was taught certain yogic secrets so that he could give the appearance to all who looked upon his body that he was deceased. The next day the man followed the instructions and his body was besieged with the wailings and sobbing of his wife and family.

The guru appeared at the door in the guise of a magician and told the family that if they loved this man so much he could bring him back to life. He said that the man would live if someone would die in his place by drinking the potion he had.

Each member of the family had an excuse that made it necessary to keep his own life, and the wife added, 'Anyway, he is already dead; we will manage.'

At this the yogi stood up and said, 'Woman, if you can live without me, then I can go with my guru.' He faced the teacher and said, 'Let us go, sir, revered master. I will follow you.'

The whole attachment to the senses is as if you *are* the senses, as if you cannot live without them, as if your whole life is confined to them. But you are not confined to them. You can renounce them, and you can live still, and live on a higher plane. Difficult! Just as if you want to persuade a seed, 'Die, and soon a beautiful plant will be born.' How can it believe? It will be dead. And no seed has ever known that by its death a new sprout comes up, a new life arises. So how do you believe it? Or say you go near an egg and you want to persuade the bird within to come out—but how is the bird to believe that there is any possibility of life without the egg? Or say you talk to a child inside the womb of a mother and tell him, 'come out, don't be afraid'—but he knows nothing outside the womb. The womb has been his whole life; he knows only that much. He is afraid. The same is the situation when, surrounded by the senses, we live in a sort of confinement, an imprisonment.

One has to be a little daring and courageous. Right now, wherever you are and whatsoever you are, nothing is happening to you. Then take the risk. Move into the unknown. Try to find out a new way of life.

Up to now you have been possessed by the material world. Once you know that you have your own energy, totally independent from the material world, you become a master. No more does the world possess you; you possess it. Only those who renounce become the real masters.

> *Only after the awareness of the distinction*
> *between* satva *and* purusha
> *does supremacy and knowledge arise*
> *over all states of existence.*

And the subtlest discrimination has to be made between *satva* and *purusha*—intelligence and awareness. It is very easy to separate yourself from the body. The body is so gross you can feel it, but you cannot be it. You must be inside it. It is easy to see that you cannot be the eyes. You must be someone hidden behind who looks through the eyes; otherwise who will look through the eyes? Your glasses cannot look. Behind the glasses, eyes are needed. But your eyes are also like glasses. They *are* glasses; they cannot look. You are needed somewhere behind to look.

But the subtlest identification is with intelligence. Your power to think, your power of intellect, understanding, that is the subtlest thing. It is very difficult to discriminate between awareness and intelligence. But they can be discriminated.

By and by, step by step, first know that you are not the body. Let that understanding grow deep, crystallize. Then know that you are not the senses. Let that understanding grow, crystallize. Then know that you are not the *tanmatras*, the energy pools behind the senses. Let that grow and crystallize. And then you will be able to see that intelligence is also a pool of energy. It is the common pool, in which eyes, ears and hands all pour their energy. All the senses are like rivers, and intelligence is the central thing, into which they bring information and pour.

Whatsoever your mind knows is given by the senses. You have seen colours: your mind knows. If you are colour-blind, if you cannot see the colour green, then your mind does not know anything about green. Bernard Shaw lived his whole life unaware that he was colour-blind. It is very difficult to come to know it, but one accidental incident allowed him to become aware. On one of his birthdays somebody presented him a suit, but the tie was missing, so he went to the market to find a tie which could fit with the suit. The suit was green, and he started purchasing a yellow tie. His secretary was watching, and she said, 'What are you doing? It won't go. The suit is green and the tie is yellow.' He said, 'Is there any difference between these two?' For seventy years he has lived, not knowing that he cannot see yellow. He sees green. Whether it is yellow or green, both the colours look green. Yellow was not part of his mind; the eyes never poured that information into the mind.

The eyes are like servants, information collectors, roaming all over the world, collecting things, pouring into the mind. They go on feeding the mind; the mind is the central pool.

First you have to become aware that you are not the eye, not even the energy that is hidden behind the eye, and then you will be able to see that every sense is pouring into the mind. You are not this mind, also. You *are* the one who is seeing it being poured. You are just standing on the bank, while all the rivers pouring into the ocean—you are the watcher, the witness.

Swami Ram has said: 'Science is difficult to define, but perhaps the most essential feature of it involves the study of something which is external to the observer. The techniques of meditation offer an approach which allows one to be external to one's own internal states.'

'The techniques of meditation offer an approach which allows one to be external to one's own internal states'— and the ultimate of meditation is to know that whatsoever you can know, you are not it. Whatsoever can be reduced to a known object, you are not it, because you cannot be reduced to an object. You remain eternally subject—the knower. And the knower can never be reduced to the known.

This is *purusha*, awareness. This is the final understanding that arises out of yoga. Meditate over it.

4

Miracles Don't Happen

Why am I always afraid of being old?
Show me how I can get rid of it.

LIFE, IF RIGHTLY lived, if really lived, is never afraid of death. If you have lived your life, you will welcome death. It will come like a rest, like a great sleep. If you have peaked, climaxed in your life, then death is a beautiful rest, a benediction. But if you have not lived, then of course death creates fear. If you have not lived, then certainly death is going to take time from your hands, all future opportunities to live. If in the past you have not lived, and there is going to be no future, then fear arises. Fear arises not because of death but because of the unlived life.

And because of the fear of death, old age also gives fear, because that is the first step of death. Otherwise, old age is also beautiful. It is a ripening of your being, it is maturity, growth. If you live moment to moment, rise to all the challenges that life gives, and you use all the opportunities that life opens, and if you dare to adventure into the unknown, then old age is a maturity. Otherwise old age is a disease.

Unfortunately many people simply age; they become old, without any maturity corresponding to it. Then old age is a burden. You have aged in the body, but your consciousness has remained juvenile. You have aged in your body, but you have not matured in your inner life. The inner light is missing, and death is coming close every day; of course you will tremble and you will be afraid and great anguish will rise in you.

Those who live rightly, they accept old age with a deep welcome, because old age simply says that now they are coming to flower, that they are coming to a fruition, that now they will be able to share whatsoever they have attained.

Ordinarily old age is ugly because it is simply a disease. Your body has not matured; it has only become more and more ill, weakened, impotent. Otherwise old age is the most beautiful time of life. All the foolishness of childhood gone, all the fever and passion of young age gone . . . serenity arises, a silence, a meditation, a *samadhi*.

Old age is tremendously beautiful, and it should be so because the whole of life moves towards it. It should be the peak.

How can the peak be in the beginning? How can the peak be in the middle? But if you think your childhood is your peak, as many people think, then of course the whole life will be a suffering because you have attained your peak— now everything will be a declining, coming down. If you think young age is the peak, as many people think, then of course after thirty-five you will become sad, depressed, because every day you will be losing and losing and losing, and gaining nothing. The energy will be lost, you will weaken, diseases will enter into your being, and death will start knocking at the door. The home will disappear, and the hospital will appear. How can you be happy? But in the East we have never thought that childhood or youth is the peak. The peak waits for the very end.

And if life flows rightly, by and by you reach higher and higher peaks. Death is the ultimate peak that life attains, the crescendo.

But why are we missing life? Why are we aging and not maturing? Somewhere something has gone wrong, somewhere you have been put on a wrong track—somewhere you have agreed to be put on a wrong track. That agreement has to be broken; that contract has to be burned. That is what I call *sanyas*: an understanding that up to now I have lived in a wrong way; I have compromised.

When you were small children, you compromised. You sold your being for nothing—what you have gained is simply nothing, just rubbish. For small things you have lost your soul. You have agreed to be somebody else other than yourself; that is where you missed your path. Your mother wanted you to become somebody, your father wanted you to become somebody, the society wanted you to become somebody—and you agreed. And by and by you decided not to be yourself. And since then you have been pretending to be somebody else.

You cannot mature because that somebody else cannot mature. It is false. If I wear a mask, the mask cannot mature. It is dead. My face can mature, but not my mask. And only your mask goes on aging. Hiding behind the mask, you are not growing. You can grow only if you accept yourself; that you are going to be yourself, nobody else.

The rosebush has agreed to become an elephant; the elephant has agreed to become a rosebush. The eagle is worried, almost consulting a psychiatrist, because she wants to become a dog; and the dog is hospitalized because he tried to fly like an eagle. This is what has happened to humanity. The greatest calamity is to agree to be somebody else: you can never mature.

You can never mature like somebody else. You can only be concerned about what people say. What is their opinion? Who are they? You are here to be yourself, you are not here to fulfil somebody else's expectations; but everybody is trying to do that. Your father may be dead, but you are trying to fulfil a promise you have given to him. And he was trying to fulfil a promise to his own father, and so on. The foolishness goes to the very beginning.

Try to understand, take courage and take your life in your own hands. Suddenly you will see an upsurge of energy. The moment you decide, 'I am going to be myself and nobody else. Whatsoever the cost, but I am going to be myself', that very moment you will see a great change. You will feel vital. You will feel energy streaming in you, pulsating.

Unless that happens, you will be afraid of old age, because how can you avoid seeing the fact that you are wasting time and not living, and old age is coming and then you will not be able to live? How can you avoid seeing the fact that death is waiting there and every day it comes closer and closer and closer, and you have not lived yet? You are bound to be in deep anguish.

So if you ask me what to do, I will suggest the basic thing. And it is always a question of basics. Never be bothered by secondary things—because you can change them, but nothing will change. Change the basic.

'Why am I always afraid of being old? Show me how I can get rid of it.' The very question is out of fear. You want to 'get rid of it', not to understand, so of course you are going to become a victim of somebody or some ideology which can help you to get rid of it. I cannot help you to get rid of it. In fact, that is the problem. I would like you to *understand* and change your life. It is not a question of getting rid of the problem; it is a question of getting rid of your mask, of your false persona—the way you have been trying to be and which is not a true way. You are not authentic. You are not sincere towards yourself. You have been betraying your being.

So if you ask—there are priests and philosophers and demagogues—if you go and ask them how to get rid of it, they will say, 'The soul never ages. Don't be worried. Just remember that you are the soul. It is the body that ages; you are not the body.' They have consoled you. Maybe for a moment you feel good, but this is not going to help, this is not going to change you. Again tomorrow, out of the influence of the priest, you will be in the same boat.

But you never look at the priest: he himself is afraid. You never look at the philosopher: he himself is afraid.

I have heard:

The new vicar had been overworking and examination revealed that his lungs were gravely affected. The doctor told him that a long rest was absolutely essential. The vicar protested and said he could not possibly afford to leave his work.

'Well,' said the doctor. 'You have the choice of Switzerland or heaven.'

The vicar walked the room for some time and then said, 'You win, Switzerland it is.'

When it is a question of life and death, even the priest, the philosopher—people you go to ask—they have also not lived. More possibility is there that they have not lived even as much as you have lived; otherwise they could not be priests. To become a priest they have completely denied their life. To become monks, sadhus, mahatmas, they have completely denied their being and they have accepted whatsoever society wanted them to be. They have completely agreed to it. They have disagreed with themselves, their own life energy, and they have agreed with false, foolish things— appreciation, respectability.

And you go and ask them! They are themselves trembling. Deep down they are themselves afraid. They and their disciples are all in the same boat.

I have heard:

The Pope lay gravely ill in the Vatican, and a message was issued that a special announcement would be made by the Cardinal from the balcony of St. Peter's.

When the day came, the famous square was packed with the faithful. The aged Cardinal spoke in quavering tones, 'His Holiness can only be saved by a heart transplant, and I am appealing to all you good Catholics gathered here today for a donor.'

He held up a feather and continued, 'I shall drop this feather among you, and on whomsoever it falls, that person is the one chosen by Holy Providence to save the Holy Father's life.'

With that he dropped the feather . . . and all that could be heard were 20,000 devout Roman Catholics gently puffing.

Everybody is afraid. I am not going to give you any consolation. I am not going to say to you, 'The soul is eternal. Don't be worried, you never die. Only the body dies.' I know that is true, but that truth one has to earn the hard way. You cannot learn by somebody else's assertion and statement about it. It is not a statement; it is an experience. I know it is so, but it is absolutely meaningless for you.

You have not known what life is. How can you know what eternity is? You have not even been able to live in time. How can you be able to live in eternity?

One becomes aware of the deathless when one has become capable of accepting death. Through the door of death, the deathless reveals itself. Death is a way of the deathless to reveal itself to you, but in fear you close your eyes and you become unconscious.

No, I am not going to give you a method, a theory to get rid of it. It is symptomatic. It is good that it goes on indicating to you that you are living a false life. That is why the fear is there. Just take the hint, and don't try to change the symptom—rather, try to change the basic cause.

From the very beginning, every child has been misinformed, misdirected and misguided. Not knowingly, because the parents are also in the same trap; they have been misguided. For example, if a child is too energetic, the family feels uncomfortable because a too energetic child is a revolution in the home. Nothing is safe, nothing at all is safe. The energetic child will destroy everything. He has to be stopped. His energy has to be blocked; his life has to be diminished. He has to be condemned, punished, and only rewarded when he behaves. And what do you expect? You expect him to be almost an old man—not doing any harm to anything that you think is very precious. Just to save a clock or crockery or furniture you destroy the child. You destroy a newly arrived being, a gift from existence. You go on scratching the being of the child just to save the furniture from being scratched.

By and by the child is forced to follow you because he is helpless. He depends on you; his survival depends on you. Just to survive, he agrees to be dead. Just to survive . . . because you give him food and milk and care. Where will he go if you are so much against him? By and by he goes on selling his being to you. Whatsoever you say, by and by he accepts. Your rewards and your punishments are the way . . . how you misguide him.

By and by he trusts you more than his own inner voice because he knows his inner voice always leads him into trouble. His inner voice has always proved to bring punishment, so punishment and his inner voice become associated. And whenever he does not listen to the inner voice and simply follows you blindly, he is rewarded. Whenever he is himself, he is punished; whenever he is not himself, he is rewarded. The logic is clear.

By and by you distract him from his own life. By and by he forgets what his inner voice is. If you don't hear it for a long time, you cannot hear it.

Close your eyes any moment: you will hear the voice of your father, your mother, your peers, teachers, but you will never hear *your* voice. Many people come to me and they say, 'You talk about the inner voice; we never hear it.' There is a crowd. When Jesus says hate your father and mother he is not actually saying to hate your father and mother. He is saying hate the father and the mother which have become consciences within you. Hate: because that is the ugliest agreement you have made—a suicidal contract. Hate: destroy those voices, so that your voice can be freed and liberated, so that you can feel who you are and what you want to be.

In the beginning, of course, you will feel completely lost. That is what happens in meditation. Many people come to me and they say, 'We had come to find a path. On the contrary, meditations have made us feel completely lost.' It's a good indication. It shows that the grip of others is loosening. That is why you feel lost—because those voices of the others were giving you guidance, and you had started to believe in them. You have believed in them for so long that they have become your guides. Now, when you meditate, those voices are taken apart. You are freed from the trap. Again you become a child, and you don't know where to go, because all the guides have disappeared. The voice of the father is not there, the voice of the mother is not there, the teacher is not there, the school is not there; suddenly you are alone. One starts feeling scared—'Where are my guides? Where are people who were always leading me to the right path?'

In fact, nobody can lead you to the right path, because all leading is going to be wrong. No leader can be the right leader, because leading as such is wrong. Whomsoever you allow to lead you will do something harmful to you because he will start forcing something, giving you a structure; and you have to live an unstructured life, a life free of all structure and character, free of all frames, references, contacts—free in this moment from the past.

So all guides are wrong, and when they disappear, and you have believed in them for so long, suddenly you feel empty—surrounded by emptiness and all paths gone. Where do you go?

This period is a revolutionary one in the life of a being. One has to pass through it with courage. If you can remain in it, unafraid, soon you will start hearing your voice which has been repressed for so long. Soon you will start learning its language, because you have forgotten the very language. You know only the language that has been taught to you. The inner language is not verbal. It is of feelings. And all societies are against feelings because a feeling is a live thing, it is dangerous. A thought is dead; it is not dangerous. So every society has forced you into the head, pushed you from all over your body into the head.

You live only in the head. If your head is cut off and suddenly you come across your body without a head, you will not be able to recognize it. Only faces are recognized. Your whole body has shrunken, has lost lustre, softness, fluidity. It is almost a dead thing, like a wooden leg: You use it, functionally it goes on, but no life exists in it. Your whole life has gone into the head. Hung up there, you are afraid of death, because the only space in which you can live has to be all over your body. Your life has to spread and stream all over your body. It has to become a river, a flow.

A small child starts playing with his genital organs. Immediately the parents are worried—'stop it!' The worry comes from their own repressions—because they were stopped. Suddenly they become anxious, because they have been taught that this is bad. They were never allowed to touch their genital organs. How can the child be allowed? They force the child not to touch the genital organs.

What can the child do? He cannot understand why the genital organs are bad. They are as much a part of him as are his hands, his nose, his toes; he can touch every place in the body, but not the genital organs. And if he is punished again and again, of course he starts forcing his energy back from the genital organs. It should not stream there because if it streams there he wants to play with them. And it is pleasant, and nothing is wrong, the child cannot see what is wrong in it. In fact, that is the most pleasant part of the body.

But the parents are afraid, and the child can see their faces and their eyes: they were normal human beings, but the moment he touches his genital organs, they suddenly become abnormal, almost mad. Something changes in them so drastically that the child also becomes afraid that there must be something wrong. The 'something wrong' is in the mind of the parents, not in the body of the child—but what can the child do?

Just to avoid this embarrassing situation, one of the most beautiful phenomena has been repressed so deeply that women have not felt orgasm. In India women still don't know what orgasm is. They have never heard about it; in fact they know that the sexual pleasure is of the man, not of the woman. This is absurd because existence is not a male chauvinist and it is not in favour of men and against women. It has given to all, equally, but girls have been prohibited more than boys because society is male dominated. So they say, 'Boys are boys; even if you prevent them they are going to do something or other.' But girls, they have to be paradigms of culture, morality, purity, virginity. They are not allowed to touch their genital organs at all. So how is it possible to achieve orgasm later on, when the energy does not move that way?

And because the energy does not move that way, a thousand and one problems arise. Women become hysterical. Men become too obsessed with sex. Women become sad and depressed because they cannot enjoy the sexual experience. And man becomes too much interested in sex because all experiences leave something out. Man goes on feeling he is missing something—so he must have more sexual experiences, have it with many more women. That is not the problem. You will go on missing with one. You will go on missing with many. The problem is within you: your energy is not flowing through the genital organs.

And this way, the whole energy by and by is forced into the head, because the head is appreciated. We have the expression 'the head clerk', 'the head superintendent', 'the headmaster'—all 'heads'. 'Hands' is used for labourers.

'Heads' are superior beings—'heads' of states. 'Hands'? Just a manual worker, worthless. In India 'heads' are Brahmins, and the poor shudras are not even hands, but legs, feet. In Hindu scriptures it is said that God created Brahmins as heads and shudras as feet and kshatriyas (warriors) as hands, arms, strength, and vaishyas (traders) as the belly. But Brahmins are heads.

The whole world has become Brahmin. That is the problem—everybody is living in the head, and the whole body has shrunken. Just stand before a mirror some time and see what has happened to your whole body. Your face looks very alive, red with life, but your chest?—shrunken. Your belly?—almost mechanical, it goes on functioning in a mechanical way.

If people stand naked, just watching their bodies you can see what types of work they are doing in their life. If they are workers, their hands will be alive, muscular. If they are just head people—eggheads, professors, vice-chancellors, and that sort of rubbish—then you will see their heads are very shiny, red. If they are postmen and policemen, their legs will be very strong. But you will never find a full body, a whole body, because nobody is living as a total organic unity.

One should live as a total organic unity. The whole body should be reclaimed. Because through the feet you are in touch with the earth—you are grounded. If you lose your legs and their strength and they become dead limbs, you are no longer rooted in the earth. You are like a tree whose roots have become dead or rotten, weak. Then the tree cannot live long, and cannot live healthy, fully, wholly. Your feet need to be rooted in the earth; they are your roots.

Try a small experiment sometime. Stand somewhere naked—on the beach, near the river, just naked in the sun—

and start jumping, jogging, and feel your energies flowing through your feet, through your legs to the earth. Jog and feel your energies going through your legs into the earth. Then after a few minutes of jogging, just stand silently, rooted in the earth, and just feel a communion of your feet and the earth. Suddenly you will feel very, very rooted, grounded, solid. You will see the earth communicates, you will see your feet communicate. A dialogue arises between the earth and you.

This grounding has been lost. People have become uprooted; they are no longer grounded. And then they cannot live—because life belongs to the whole being, not only to the head.

They are doing experiments in a few scientific labs in the West where only heads have been kept alive. The head of a monkey has been cut from the body, and the head is attached to mechanical devices which function as the body. The head goes on thinking, dreaming. The head is not affected by it, not at all.

This is what has happened. Not only in some labs in the West—it has happened to every human being. Your whole body has become just a mechanical thing; only your head is alive. That is why so many dreams, so much thinking, so much traffic in the head. People come and ask me, 'How do I stop it?' The problem is not how to stop it. The problem is how to disperse it into the whole body. Of course, it is crowded, because the whole energy is there—and it is not meant to carry that much energy, so you go crazy.

Insanity is a disease produced by our culture; it is a cultural disease. There have existed on earth a few cultures, primitive, where madmen were not known at all, where insanity has not existed at all. You can notice it even now— insanity rarely happens in societies which are not economically very prosperous, educationally where the calamity of universal education has not happened yet, where people are still not just in their heads but in other parts also. The more a society becomes head-oriented, the more insanity there is.

It is as if in a 110-volt wire you are trying to force a 1000-volt current—everything will go berserk. The head needs a small energy to function well. If there is too much energy in the head, then it continues working, it knows no end, because how do you dissipate that energy? It goes on thinking and thinking and thinking, and dreaming and dreaming, day and night, year in, year out it goes on and on. Just think: only this much is your life.

Then of course one becomes afraid of old age. Time is passing. Of course one becomes naturally afraid of death. Death is coming any moment and you have been just revolving in the head. Nowhere else have you moved; the whole territory of life has remained untouched.

Live; move all over the body. Accept it with deep love; almost fall in love with your body. It is a divine gift, a temple where existence has decided to reside. Then there will be no fear of old age; you will start maturing. Your experiences will mature you, and then old age will not be like a disease. It will be a beautiful phenomenon. The whole life is a preparation for it. How can it be a disease? Your whole life you move towards it. It is a crescendo, the last song and dance you are going to do.

And never wait for any miracle. You will have to do something. The mind says something or other will happen and everything will be okay. It is not going to happen that way. Miracles don't happen.

Let me tell you a story:

Abe Cohen had both his legs broken in an accident.

The bones mended and Abe sued the responsible company for damages, alleging that he was permanently crippled and would have to remain in a wheelchair all his life. The insurance company employed surgeons to assess the situation. They reported that the bones had healed perfectly, that Cohen was well able to walk and that he was simply malingering.

However, when it came to court the judge took pity on the boy in the wheelchair and awarded him 10,000 pounds in damages. Abe was later wheeled up to the head office, to collect his check.

'Mr Cohen,' said the manager. 'Don't think that you will get away with this. We know that you are malingering. And let me tell you that we are going to keep a huge dossier on you. We are going to watch you night and day. We are going to photograph you, and if we produce evidence that you can walk, not only will you have to repay the damages but you will also be had up for perjury.'

'Mr Manager, I am permanently crippled and in this wheelchair.'

'Very well, here is the check for 10,000 pounds. What do you intend to do with it?'

'Well, Mr Manager, my wife and I, we have always wanted to travel. So we are starting out at the top of Norway and going through Scandinavia,' he motioned down with his fingers for effect. 'Then Switzerland, Italy, Greece—and I don't care that your agents and spies are following after me; I am crippled and in my wheelchair. Naturally we are going to Israel, then Persia and India and across to Japan,' he motioned for effect. 'And then Philippines—and I am still in my wheelchair so I don't care about your spies that are following me with their cameras. And from there we are going all across Australia and then to South America and all the way up to Mexico,' he motions the route. 'And the US—and remember that I am still crippled and in my wheelchair, so what is the use of your spies with their cameras?—and Canada. And from there we are going across to France, where we are going to visit a place called Lourdes, and there you will see a miracle!'

But in actual life, miracles don't happen. There is no Lourdes for you. If you are crippled you have to do something—because it is you who have crippled yourself, by accepting something which is absolutely foolish.

But I know you had to accept it. To survive, you decided to remain dead. To survive, you sold your being.

But now there is no need to continue in that stupid thing. You can come out of it.

> *Most of the time I feel sexual and my eyes*
> *remain seeking the other.*
>
> *And also I am too much in the mind.*
> *As far as I understand myself these three are*
> *my basic problems. I remain covered in the*
> *clouds of these problems so that I cannot listen*
> *to you as I should.*
>
> *Please guide me.*

These are not problems. You have made them problems. And once you look at a simple thing as a problem, it becomes a problem—not that it is. *Your* look, *your* attitude makes it a problem.

'Most of the time I feel sexual and my eyes remain seeking

the other.' So what is the problem in it? Where is the problem? It is as if a hungry man thinks of food and goes on looking for restaurants. What is wrong in it? Will you say that he is in a problem and he has to get out of it? He will die if he gets out of his problem; he has to find food. Love is food, a very subtle food.

'Most of the time I feel sexual and my eyes remain seeking the other'— it is natural! You are searching for food, and you are hungry. But people have taught you that sex is a problem. It is not. It is pure energy. It is divine. It has nothing like a problem in it.

You can create a problem if you don't accept the energy, if you don't flow with it. And I know that if you flow with it, one day you will transcend. You will go higher, you will ride on it and you will reach higher and higher. It is a beautiful energy, which can take you to the very ultimate. But if you make a problem of it, you will remain obsessed with it forever. And the more you fight with it, the more the sexual energy will fight back. It has to fight back, because it is survival energy.

You are made of sexual energy. If your father and mother had thought that it is a problem, you would not have been here. You are out of a 'problem'; you exist because of a 'problem'. Because your father and mother could not solve the 'problem', that is why you are here.

My observation is that people who think of sex as a problem can never be respectful to their parents. How can they be? Just look. It is simple arithmetic. How can you be respectful to your father? He was doing something nasty to your mother! In fact, you would like to kill the guy immediately. And how can you respect your mother? She is also a sexual being, as any ordinary woman, just animalistic. How can you touch the feet of your mother? Impossible!

Unless you accept your sex as a gift, a divine gift, you cannot respect your father and mother.

Gurdjieff used to say to his disciples—he had written it on his house—that unless you respect your father and mother, don't enter here. Looks very ordinary—could not a man like Gurdjieff find a better thing to write? But he has said many things in a simple way. Only a person who accepts sex energy totally can respect his father and mother. Otherwise you can pretend; you cannot respect.

And if you think sex is a problem, a disease, something to get rid of, will you be able to love your children? How can you love your children? They come out of a problem, out of a disease. You will hate them. You may pretend that you love them, but you know that they are actualizations of your problem. They will always indicate towards you as a sexual being. They will always go on as a proof in the world that you were animalistic, that you could not get beyond sex. They will be a proof, a permanent proof of your degradation.

No, I would like to tell you, sex is not a problem. It is pure energy. And if you avoid it, then of course you will be continuously looking. Then it will become an obsession. Then you will be completely possessed by it and it will become a perversion; then whatsoever you will see, you will see only sex in it, nothing else. And you can get so obsessed you can go mad.

Freud has said that out of every 100 people who go insane, at least ninety are certainly because of sex—repressed sex. Sex has to be understood, has to be creatively used. It is vital life, fire, alive. You are made of it, everybody is made of it.

To avoid this, Christians have been trying to prove that Jesus came out of a 'virgin' Mary—just to avoid answering how Jesus can come out of an ordinary sexual love affair. And they know that they have not been able to prove it.

I was reading a story:

A young, beautiful woman came to a physician. The physician examined her and said, 'Miss, you are pregnant.'

The woman said, 'No, never, it cannot be. It is impossible; I have never been with a man, so how can it be?'

The physician said, 'But it is absolutely certain.'

The woman denied it. She said, 'It is impossible, it cannot be. I have never been with any man.'

Then the physician said, 'Wait, let me pack up my things. I am coming with you.'

The woman said, 'What? For what?'

He said, 'I have heard that three wise men from the East had come to see the Virgin Mary. I'm not going to miss it! I am coming; I want to see those three wise men.'

Just to avoid an embarrassing situation . . . Jesus, out of a sexual love affair? But this simply shows the foolishness of the followers.

We have never done that in India. We accept Buddha, Mahavira, Ram, Krishna—all were born out of sexual love affairs. We have never thought in terms of sex being animalistic. Even a Buddha is born out of it. We know that a lotus is much different from the mud out of which it comes, but it comes *out* of the mud. The mud has to be respected; otherwise all lotuses will disappear. Yes, the water is muddy, but you have to live it, you have to go through it, you have to pass through it, to flower like a lotus on top of it, far away. Nobody can imagine that the lotus comes out of the dirty mud. It is a transformed form.

This is the whole effort of Patanjali: to tell you that from the sex centre to the *sahasrar* it is the same energy—moving through new transformations, at each centre achieving a new vision, a new potentiality, a new wing, flowering, with more and more petals. At the sex centre there is a lotus—a lotus with four petals, but a lotus. At the *sahasrar* it becomes a lotus with a thousand petals, but still a lotus—a thousand petals, as if millions of suns and moons were meeting. A great communion and synthesis of energy—but of the same energy. The same energy has come of age, has grown, flowered.

So the first thing I would like to say to you: please, don't take sex as a problem. It is not. Otherwise it will become a problem.

If you try to avoid it in your life because of some stupid teachings that have been thrown at you and you have been conditioned by them, it will become a problem. It will haunt you. It will become a ghost, continuously with you and talking to you. It will become an inner talk; and you will be looking everywhere with a deeply dissatisfied being. You will become a beggar, begging and begging—and feeling guilty and feeling bad, like a criminal. Just because of an attitude. It seems that you have been influenced too much by religious people, by the church, by the temple, by the priest.

Let me tell you an anecdote:

An old-time physician whose son had just graduated from medical school decided to pass on some tips about the profession. One day his son accompanied his father while he was making his hospital rounds. The first patient they called on was advised by the father to cut down on smoking. 'How did you manage to come to that conclusion?' asked the son.

'Just look around the room and observe the large number of cigarette ends,' was the answer.

The second patient was told to stop eating so much chocolate. Again, the new doctor was bewildered. 'How come?' he said.

'You don't look,' said the father. 'If you did, then you would notice the large number of chocolate boxes all over the place.'

'I think I have got the idea now,' said the son. 'Let me try the next one.'

A woman, who was the third patient, was informed by the son to cut down on things involving the church, religion and priests. The amazed father asked his son what led him to that strange conclusion, since the church had not even been mentioned in the conversation, and you cannot find churches all over the place.

'Well, Dad, it was like this,' said the son. 'Did you notice that I dropped the thermometer? When I bent down to pick it up, I could not help noticing the preacher under the bed.'

That is what I also notice: under your bed is the preacher, over your bed is the preacher, all around the place are temples and churches. Cut down, become a little freer.

'Most of the time I feel sexual and my eyes remain seeking the other. And also I am too much in the mind.' You have to be then, because if you fight with sex, where else will you go? Then sex will become a mind thing. It will move into the head. You will think about it, fantasize about it, dream about it. And those dreams cannot be satisfying because just dreams cannot be satisfying. You can go on fantasizing about food and being invited to the palaces of the kings, but that is not going to help. When you will be out of a dream you will again feel hungry; in fact, even more so.

After the dream you will feel more dissatisfied because you are avoiding an actuality, a reality of life; a fact, which has to be accepted, used and creatively transformed.

I know one day it is possible your energy will move in *sahasrar* but let it move as a mature energy. One day sex will simply disappear from your life; then you will not think about it. Then it will no longer be a fantasy to you. It will simply disappear. When you have achieved the higher orgasm of the same energy, the lower orgasms have no appeal. But up to then it is going to become a head thing.

And it is good if sex is in the genitals because that is the right place for it to be. If it is in the head, then you are in a mess. Gurdjieff used to say to his disciples that if each chakra functions where it should function, a man remains healthy. When chakras overlap, the natural locus is lost and energy moves in a haphazard way. If you make windows in people's heads, you will find their genital organs, because sex has moved there; and of course if you are in a mess, there is no wonder about it. It has to be so.

Bring your energy to the natural centre: then it functions well, and then you can even hear the humming sound of the whole functioning of the organism. It is just like a beautifully functioning car: you drive and you can feel the humming sound surrounding you.

But when things go wrong, then of course you are topsy-turvy, upside down. Nothing is where it should be. Everything is missing from its natural centre and is found somewhere, overlapping, hiding, escaping. You become a chaos. And this is what insanity is.

I have heard:

A priest died and found himself at the Pearly Gates. As they slowly opened to admit him, a tremendous fanfare was sounded, and all the angels and archangels, cherubim and seraphim, thrones and dominions, saints and martyrs, were paraded in serried ranks to do him honour.

'Well, I am flattered,' said the priest to St. Peter. 'Do you arrange this reception for every priest who comes to heaven?'

'Oh, no,' said St. Peter. 'It is just that you are the first one to get here.'

Even I suspect that. Priests cannot enter into paradise, because priests cannot be whole. So how can they be holy? Impossible!

And now you ask me: 'I remain covered in the clouds of these problems so that I cannot listen to you as I should. Please guide me.' You are not fed up with guides yet. They are your problem. And you are not fed up with 'shoulds' yet. That is your misery, the whole misery. Drop all 'shoulds', drop all guides. That is the only guidance I can give to you. Just be totally alone, and listen to your own inner voice. Trust life and nobody else. And life is beautiful, intrinsically valuable. And if you listen to anybody else, *against* life, then you will go astray.

So I call that man a real master who helps you . . . to give back to you your inner voice. He does not give you *his* voice. He simply helps you to reclaim your own lost inner voice. He does not guide you; in fact, by and by he takes all guides away from you so that you can become your guide and you can take your life in your own hands and you can become responsible.

It is irresponsibility to repeatedly ask somebody, 'What should I do?'

And that is why you feel continuously in trouble with me. You would like me to spoon-feed you, so that you have not to do anything. I should do everything—the chewing and everything—and I should spoon-feed you. That I am not going to do, because that is what others have done, and destroyed you.

I love you. I cannot do this. I love you tremendously; it is impossible for me to do that. I would like to make you responsible, to take charge of your life. When are you going to take charge of your life? You are not children. You are not helpless.

This is how I am going to help you: to make you just yourself, to help you to move towards that direction which is your destiny.

✻

You have spoken of the union of the sun and moon within oneself and going beyond. It feels like having a mate outside oneself may be more complication and trouble than it is worth.

Will you please speak on how having a mate or not enhances or detracts from one's inwardness and spiritual development.

The question is not of complication. The question is of richness of experience. It is going to be complicated. Alone you are complicated; when you find a girlfriend or a boyfriend, a man or a woman, of course two complicated beings come together. And it is not going to be a simple addition; it is going to be a multiplication. Things become complicated, certainly.

But through that complexity you have to find a way. It is a challenge. Each woman or man you come in contact with is a great challenge. You can avoid those challenges.

That is what monks have always been doing—escaping from the world, avoiding the challenge. Of course you will be more still, silent, your life will not be complicated; but you will be poor. And when I say 'poor', I mean you will be very, very inexperienced, immature. Because from where will you get the maturity? From where will you get that enrichment that life and experience bring? And there is no other way—it cannot be purchased, it cannot be borrowed. It is not hidden in the Himalayas so you can go and dig it up. It is not there—it is in life, it is with people, it is in relationship.

So I know it is complicated, but just for complications' sake if you think that it will be better to be alone, your aloneness is not going to be spiritual. It will be the aloneness of a coward, not of a brave man.

Let me tell you an anecdote:

A man who was very hard of hearing went to see his doctor, who examined him thoroughly and told him he was in good shape for a man of seventy.

'Do you smoke?' asked the doctor.

'What do you say?' asked the old man.

'I said, do you smoke?' yelled the doctor.

'Oh, yes.' said the old man.

'Much?' inquired the doctor.

'Who?' said the old man.

'Do you smoke much?' said the doctor.

'Cigarettes, cigars and sometimes a pipe. Yes, I am smoking all the time.' he told him.

'Drink?' asked the doctor.

'It is after nine.' replied the old man.

'No, no,' said the doctor. 'Do you drink?'

'Oh, yes, I will drink anything.' he said.

'I suppose you keep late hours? Lots of parties? Like

girls?' The doctor was getting a little annoyed by now.

'Sure thing! And I intend to carry on like it for a long time.'

'Well,' said the doctor. 'I am afraid you will have to cut it all out.'

'What?' yelled the old man, more in surprise than lack of hearing.

'You will have to cut it all out!' the doctor yelled.

'Just to *hear* better?' said the old man. 'No thanks!'

Just to avoid complexities? No, never. That is the way of the coward. Never escape from problems. They are helpful, tremendously helpful. They are growth situations.

And if you are going to find a girl, don't try to find a cow. It will again be less complicated. Find a real woman, who will give you all sorts of troubles. Your mettle will be tested there.

A young man once asked Socrates, 'Should I get married, sir?' And of course he asked Socrates because he must have been thinking not to get married. And, then, he found the right man to ask because Socrates had suffered so much with his woman. She was really terrible—a crocodile. She had been beating Socrates, she had poured a kettle of tea over his face and had burned him, and half his face remained burned his whole life. Such a beautiful person like Socrates had found a very terrible woman. So this young man asked.

Socrates said, 'Yes, if you listen to me, get married. There are two possibilities. If you get a wife like mine, you will become a great philosopher like me. And if you get a beautiful wife, of course, you will enjoy your life. Both the possibilities are good.'

Just a continuous nagging—it is a great help to meditation.

By and by one starts feeling unattached. One has to. One starts feeling 'this is all illusion—maya.' So don't avoid complexities in life, because life *means* complexities. Learn and pass through them, because that is the only way to grow.

A tramp knocked at a door which was opened by a large, muscular, hard-faced woman.

'Get out of here, you miserable tramp!' she yelled. 'If you don't clear off I will call my husband.'

'I think not,' was the calm response of the tramp. 'He is not at home.'

'How do you know that?' asked the woman.

'Because,' said the tramp. 'When a man marries a woman like you, he is at home only at meal times.'

The question is from Alok. Alok, find a really terrible woman.

*

Now I feel, unless one is ready, nothing is possible.
I have been seeking the key for many years; I asked you also many times, but you remained silent.

One day suddenly you delivered me the key, Osho.
Now the key is with me. But I am finding myself unable to unlock. Blocks are in me. I have the key, I have the locks before me, and even then what is this happening?

You are present; see my helplessness.
Once I used to think that I had not the key, and was disturbed; now I have the key and am more disturbed.

Please help, Osho; I know you are always helping.
Obstacles are in me. Please tell me how to remove
those, so that . . . so that . . .

The first thing: the key that I have delivered to you is a false key—because the real key cannot be delivered. You have to attain it, earn it. Because you were after me so much, so I said, 'Okay, have this.' Now don't go on knocking your head against the wall. Throw that key away. Nothing is wrong with you; the key is false.

All keys are false—because the lock is *yours*. How can you find the key from somebody else? The lock is *you*! *You* have to create the key within you, as you have created the lock.

And once you have created the key, the lock disappears; it is not that the key has to open it. Once you know, the problem disappears. Not that you have to bring your knowledge to solve the problem. Once the understanding is there, the problem is not. The key never meets the lock. The lock is there because the key is not. When the key is there, the lock simply disappears.

I cannot deliver that key. And all that is borrowed is going to create more trouble, because you are already complicated, and now this borrowed thing complicates you more.

I have heard:

An overworked business executive went to the doctor and was told that he was overdoing things and must get far more exercise.

'Get yourself a hoop and roll it to and from the office each day, instead of relying on a car. It will make a new man out of you,' said the doctor.

So he bought a hoop and did what the doctor ordered. He rolled it to the office every day, and the garage housed it during working hours. However, one evening he found that the hoop was missing. The garage hand told him that due to an error it had been returned to someone else. 'But don't worry, sir,' he said. 'We will replace it free of charge tomorrow.'

The executive said, 'Tomorrow? What do you mean, tomorrow! How am I going to get home tonight?'

If the understanding is not there, then all methods, rather than becoming a help, become hindrances.

And if the understanding is not there and you start looking through my eyes, your eyes are not going to stop seeing. They will go on seeing through my eyes. It is going to be a great complication.

Another anecdote:

'I hear that your husband had his eyebrows all burnt off in a fire at home?' the woman asked her friend.

'Yes,' came the reply, 'but the doctor was so wonderful to him. He actually grafted new eyebrows on him, from the hair taken from the hind leg of a dog.'

'That is fantastic!' her friend said. 'How is he now?'

'Oh, he is not too bad,' she said. 'Mind you, he does have a little problem still. Every time he passes a lamp post, he looks surprised.'

5

The Seed of Liberation

By being non-attached to even these powers,
the seed of bondage is destroyed.
Then follows kaivalya, *liberation.*

There should be an avoidance of any
attachment or pride to
invitations from the superphysical entities
in charge of various planes
because this would bring the possibility
of the revival of evil.

The first sutra: *Tad vairagyatapitosh bikshaye kaivalyam.*

IT IS VERY difficult to be non-attached in the world, but it is even more difficult to be non-attached when the spiritual world opens its doors. The difficulty of the second is a million-fold because the worldly powers are not real powers. They are impotent and they never satisfy you, they never make you contented. In fact, every new achievement in the world creates more desires. Rather than satisfying you it sends your mind into new trips, so whatsoever power you attain in the world, you use it only to create new desires.

Whatsoever money you can gather in the world, you

invest it to gain more money. Then more money comes, you invest it for still more money, and this way it goes on. Only means and means and means, and never does the end come closer. So even a stupid person becomes aware sooner or later that he is moving in a vicious circle and there seems to be no way out of it—except to drop out. For an intelligent person—who thinks about his life, meditates about it—it is very obvious.

So non-attachment is not so difficult in the worldly things, but when it comes to the inner powers, the psychic powers, they are so close to your being and so infinitely satisfying, it is almost impossible to be non-attached to them. But if you are not non-attached, then you have again created a world and you will remain far, far away from the ultimate liberation.

Because whatsoever you possess possesses you, the sacrifice has to be total, utterly total. You have to drop everything that you can possess—except your nude nature. That which cannot be sacrificed, only that can be left. That which can be sacrificed *should* be sacrificed.

In this sutra Patanjali is asking almost the impossible, but that, too, becomes possible through understanding. It is very satisfying, gratifying, to have spiritual powers, and it gives you such a subtle joy of the ego, so pure that you cannot feel any sting in it. It never frustrates you. In the worldly things there is much frustration—in fact, nothing *but* frustration. It is a miracle how people can avoid seeing this. It is a miracle how people can go on deceiving themselves and believing that there is some hope. The outside world is hopeless, it is doomed.

Howsoever big a house you can make, or howsoever powerful you become politically, economically, socially, death is going to take them all away from you—and not much intelligence is needed to understand this. But the inner powers, death cannot take them away. They are beyond death and they never frustrate you. They are your powers; your potentialities come to flower. There seems to be no need to sacrifice them, no need to renounce them. But Patanjali is saying that they have also to be renounced, otherwise you will start living in a world of visions—again the power trip. And religion is not a power trip.

You are not seeking the ego, but you are trying to find out the whole—and the whole is possible only when all sorts of egoistic trips are dropped and sacrificed. When you are not, the divine is.

Let me tell you a very famous Sufi story, *The Holy Shadow*:

There once lived a saint so good that the angels came from heaven to see how a man could be so godly. This saint went about his daily life diffusing virtue as the stars diffuse light and the flowers scent, without being aware of it. His day could be summed up by two words—giving and forgiving—yet these words never passed his lips. They were expressed in his ready smile, his kindness, forbearance and charity.

The angels said to God, 'Lord, grant him the gift of miracles.'

God replied, 'Ask what it is that he wishes.'

They said to the saint, 'Would you like the touch of your hands to heal the sick?'

'No,' answered the saint. 'I would rather God does that.'

'Would you like to convert guilty souls and bring back wandering hearts to the right path?'

'No, that is the angels' mission. It is not for me to convert.'

'Would you like to become a model of patience,

attracting men by the lustre of your virtues, and thus glorifying God?'

'No,' replied the saint. 'If men should be attracted to me, they would become estranged from God.'

'What is it that you desire, then?' asked the angels.

'What can I wish for?' asked the saint smiling. 'That God gives me his grace; with that would I not have everything?'

The angels said, 'You must ask for a miracle, or one will be forced upon you.'

'Very well,' said the saint. 'That I may do a great deal of good without ever knowing it.'

The angels were perplexed. They took counsel and resolved upon the following plan: every time the saint's shadow fell behind him or to either side, so that he could not see it, it would have the power to cure disease, soothe pain and comfort sorrow.

When the saint walked along, his shadow, thrown on the ground on either side or behind him, made arid paths green, caused withered plants to bloom and gave clear water to dried-up brooks, fresh colour to pale children and joy to unhappy men and women.

The people, respecting his humility, followed him silently, never speaking to him about his miracles. Soon they even forgot his name, and called him 'The Holy Shadow'.

This is the ultimate: one has to become a holy shadow, just a shadow of the divine. This is the greatest revolution that can happen to a human being: the transfer of the centre. You are no longer your own centre; the divine becomes your centre. You live like its shadow. You are not powerful, because you don't have any centre to be powerful. You are not virtuous; you don't have any centre to be virtuous. You are not even religious; you don't have any centre to be religious. You are simply *not*—a tremendous emptiness, with no barriers and blocks, so the divine can flow through you without being hindered, interpreted or touched—so the divine can flow through you as He is, not as you would like Him to be. He does not pass through your centre—there is none. The centre is lost.

This is the meaning of this sutra: that finally you have to sacrifice your centre, so you cannot think in terms of the ego again, you cannot utter 'I'—to annihilate yourself utterly, to erase yourself utterly. Nothing belongs to you; on the contrary, you belong to the divine. You become a holy shadow.

It is difficult to conceive it because it is so difficult to be unattached to useless rubbish. You go on collecting in the hope that whatsoever you accumulate can fulfil you. You go on accumulating—knowledge, money, power, prestige. You go on just accumulating. Your whole life is a stuffing in. And, of course, if you become a dead weight, there is no wonder in it. That is what you have been doing: collecting dust and thinking of it as if it were gold.

The valueless becomes of immense value if seen through the ego. The ego is a great falsifier, the great deceiver. It goes on lying to you, and it goes on creating illusions, dreams and projections. Watch it: it is very subtle. Its ways are subtle and it is very cunning. If you stop it in one direction, it moves in another direction. If you stop one path, it finds another path, and in such a cunning way that you cannot think that the other path is also of the ego.

I have heard about an old woman who had fallen down the stairs and broken her leg:

The doctor put it in a cast and warned her not to walk

up and down the stairs. It finally mended after six months and the doctor announced the cast could be removed.

'Can I climb the stairs now?' asked the old lady.

'Yes,' said the doctor.

'Oh, I am glad,' she giggled. 'I am sick of going up and down the drainpipe.'

If you block the ego coming from the staircase, it comes from the drainpipe—but it comes!

See your so-called religious men. They have renounced all—but they have not renounced renunciation. They have renounced all; now they are clinging to their renunciation. That renunciation has become their wealth, the drainpipe. Now they are climbing to the same ego but in a more cunning and subtle way—so subtle that not only are others deceived, but also they themselves are deceived.

You are a worldly man; then one day you feel the frustration. One day *everybody* feels it; there is nothing special in it. Then you start becoming religious and you start feeling very egoistic about it. You are becoming 'religious'. You look at others as sinners, worldly people. You are religious: you have become a sanyasin, you have renounced.

But the enemy has entered from another door. The world is not to be renounced; the ego has to be renounced. So you have to be very, very careful not to allow it to deceive you.

The ego cannot be repressed, remember. It has to be simply evaporated—through the heat of understanding, through the fire of understanding. If you repress it, it is easy. You can become humble, you can become simple, but it will hide behind your simplicity.

A woman told her doctor that she was convinced she had a

very dangerous illness. He advised her not to be so foolish, that she could not possibly know whether she had it or not because, 'the disease,' he added, 'carries with it no discomfort whatsoever!'—so there is no way for her to know.

The lady said, 'But doctor, that's exactly how I feel—no discomfort whatsoever! The disease is there!'

You can go on deceiving yourself and you can find rationalizations, and on the surface they look very reasonable—but look into them. And remember—it is nobody else's business. It is for you to see. The whole world can see it, but if you have not seen it, that is useless.

Now modern psychology is by and by turning from individual therapy to group therapy, and the only reason for it is this: it is very difficult for the psychoanalyst to convince the patient one on one about what he is doing to himself. About the patient, about his complexes, about his rationalizations, repressions, deceptions, stupidities—it is very difficult to convince him one on one. But in a group it becomes easier because the whole group can see the foolishness, the obviousness of it—that he is clinging to something and unnecessarily becoming miserable. The whole group can see it and the understanding of the whole group functions more tremendously and deeply than the understanding of one person can function. That is why group therapy is growing and individual therapy disappearing.

Group therapy has a tremendous advantage. Twenty persons working in a group, and nineteen become alert that you are doing something which you don't want to do . . . and still you are clinging to it!

A sanyasin came to me, a very good man, but he was feeling very, very happy because I had given him a beautiful name. I give beautiful names to everybody. He had made an ego trip out of it. He said, 'Osho, you are wonderful. You have given me such a beautiful name—it exactly represents me.' Your names don't represent you. These are my hopes and dreams, not realities. I called that sanyasin 'Satyananda'—the bliss that arises out of the experience of truth. That is the ultimate. But he said, 'Osho, with "Satyananda", you have exactly, exactly got me. I am so impressed by your understanding.'

Now I became alert that this had been very, very wrong. It had been a misunderstanding. I should not have given him this name. I wanted to pull him down from his euphoria, so when after a few minutes he started saying, 'I don't want anger, greed, this and that; these are all animalistic'; I said, 'Don't be a coward.' Immediately he exploded: 'Coward? You call me a coward?' He was almost ready to hit me—screamed, completely forgot about Satyananda—and he started defending himself. 'Why have you called me a coward? I am not a coward.' And I told him, 'If you are not a coward, then why are you defending? Then simply you can say, "You are wrong." Or even that is not needed. You are not a coward; why are you worried about it? Why have you got so red hot? Why are you screaming at the top of your voice? Why have you got so mad? I must have touched something.'

Now everybody who was present became aware that the man was defending something, and defending very fanatically; but only he could not see it.

In a group, if you work for a longer time, by and by you have to become aware that the whole group is seeing that you are doing something foolish, stupid, contrary to your own wishes—against your own fulfilment, against your own growth. You are clinging to a disease and you go on saying, 'I want to get rid of it.'

Almost everybody knows where you are doing wrong—

except you. Everybody knows that you are an egoist—except you. Only you think you are a humble man, a simple man. Everybody knows your complexity. Everybody knows your double bind. Everybody knows your madness except you. You go on defending it. And because of politeness, etiquette, formalities in the society, nobody will tell you. Hence, the group is helpful because it is not going to be polite. It is going to be truthful. And when so many people say that this is your problem, pinpoint it and finger it and put their fingers on your wound, it hurts. It is very difficult to make you alert one on one because you can think this man may be wrong, but twenty persons? The possibility of twenty persons being wrong is less, and you have to fall back upon yourself and see the point of it.

That is why Buddha created a great *sangha*, a great order of monks—10,000 monks. It was the first experiment of group therapy. It was a great experiment.

That is what I am doing—16,000 sanyasins—one of the greatest experiments in therapy. A community, a commune, in which you have to become aware—because otherwise you will not be part of this commune where everybody is understanding and seeing your error and showing it to you. Sanyasins are not meant to be polite or formal; none of that rubbish! Sanyasins are here to transform themselves and become situations for others' transformation.

See, whenever somebody points at some fault of yours, don't get angry; that is not going to help you. Try to see the point. Maybe the other is true; and there is more possibility for the other to be true because he is so detached from you, he is so far away from you. He is not involved in you. Always listen to what people are saying about you. 99 per cent of the time they will be right. How can they be wrong, when they have a detached view about you?

That is why a master is needed: to show you your wounds. And it is possible only if you are in deep respect and trust. If you get angry and you start fighting, then there is no trust and no respect. If you are here to defend your illnesses and diseases, then it is for you—don't be here. What is the point of wasting your time here?

When I say that you are a coward and you cannot see the point, if you have to fight and prove to me that you are not, then there is no point in being here. The relationship is finished with me. Now I cannot be helpful to you. When I say something to you, you have to look into the fact. Why should I call you a coward? There is no investment with you, and with your cowardliness I have not invested anything. I simply said so because of compassion, because I see the illness is there. And unless you know it, unless it is diagnosed, how are you going to get rid of it?

If the doctor puts his hand on your pulse and says that you have fever and you jump on him and start fighting and saying, 'What are you saying? How can I ever have any fever? No, you are wrong, I am perfectly healthy', then why in the first place had you gone to the doctor? Just to get a certificate of health?

You are here—remember it—you are here not to get recognition for your illnesses, and certificates that they don't exist. You are here to be diagnosed, dissected and destroyed so that your real nature can bloom. But if you are defending, then it is for you to defend. It is none of my business; defend it. But then you will suffer. Then don't come and tell me, 'I am suffering, I am tense.'

It is very difficult to move inwards from the world, because inside you have been hiding illnesses and diseases. They force you to go out. That is a way of diverting the attention. That is why so many masters have been teaching you, 'Go in. Know thyself'—but you never go there! You talk about it, you read about it, you appreciate the idea, but you never go in—because there you have only darkness and wounds and diseases. You have been hiding things which are not good or healthy for you. You have been, on the contrary, protecting them rather than destroying them. Now you open the door . . . and you start feeling such stinking, such dirt, such ugliness; a hell opens. You immediately close the door and you start thinking, 'What is the matter?'

Buddha, Jesus, Krishna, they all have been teaching, 'Go in and you will be tremendously blissful, eternally blissful', but you open the door and you move into a nightmare. This nightmare is created by your repressions. On the surface you are simple; deep down you are very complex. On the surface you have a face of a very innocent person; deep down you are very ugly.

Because of that 'repressiveness' you cannot look within and you have to continuously divert yourself into something—listening to the radio, watching TV, reading the newspaper, going to see friends; just wasting time somewhere until you fall asleep. The moment you are awake you start running again. From whom are you running? You are running from yourself.

Give space to yourself to see your being; then suddenly you will see that there is no attachment with things. How can it be? It is absurd.

I have heard a very beautiful story—a Sufi story, *The Golden Door*:

Two men prayed, and went their separate ways. One gathered wealth and power, people said he was famous, but there was no peace in him. The other saw the hearts of men—glowing as lamps even in the darkness of their own secret fears. He too had found richness and power; and his wealth, his power, was love. When simply, kindly, tenderly, he touched his fellowmen with all the richness and power of this love, the light within grew clear and bright with courage and with peace.

Both men one day stood before that golden door through which all men must pass to the greater life beyond. The angel in the soul of each asked, 'What do you bring with you? What have you to give?' . . .

God always asks, 'What do you bring with you? What have you to give?' God goes on giving to you, but finally, the last day before you enter into his innermost shrine, he asks, 'Now, what have you brought for me? What is your gift for me?'

. . . The one who was famous recounted his exploits. Why, there was no end to the people he knew, the places he had been, the things he had done and the things he had accumulated.

But the angel answered, 'These are not acceptable. These things that you did, you did for yourself. I see no love in them.' . . .

If there is ego there cannot be love. Remember this. I am going to discuss it later on, because it is one of the most important things: if there is ego, there can be no love.

. . . And the famous one sank outside the golden door and wept . . .

For the first time he could see the whole futility of all his efforts. It was like a dream that has passed and his hands are empty.

If you are too full of things, one day or the other you will see your hands are empty. It was dream stuff that you were carrying in your hands; they have always been empty. You were just dreaming that something is there. Because you were afraid of emptiness, you had projected something, you had believed. You have never looked deeply whether it is really there or not.

. . . And the famous man sank outside the golden door and wept. He had been too busy to be kind . . .

Too occupied to love, too engaged to be himself, too concerned with futile things to be concerned with the essential.

. . . Then the angel in the soul of the other asked, 'And what do you bring? What have you to give?'

And he answered, saying, 'No one knows my name. They called me the wanderer, the dreamer. I have only a little light in my heart, and that which I have, I have shared with the souls of men.' . . .

The real people look like dreamers in this world of mad people. The sages have always been known as wanderers, dreamers, poets, imaginative, living somewhere, lotus-eaters, navel-gazers. These types of labels have been given to real people because the world belongs to paper people. They are not real. Paper people, whenever they come across a real person, call him 'dreamer' or 'poet'. That is their way of condemning him, and that is their way of defending themselves.

. . . Then the angel said, 'Oh, blessed one, you have the

greatest gift of all. It is love. Always and always, there is enough and to spare. Enter.' . . .

That is the beauty of love: the more you give, the more you have it. Let this be a criterion in your life: Don't accumulate that which by giving disappears. Only accumulate that which by giving accumulates. Only accumulate that which by sharing increases and grows. That is worth: which you can share and by its very sharing it grows and you have more than before.

. . . Then said the wanderer, 'But first let me give the extra measure to my brother, that we may both walk through the door.'

The angel was silent; for in that moment a great light shone around the simple wanderer like a radiant mantle, enveloping both himself and his friend.

The golden door was opened wide and they walked through it together.

He shared at the very last moment also. This is real richness. A miser is never rich; if you are attached to things in the world, you are not rich. Richness arises out of the heart. Richness is a quality of the heart, glowing with love.

One of the greatest poets of India, Rabindranath Tagore, has written a poem, *Beloved of My Heart*. This is not only a poem; it is based on a real incidents. In essence, the poem means this:

'One day in a small village in Bengal an ascetic woman from the neighbourhood came to see me. She had the name of Sarvakhipi, given to her by the village people, the meaning of which is "the woman who is mad about all things" . . . '

Sarvakhipi: one who is mad about all things—absolutely mad.

' . . . She fixed her star-like eyes upon my face and startled me with the question: "When are you coming to meet me underneath the trees?" Evidently she pitied me, who lived, according to her, imprisoned behind walls, banished away from the great meeting place of the all, where she had her dwelling.

'Just at that moment, my gardener came with his basket, and when the woman understood that the flowers in the vase on my table were going to be thrown away to make place for the fresh ones, she looked pained and said to me, "You are always engaged in reading and writing. You do not see." Then she took the discarded flowers in her palms, kissed them, and touched them to her forehead, and reverently murmured to herself, "Beloved of my heart."

'I felt that this woman, in her direct vision of the infinite personality in the heart of all things, truly represented the spirit of the East.'

Love is the spirit of the East. Love is the spirit of man. Love is the spirit of godliness. Love is the only richness there is, the only happiness there is.

Now, if you are attached to things, you cannot be a lover. Only a non-attached man can raise himself towards that sky which we call love. There is much misunderstanding about it. People who leave the world and become detached almost simultaneously become loveless as well; then something has gone wrong because love is the criterion, the very test, the touchstone. If your non-attachment to the world makes you loveless, something has gone sour. Your non-attachment is not true, authentic or real. It is 'pseudo'.

Because you are afraid of love, it shows you are afraid of being attached, so you avoid all situations where love can flower—because you are afraid deep down that if love flowers you will become attached again.

That is why your so-called mahatmas are so afraid of love. They will not stay in one place for more than three days. Why so much fear? Because, if you remain in one place for many more days, you will start feeling love for people. Somebody will come every day to massage your feet, and you will start feeling love for him. Somebody will bring food for you every day, and you will start feeling love for her. Certain affections will arise, as will the fear of being attached again: move before you become attached.

These so-called non-attached people are simply afraid. They live in deep panic. They can never touch the real core of life, because that is always touched by love.

Remember, if your non-attachment to things is true, and it has come out of understanding and has grown out of awareness, you will become more loving—because the same energy that was involved in attachment will be released. Where will it go? You will have more energy at your disposal. Attachment is not love. It is an ego trip—to possess, to dominate, to manipulate. It is violence; it is not love. When this energy is relieved, suddenly you have much more energy to love. Really non-attached people are full of love, and they always have more and more to give and always go on finding new sources of love. Their sources are infinite.

And the ultimate non-attachment comes when you have attained some miracles, *siddhis*, powers; when you can do things—things which are miraculous, things which are unbelievable. If you become attached to them, sooner or later you will be back in the world again. Beware! It is the ego's last attack on you; don't be caught. The ego is throwing its last net on you.

By being non-attached to even these powers, the seed of bondage is destroyed. The seed of bondage is attachment. And the seed of liberation is love. And how alike they look! They are diametrically opposite: attachment is lovelessness; love is always non-attached.

You love a woman or a man and you feel attached. Why do you feel attached? Attachment means that tomorrow also you would like to have this woman or man with you—that is all. Tomorrow and again the day after tomorrow you would like to have this woman or man in your possession. That simply shows you have not been able to love today; otherwise the tomorrow never enters. Who bothers about tomorrow? Who knows about tomorrow? Tomorrow never comes. It enters only into the minds of those who have not been living today. You have not loved this woman or man today, so you are waiting for tomorrow to come so that you can love. Your love is incomplete, unfinished. For that unfinished love attachment arises. Then it is natural, logical. If you are painting, but the painting is incomplete, you would like to have the canvas tomorrow also, to complete it.

There is a very deep law in life: it wants to complete everything. The bud wants to flower; the seed wants to become a sprout.

Everything is moving towards completion, so whatsoever you leave incomplete becomes a desire in the mind and says, 'Possess this person. You have not loved yet; you have not yet travelled through their being, through and through. Still much unknown territory remains in them. Still much potentiality which has not been actualized is there—many songs of being and many dances to be danced.'

Attachment arises. Tomorrow is needed, the day after

tomorrow is needed—future is needed. And if you are really incapable of living in the present, then a future life is also needed, and people go on promising each other, 'We will remain spouses in the future life also.' That simply shows these people have become absolutely incapable of living. Otherwise this day is enough unto itself.

This moment, if you complete your love, if you have loved with your full heart—totally, surrendered, dissolved into it; you have not been holding anything back—then the idea of tomorrow *never* arises. It is impossible for the idea of tomorrow to arise. It always comes when something is unfulfilled; then you hanker for the future. If you have loved your woman or your man today and death comes, you will accept it. Or, if the woman or man falls in love with somebody else, you will say a good-bye—sad, but not miserable. Sadness has a beauty, but misery is ugly. Sad . . . not because of attachment; sad because your love is still there arising in you and the person is going away who could have understood it. Sad, but fulfilled; there is no complaint, no grudge.

But if you have loved totally, your partner will never want to leave. If you have loved totally it is impossible, because that total love satisfies so deeply. One cannot even think of some other. It is impossible to dream of the other. The dream arises only because of dissatisfaction with this one. You think of other women because with your own woman it has not been a satisfactory relationship. You think of other men because your mind wants to free itself and this has not happened in this relationship. So the mind goes on wandering all over the place. You start feeling love for any woman or man who passes by.

And if your love has become frustrated so much so that you cannot imagine now that it is possible to love any human being, you start loving dogs and cats. Seems to be less complicated—Alok should make a note of it.

Loving a dog is very simple . . . loving a cat a little more difficult. That is why men call women 'cats'. A cat is less predictable than the dog, cleverer than the dog. You can kick the dog and he will come again; you kick the cat, she will not come again. Finished! Always ready for the divorce.

People fall in love with animals. How unfortunate. I am not saying don't love animals. What I am saying is that don't make them substitutes for human beings. You should love human beings so deeply that your love starts overflowing and it reaches animals as well. Then it is totally different. Then it also reaches the trees and the rocks, because you go on overflowing. An infinite source of love . . . nobody can contain your love. It goes on overflowing. Then it has a totally different quality to it.

But the doors with humans are closed and you have to find someone to love, otherwise you feel very frustrated, a relationship is needed—then you relate with dogs, cats.

Even that, too, sometimes proves to be unsatisfactory, because dogs and cats are living beings—they also have their own ideologies, their own ideas, and they want to do *their* thing. No dog is there to fulfil your desires. You may be thinking while you are taking a dog for a walk that you have tamed him, because you have never asked the dog what he thinks. He thinks he possesses you, and he has tamed this man. I have heard dogs talking to each other!

When it becomes difficult even to love animals, then people start loving things—a house, a car, a bike. And they become much too romantic about these things.

I have seen a man who used to live just in front of my house. He loved his scooter so much that I have seen him cleaning his scooter almost in a romantic way—as if he is cleaning his woman. Looking from this side and that, and feeling so happy. And he would never use it because it may get dirty. He would go on his old bike.

I told him many times, 'What are you doing? You have got a beautiful scooter.'

He would say, 'But there is a possibility of it raining. You see, there are clouds.' Or it is too hot and his scooter may lose its shine . . . no, I have never seen him using it. He simply cleans it and cares for it. The scooter is the beloved.

This is a degradation of human consciousness. The more attached you become, the more degraded you become; the less the attachment, the higher you rise and soar.

And there comes a moment Patanjali is talking about when spiritual powers happen to you. Remember, don't get attached to them, because they are *really* beautiful, very fulfilling. You would like to possess them. Many people become interested in yoga not because of yoga, not because of *kaivalya*, liberation—but only because of *vibhutis*, *siddhis*. They study yoga, they go to the masters. They want to do miracles.

By being non-attached to even these powers, the seed of bondage is destroyed. This is the last possibility of getting caught into bondage again. If you can cross this, the seed is burned.

Then follows kaivalya—then follows liberation. Then you are totally free—freedom, absolute freedom—not attached to anything and full of love, showering your love on the whole of existence . . . a benediction to existence and to yourself, a blessing.

But one has to be alert on each step. The mind is cunning. And you may be thinking, 'Yes, when miracles come I am not going to be attached to them.' Think again. You will find in yourself somewhere a desire lurking, 'Let them come, then we will see. First let them come.' Who bothers about *kaivalya*, liberation? Does not seem to be like a goal: just to be liberated, free? What is the point in it?

People come to me and they say, 'What are we going to get out of meditation?' I say, 'More meditation.' They say, 'But what is the point? Peace? Peace is okay, but what *real* power are we going to get out of it?'

Peace doesn't look like a goal. But *power* is something that you can *do* things with, something through which you can prove.

I have heard an anecdote:

'Tell me, where do you Catholics get all the money to build cathedrals?' a rabbi asked his friend, a priest.

'Well, Abe, you see, we Catholics have a system called Confession. Whenever anybody does something wrong, he comes to church, confesses his sin, puts a little in the kitty, and is forgiven; and in this way we can collect large amounts of cash.'

'Really? What a wonderful system. Maybe we could adopt it for use in our synagogue. But let me go along with you tonight so I could get an example of how you work.'

'Well, Abe, it is strictly forbidden for me, as a priest, to have you along, but seeing as how you have been such a good friend all these years, I will permit it just this once.'

That evening they are seated in the confessional box, the priest in front and Abe, all agog, behind. Presently a man's voice is heard from behind the curtain:

'Father, I have sinned grievously.'

'What have you done, my son?'

'Last night I consorted with two women.'

'Well, then, put two pounds in the kitty and your sins

will be forgiven.'

Abe is very excited. Presently another man's voice is heard: 'Father, I have sinned grievously.'

'What have you done, my son?'

'Last night I consorted with three women.'

'Well, then put three pounds in the kitty and your sins will be forgiven, my son.'

Abe can contain himself no longer:

'What a way to make money; what a wonderful system. Do me a favour. Let me do the next one, just to get some practice.'

'Well, Abe, strictly speaking it is not permitted, but seeing as how you have been such a good friend all these years, I will permit it just this once.'

So they exchange places and Abe sits in front waiting. Presently a woman's voice is heard:

'Father, I have sinned grievously.'

'Now, now, what is it that you have done?'

'Last night I consorted with four men.'

'Now, put five pounds in the kitty and I will give you a credit for one.'

Watch out! The mind is very greedy; the ego is nothing but greed.

Patanjali wrote this chapter; many have felt it would have been better if he had not written it. But he has a very scientific mind. He wanted to map out the whole thing that is possible, and he wrote this chapter just to make people aware that these things happen. As far as I am concerned, I think it has been perfectly good that he has included it, because in ignorance there is more possibility for greed to take possession of you. If you know and understand the territory and you know where the last attack of the ego is going to come, you can prepare more cautiously, and when it happens you will not be caught unawares.

I am perfectly happy that he included *Vibhuti Pada*, this chapter about *siddhis* and powers, because even if you are not looking for them they happen on their own. The more you grow inside, many things start happening by themselves. Not that you are seeking or looking for them—they are consequences. Each chakra has its own powers. When you pass through them, they become available to you. It is good to be alert and move knowingly where one is going.

> *There should be an avoidance of any attachment or pride to invitations from the superphysical entities in charge of various planes because this would bring the possibility of the revival of evil.*

When these powers start happening, you start receiving invitations from higher entities, superphysical entities. You must have heard or you must have read about the Theosophists. Their whole work consisted of these superphysical entities. They used to call them 'the Masters'. There are superphysical entities that go on communicating with human beings, and whenever you rise high, you become available to them; you become more in tune with them. You receive many invitations, many messages.

That is what Mohammedans call *paigam*, the message; and they call Mohammed *paigambar*, one who received the message. They don't call him an avatar; they don't call him God reincarnate. They don't call him a Buddha, one who has become enlightened. They don't call him a *jina*, one who has conquered. They don't call him a messiah, a Christ—

no. They have a very, very perfect scientific terminology for it: they call him 'the messenger'—*paigambar*. It means simply that he has risen high and now he is functioning no more; some other entities, higher entities, have taken possession of him. He has become a medium.

And it is so. Mohammed was illiterate; it is almost impossible to imagine that he could have given birth to the beautiful poetry of the Koran. It is incomparably beautiful, it is one of the greatest songs, and if you can hear somebody singing it, you will be affected by it immediately. Even if you don't understand its meaning, it has tremendous power. The very sound has tremendous power to stir you.

Mohammed was illiterate, not knowing anything about literature and the world of letters. Then, while meditating on a mountain, he heard, 'Read!' The word 'koran' means read. 'How can I read? I don't know how to,' said Mohammed. He became very bewildered, and wondered who said that. He could not see anybody anywhere. Again this voice came, 'Read!' It was coming from his own heart; he had become a channel. And, of course, he was thinking about his past, and the voice was saying something about his future. The voice was saying, 'I can read, don't be worried. Just read—I will be reading through you. You recite—I will be reciting through you. You say—I will be saying through you. Just put yourself out of the way.'

It was so strange, so unexpected, that he got a high fever. He became very puzzled and went home, ill. His wife asked, 'What has happened? Just in the morning you were perfectly well, and now such a high fever?' He said, 'I will tell you one thing. Either I have gone mad or something has happened from the beyond. I cannot believe that I am capable of anything, but I have heard a voice which says, "Read! Recite!" and I don't know what to recite—and not only that, I started reciting! I heard myself saying things I have never thought about, and they were coming in perfect poetry, with metre, rhythm and everything. I cannot believe it. Either I have gone mad or I have been taken possession of by somebody—but I am no longer the same, your husband. Run and fetch a physician. I will need treatment. I am going mad, and I am still hearing this voice, "Recite!"— and beautiful poems are descending in me and filling my heart.'

His wife was his first disciple. She touched his feet. She could see the radiance all around him. It was not fever; it was the first explosion of his aura. He was feeling feverish because it was so hot, so new, and he was disturbed because he was not ready; he wasn't expecting it and had not planned for it.

This would not have happened if he had known about Patanjali. Patanjali has noted everything; he has mapped the whole journey, the inner journey. Then he would have understood this sutra. This sutra was needed.

But Patanjali says to remember that when you become a vehicle of higher planes, don't start feeling proud, and don't start thinking yourself to be the chosen few or the chosen one. Don't start feeling that you have been elected, selected, chosen and you are special. Otherwise that will be the cause of your fall.

There is a Sufi story:

The Murshid was speaking to a group of people when he was still a young man. In the group was a wide-eyed dervish dressed simply in brown clothes. This dervish looked continuously at the speaker. He looked with such a knowing stare that the speaker was embarrassed and turned away. At the end of the talk the dervish approached him and told him that he had been sent to initiate him. 'That cannot be so. You see, my father has already arranged for my initiation.'

'I told you that I have been *sent*,' said the dervish.

'No matter, I must obey my father's wish.' With this insistence of the young man, the dervish departed.

That night the man dreamed that his father was instructing him to be initiated by the dervish. In the morning the dervish came to his room, saying that he was there to initiate him.

'Do you not remember from day to day? Go, my father is arranging my initiation.'

The dervish looked at him, smiled with his eyes, and said, 'Have you already forgotten your dream?'

At this the man bowed and was initiated by the dervish.

For days afterwards the man put all kinds of spiritual questions regarding life and holy scriptures to the dervish, who simply shrugged them off unanswered. One night the young man was sitting in his room thinking that surely he would get nowhere with this teacher who seemed so lacking in knowledge regarding his questions.

As he thought this the dervish appeared and said in a whisper, with great conviction, 'I am the answer to your questions.'

Now these stories look just like stories—mythological, fantasies, allegorical, or at the most, symbolic. It is not so. They are factual. If you are ready, immediately, from the higher plane messages and messengers start coming to you. They have been waiting long for somebody to become a receptive centre. When this happens, don't deny them. When this happens, become vulnerable. The first thing: open your heart and trust. And the second thing: don't feel proud. If you can do these two things, truth starts functioning through you. You become like a flute, a hollow bamboo. It starts singing through you.

But once the pride enters, the song stops. Once you start feeling superior, the song starts faltering. It has happened to many people. They had come in contact with the superior world, the higher world, the superphysical world, and then they started feeling proud. Sooner or later that contact was lost again; they became ordinary.

But then they become great pretenders because they cannot accept this, that now the contact is lost. I have seen a few people who really came to have miraculous powers, but then they became proud. Then the powers were lost, and then they became just ordinary magicians, because they cannot accept the idea that they cannot do it. They used to do it, it had happened once.

This is what has happened to Satya Sai Baba. He had come in contact. The first things that he did were not from him, but now everything is from him. The first things had just happened, but he got proud, special, a miracle-monger. Now whatsoever he is doing is just pretension; now he has to keep his prestige. Now he is even lower than an ordinary magician because at least the ordinary magician accepts that he is doing just tricks.

But this seems logical. Once you can do something and then you cannot do it, what to do then? You substitute it with something. You start learning something and doing something, somehow to manage your status that you have created around you, your image that you have created around you.

Whenever something happens to you—and it is going to happen to many, because I have made available many techniques to you; if you go on deeply in them, many things are going to become available to you—the first thing is to remain available. The second thing is to not get proud about it. Take it as a matter of fact; never exhibit it.

And if it is forced on you, then ask the forces that you should be made just a shadow, that you should not be in any way aware of what is happening through you. Because if you are aware, there is every possibility you may fall. You may start accumulating the ego—I can do this, I can do that—and lower you start slipping.

6

Your Problems Are All Bogus

*The body is becoming more and more sensitive;
it seems to vibrate at a faster rate. The more
work on consciousness and awareness, the less
conscious awareness is there.*

*Meditation seems to be taking a new form
unrecognizable and incomparable to the
previous meditation states or experiences.*

*There is less time and space and tranquil
conditions for passive, receptive meditation in
the midst of noise and physical chaos, yet
something is happening.*

*Immense trust in you is there in the face of this
loss of rational understanding.*

*Please explain, if you will, what indeed is
happening and how it is possible to go deeper
and deeper in the midst of apparently chaotic
conditions.*

THE FIRST THING and one of the most basic to be remembered

always is that only out of chaos is one reborn. There is no other way. If you want to be reborn, you will have to move in complete disorder because your old personality will have to be taken apart. You will fall apart. All that you have believed yourself to be will start disappearing by and by. All that you have always identified yourself with will become dim, cloudy. The structure that the society has given to you, the character that the society has forced upon you, will fall into pieces. Again you will be standing without a character, as you were when you were born, on the first day.

Everything will be a chaos, and out of that chaos, out of that nothingness, you will be reborn.

That is why I say again and again that religion is a great daring. It is a death, a great death, almost a suicide. Voluntarily you die, and not knowing what is going to happen . . . because how can you know what is going to happen? You will be dead. Hence, trust is needed.

So if, continuously, side by side with the chaos, a trust is growing in me, then there is no need to be afraid. That trust will take care. If the trust is not growing by the side, side by side, then there can be danger, then one can become mad. So people who don't have trust, in fact, should not move into meditation. If they move into meditation, they will start dying. They will not find any ground to stand upon, any supportive environment.

Many people come and ask me, 'If we don't take sanyas, are you not going to help us?' I will be ready to help you, but you will not be ready to take it—because it is not only a question of my giving, but also a question of your taking. I will be pouring, but if there is no trust, you will not receive it. And then there is no point in pouring in you if there is no trust. You will receive in the same amount as you are receptive. Sanyas is simply symbolic of your deep trust, symbolic that now you are going to be with me—even when all reason says don't go, even when your mind resists and says, 'This is dangerous. You are moving into a world of insecurity.' If you are ready to go with me even when your mind tries to protect you, then you have trust.

Trust is not just an emotion; it is not sentimental. People think it is only for sentimental people. They are wrong. In a deep sentiment you can say, 'I trust', but this is not going to be of much help because when everything will be disappearing, the first thing to disappear will be your sentiment. It is a very weak thing, impotent. Trust has to be so deep and solid that it is not like a sentiment, it is not a mood; it is something permanent in you, that whatsoever happens, at least you will not lose trust.

That is why I tell you to do small things. They don't look meaningful. I insist on ochre robes. Sometimes you think, 'Why? What is the point? Can't I meditate without ochre robes?' You can meditate without ochre robes—that is not the point at all. I am putting a few things to you which are not rational. There is no reason for ochre robes; there is no scientific reason for it. One can meditate and become enlightened dressed in any colour. I am giving you something irrational just as a test to see whether you are ready to go with me. I put a mala around your neck just to make a fool out of you, so you go into the world like a fool. People will laugh at you. They will think you have gone crazy. That is what I want, because if you can go with me even while I am making you almost mad, then I know that when the real crisis will come, you will have trust.

These are crises artificially created around you. They are tremendously significant, with no reason—their significance is deeper than reason. All the masters have done that.

When Ibrahim, a Sufi master, came to his master to be initiated, Ibrahim was a king; and the master looked at him and he said, 'Drop your clothes. Take my shoe, go into the marketplace, naked, and beat your head with my shoe.' His old disciples, who were sitting around, said, 'This is too hard. You never asked this from us. You never told us to take off our clothes and go into the marketplace and beat our head with our shoe. Why are you so hard with King Ibrahim?'

The master said, 'Because his ego is bigger than yours. He is a king, and I have to drop it, otherwise further work will not be possible.'

But Ibrahim didn't ask a question. He simply dropped his clothes. It must have been very, very difficult for him—in the same capital where he has always been a king, almost always been thought of as a superhuman being—moving on the street where he has never moved, naked, and with a shoe beating his head. But he moved, he went into the town. He was laughed at, children started throwing stones at him—a big crowd gathered, laughing and ridiculing him, saying that he has gone mad. But he went around the town, came back. The master said, 'You are accepted. Now everything is possible; you are open.'

Now what is the reason of it? If you understand, you will understand that this was a way to break down his ego. When ego is gone, trust arises.

Sanyas is just a method, a means, to see whether you can come with me. I have made it difficult for you. There are rumours about me all around, and I go on helping them. And I will tell you also to create as many rumours as you can. Don't be bothered about truth; create rumours. People who will be able to make contact with me in spite of the rumours will be the right people—daring, courageous. Much is possible for them.

So the first thing, chaos is created here very knowingly. So don't think that it is some sort of a problem. No, it is a device.

And don't go and ask anybody about the chaos, otherwise he will think that you are going mad. Don't go to a psychiatrist and ask him, because the whole of psychiatry, psychoanalysis, has been trying to help people in a very, very wrong way. They try to make you an adjusted being. Here, my whole effort is to break all your adjustment. What I call 'creative chaos' they will call 'maladjustment', and they want everybody to become normal, without ever thinking who is normal.

The society, the majority, the mob is normal? Where is the criterion? Who should be thought of as the norm? There is no criterion. If in India something is thought normal, it is possible that the same thing will not be thought normal in China. Something which is thought normal in Sweden will not be thought normal in India. Each society believes that the majority of the people are normal. It is not so. And to force a person to adjust with the crowd is not creative; it is very deadening.

Adjustment may be good for those who are dominating the society, but it is not good for you. Every society has been using priests, teachers, psychoanalysts to put rebellious people back, force them back into the so-called normality and adjustment. They all serve the establishment, the status quo. They all serve the class which is dominant.

Now they are doing the same in Soviet Russia. If somebody is not a communist, he is maladjusted. They put him into the mental hospital. Now not to be a communist in Soviet Russia is a sort of illness. What nonsense! But they have power: They will give you electric shocks, they will brainwash you, they will give you tranquilizers so you become dull. And when you have lost your radiance, your radicalness, when you have lost your individuality and you have become faceless, they say to you, 'Now, you are normal.'

Remember, I am not here to make you normal or adjusted. I am here to make you individuals. And you are not to fulfil any criterion other than your own destiny. I am looking at you directly. I am not saying that you have to be like 'this', because that is how you have been destroyed, that is how your so-called character has been created. The character is disease, it is illness, it is how you are suffering, imprisoned. I have to take it apart, destroy it, so that you can become free. So that again you can start soaring high, again you start thinking in terms of your own being, again you can become an individual.

The society has polluted it too much, corrupted you too much, and so whenever the chaos starts you become afraid—'What is going on? Am I going crazy?'

I have heard a very famous story of when Queen Marie visited the US and asked to meet a most famous psychiatrist.

The nurse ushered in Queen Marie and said to the psychiatrist, 'I would like you to meet the Queen of Romania.'

The psychiatrist looked at the queen and asked, 'How long does she think she has been a queen?'

A psychiatrist is always treating people of whom somebody thinks he is Alexander, somebody thinks he is Genghis Khan, somebody thinks he is Hitler, somebody who thinks she is Cleopatra . . . and so on. So of course he couldn't think that Queen Marie, Queen of Romania, herself has come. He thought, 'Must be some other woman gone crazy. How long does she think she has been a queen?'

Another story I have heard:

A patient was brought to a psychiatrist by friends, who told the doctor that the man was suffering from delusions that an enormous fortune was awaiting him. He was expecting two letters which would give him full details involving a rubber plantation in Sumatra and titles to some mines in South Africa.

'It was a difficult case and I worked hard on it,' the psychiatrist told some of his colleagues, 'and just when I had the man cured, the two letters arrived.'

Be alert. Those two letters may be really coming.

And don't be afraid. The fear arises whenever you start walking alone. One feels insecure. The doubt arises—'Am I right?'—because the whole crowd is going in one direction, but you start walking alone. With the crowd, the doubt never arises because you think, 'Millions of people are going in this direction; there must be something in it, has to be.' The crowd-mind prevails over you; the collective mind prevails over you. So many people cannot be wrong; they must be right.

I have heard about one psychoanalyst who went on a picnic. They were trying to find a right spot; then one member of the group found a place. 'This is a beautiful place,' he said. 'The right spot. Big trees, shade, the river flowing by and absolutely silent.'

The psychiatrist said, 'Yes, ten million ants can't be wrong.'

Ten million ants can't be wrong. Ants gather together wherever there is a picnic spot—flies and ants. That is our inner mathematics, that if there are so many people, then they cannot be wrong. Alone one feels dizzy. With the crowd, people all around—a whole ocean of people, one feels perfectly right. So many people are going: they must be going in the right direction. And everybody is thinking the same.

Nobody knows where they are going. They are just going because the whole crowd is going. And if you ask everybody individually, 'Are you going in the right direction?', they will say, 'I don't know. Because the whole world is going, I am going.'

My whole effort here is to bring you out of the collective mind, to help make you an individual. In the beginning you will have to face chaos. And great trust will be needed, tremendous trust will be needed. Otherwise you can get out of the collective mind and you may not get into the individual mind; then you will be mad. That is the risk. Without trust, moving into meditation is risky. I will not tell you to move into it; I will tell you it is better to remain normal, whatsoever 'normality' means. Remain adjusted with the society. But if you are really ready to go on a great adventure, the greatest, then trust. And then wait for chaos.

The more aware you become, the less, of course, you are conscious of it—because there is no need to be conscious of it. Awareness is enough. Consciousness of awareness will be a strain. In the beginning it is so. You start learning to drive a car. Of course you are much troubled; you have to manage so many things—the wheel, the gear, the clutch, the accelerator, the brake, the road and so on. One has to be very, very conscious because so many things have to be managed together. It seems almost impossible in the beginning. By and by everything drops; you simply go on driving. You can talk to a friend, you can listen to the radio, you can sing a song, or you can meditate, and then there is no problem. Then driving has become a spontaneous thing. You know it, so there is no need to be self-conscious about it.

The same happens when you meditate. In the beginning you have to be conscious about consciousness. It brings a strain, tiredness. By and by, as consciousness grows, there is no need to be conscious about it. It goes on flowing on its own, like breathing. You need not be conscious about it; it goes on its own. In fact, at the later stages of meditation, if you are concerned too much about your awareness, it will be a disturbance; just as, if you become conscious of your breathing, you will immediately disturb its natural rhythm. It flows naturally. There is no need for you to come in.

And awareness has to become natural, only then is it possible: even while you are asleep, the light of awareness continues burning, the flame remains—even while you are fast asleep.

And the last thing about the question: 'Immense trust in you is there in the face of this loss of rational understanding.' Rational understanding means not understanding at all. It is a misnomer. Through reason one never understands anything. One simply comes to feel that one understands. Reason is a lie. It gives you a false feeling, 'Yes, you have understood.'

Only through experience does one understand; only through existential experience is understanding possible.

For example, if I talk about love, you can understand it rationally, because you know the language, you know the semantics, you know the meaning of the words, you know the construction of the sentences and you have been trained— so, you can understand what I am saying. But your understanding will be 'about' love. It will not be *exactly* the understanding of love. It will be 'about' love, it will not be direct. And howsoever you go on collecting facts and information about love, you will never be able to know what love is only through this accumulation. You will have to move into love, you will have to taste it, to dissolve into it, to dare . . . and only then will you know.

Rational understanding is just a very superficial understanding. Become more existential. If you want to know about love, it is better to go into love rather than going into the library and consulting what others have said about love. If you want to meditate, rather than going into the books and learning what meditation is all about, go directly into meditation. Feel it, enjoy it, enter into it, allow it to happen around you, allow it to happen within you; then you will know.

How can you know what dancing is without dancing? It is impossible to know from the books, and it is difficult to know even seeing a dancer dance. Then too it is not 'knowing', because you see the outer form of it, just the movements of the body. You don't know what is happening inside the dancer, what harmony is arising in him, what consciousness, what awareness is arising in him, what crystallization, what centring. You cannot see it, you cannot infer it. From the outside it is not available, and you cannot enter into the inner world of the dancer. The only way to enter there is to become a dancer.

All that is beautiful, deep and great has to be lived.

Trust is one of the greatest things in life—greater than love, because love knows of hate. Trust does not know anything about it. Love is still a duality. The hate part remains hidden; it has not been dropped. You can hate your lover within a second. Anything can cause it, and the hate part comes up and the love part goes down. In love it is only half of what you call love; just beneath the surface the hate is always waiting to jump over and possess you. And it possesses you. Lovers go on fighting: continuous conflict. Somebody has written a book about love. The title is beautiful: *The Intimate Enemy*. Lovers are enemies also.

But trust is higher than love; it is non-dual. It knows no hate. It knows no polarity, no opposite. It simply is one. It is the purest love—love purified of hate, love which has dropped the hate part completely, love which cannot turn into a sour or bitter experience; love which has become almost unearthly, other-worldly.

So only those who love can trust. If you want to avoid love, and only trust, your trust will be of a very lower status because it will continue to have the hate part. You have to move your energy first through love so you can become aware of the hate and love duality. Then is the frustration that comes out of the hate part, then an understanding through experience, and then dropping the hate part. Then pure love, the very essence, survives. Even the flower is not there, only the fragrance; then you rise into trust.

Of course it has nothing to do with rational understanding. In fact, the more rational understanding disappears, the more trust will arise. Trust is in a way blind; in a way trust is the only clarity of vision there is. If you think from reason, trust will look blind. Rationalists will always call trust blind. If you look through the experience of trust, you will laugh; you will say, 'I have got my eyes for the first time.' Then trust is the only clarity there is. The vision is so clear, without any cloud of anger and hate, so transparent.

✽

Two or three months back, during the lecture I
used to weep a lot. Now even if you are not
saying anything funny, in the moments when I
feel closer to you, I just want to laugh and
laugh and laugh. Why is it so?

But why 'why?'—laugh! Why make it a question and a
problem?

This is from Krishna Radha. First she used to ask, 'Why
am I crying?' Now, somehow, by some miracle, she is not
crying, but laughing; but the problem continues.

Why do we cling to problems? Even if you feel happy,
suddenly the mind says, 'Why?' As if happiness is also a
disease. A rational explanation is needed; otherwise even
happiness will not be worth it.

This goes on and on. I see people come to me—they are
miserable; they ask 'why'— if one is feeling miserable, I can
understand that one asks 'why'. But I know their 'why' is
deeper than their misery. Soon they start feeling happy, and
again they are there—very miserable because they are happy.
Now the misery is 'Why?'

Let me tell you an anecdote:

A man walks into a psychiatrist's office and says, 'Doc,
I am going out of my mind. I keep thinking I am a zebra.
Every time I look at myself in the mirror my entire body is
covered with black stripes.'

The psychiatrist tries to calm him down. 'Steady, steady,'
he says. 'Now just calm down, go home and take these pills,
get a good night's sleep, and I am sure the black stripes will
completely disappear.'

So the poor man goes home and returns two days

after. He says, 'Doc, I feel great. Got anything for the *white* stripes?'

But the problem continues.

Once, somebody brought a mad young man to me. The young man had a crazy idea that flies had entered into his body, through his nose or mouth in his sleep, and that they go on whirling inside. So of course he was in much trouble. He would turn this way and that. He could not even sit rightly because of those whirling dervishes inside; he could not sleep. A continuous agony . . . what can be done with this man? So I told him, 'You lie down on the bed and have a good ten minutes' rest; we will do whatsoever can be done.'

So I covered him with a sheet so that he could not see what was happening and ran around the whole house to catch a few flies. It was difficult because I had never done that before, but my experience of catching people helped. Somehow I could get three flies. I put them in a bottle, brought them to the man, made some hocus-pocus passes over him, then told him to open his eyes and showed him the bottle.

He looked at the bottle. He said, 'Yes, you have got some, but only the smaller ones. The big ones are still there— and they are so big.' Now from where do I get such big flies? He said, 'I am very, very grateful to you. At least you got rid of the smaller ones; but the big ones are really very big.'

People go on. If you help them from one side, they will bring the same problem from another side—as if there is a certain deep necessity. Try to understand it.

To live without a problem is very difficult, almost humanly impossible. Why? Because a problem gives you a distraction. A problem gives you an occupation. A problem gives you a busy-ness without any business. A problem engages you. If there is no problem, you will not be able to cling to the periphery of your being. You will be sucked by the centre.

And the centre of your being is empty. It is just like the hub of a wheel. The whole wheel moves on the empty hub. Your innermost core is empty, nothing, nothingness, *shunyam*, void, abyss-like. You are afraid of that emptiness, so you go on clinging to the rim of the wheel or, at the most, if you are a little daring, then you go on clinging to the spokes; but you never move towards the hub. One starts feeling afraid, shaky.

How can you go within? People come to me and they say, 'We want to go within, but there are problems.' They think because of the problems they are not going within. The real case is just the opposite: because they don't want to go within, they are creating problems.

Let this understanding become as deep in you as possible: your problems are all bogus.

I go on answering your problems just to be polite. They are all bogus—basically meaningless—but they help you to avoid yourself. They distract you. How can one go in? There are so many problems first to be solved. But if one problem is solved, immediately another bubbles up. And if you look, you will see the other problem has the same quality as the first. Try to solve it and a third one comes up, which in turn is immediately substituted.

Let me tell you an anecdote:

Psychiatrist: 'You teenagers are a menace. You have no

sense of responsibility. Forget about the material things and think of other things like science, mathematics and the like. How are you at maths?'

Patient: 'Not very good.'

'I will give you a test for your factual information. Now give me a number.'

'Royal 3447. That is the store where my girl works.'

'I don't want a phone number, just an ordinary number.'

'All right. Thirty-seven.'

'That's better. Now another number, please.'

'Twenty-two.'

'And again.'

'Thirty-seven.'

'Fine, fine. See, you can get your mind working in other directions if you want to.'

'Correct. 37-22-37! Boy, what a figure.'

Back to the girlfriend, if not through the phone number, then through the figure.

This goes on and on, ad infinitum.

Look at the essential thing. Why do you want to create problems in the first place? Are there really problems? Have you asked the most essential question to yourself: are there really problems, or are you creating them and you have become habituated to create them and you keep their company and it feels lonely if there are not problems? You would even like to be miserable, but you would not like to be empty. People cling to their miseries even, but are not ready to become empty.

I see it every day. A couple comes. Both are fighting for years, they say for fifteen years they have been fighting. Married for fifteen years, and continuously fighting and creating hell for each other. Then why don't you separate?

Why are you clinging to misery? Either change or separate. What is the point of wasting your whole life? But I can see what is happening. They are not ready to be alone. At least misery gives them company. And they don't know now, if they separate, how they are going to manage their lives. They have become adjusted to a particular pattern of continuous conflict, anger, nagging, fighting, violence. They have learned the trick of it. Now they don't know how to be in another situation with somebody else with a different personality. How to be with somebody else? They don't know anything else. They have learned a particular language of misery. Now they feel skill, efficiency in it. To move with a new person again will be starting things from the beginning. After fifteen years of remaining in a certain business one hesitates to move in another.

I have heard about a great film star who went to a psychiatrist and said, 'I have no talent for music, no talent for acting. I am not a handsome person. My face is ugly, my personality is very poor. What should I do?' And he is a famous actor.

So the psychiatrist said, 'But why don't you leave acting? If you feel you don't have any talent, no genius, and this is not the work you are meant to do, why don't you get out of the work?'

He said, 'What? After twenty years working in it and becoming a famous star?'

You invest in your miseries also. When one problem drops, just see, the real problem will shift immediately to something else. It is like a snake that goes on slipping out of its old skin—but the snake remains. The 'why?' is the snake. It was concerned when you were crying. Now the crying has stopped; you are laughing. The snake has slipped out of the old skin. Now the problem is the laughing.

Can't you think of a life without any 'why'? Why do you make life a problem?

A man was talking to a Jew, and was feeling very annoyed by the Jewish habit of answering questions with other questions. Annoyed, the man finally said, 'Why do you Jews go on answering questions with questions?'

Said the Jew, 'Why not?'

People go on moving in a circle. 'Why not?' Again, a question.

Just look into it. If you are laughing, it is beautiful. In fact, if you ask me, even crying was beautiful; nothing was wrong in it. If you really ask me, then I will say accept whatsoever is. Accept the real, and then crying is also beautiful. And there is no need to go into the inquiry of 'why'—because that inquiry distracts you from the factual. Then crying is not important, but why you are crying is. Then the real disappears and you go on chasing the cause. Where can you find the cause? How can you find the cause? You will have to go to the very beginning of the world—and there has never been any beginning. The world has been here always.

No question is needed to live. And don't wait for answers; start dropping questions. Live with the fact. If you are crying, cry. Enjoy it! It is a beautiful phenomenon—relaxing, cleansing, purifying. Laughter is beautiful. Laugh, and let laughter take possession of you. Laugh, so your whole body throbs and pulsates with it. It will be purifying, it will be vitalizing; it will rejuvenate you.

But remain with the fact. Don't move into causes. Remain with the existential. Don't be bothered *why* it is so, because it cannot be answered. Buddha has said many times to his disciples, 'Don't ask questions, and at least not metaphysical ones, because they are foolish.' Just remain with the fact.

Life is so tremendously beautiful, why not live it right now? Crying, it is a gesture of life. Laughing is also a gesture of life. Sometimes you are sad. It is a gesture of life, a mood. It is beautiful. Sometimes you are happy and bubbling with joy and dancing. That too is good and beautiful. Whatsoever happens, accept it, welcome it, and remain with it; you will see by and by you have dropped the habit of asking questions and creating problems out of life.

And when you don't create problems, life opens all its mysteries. It never opens before a person who goes on asking questions. Life is ready to reveal itself to you if you don't make a problem. If you make a problem, your very creating of the problem closes your eyes. You become aggressive towards life.

That is the difference between scientific effort and religious effort. The scientist is like an aggressive man, trying to snatch away truths from life, forcing life to deliver truths almost violently. A religious man is just standing before life and asking questions. A religious man simply relaxes with life, floats with it; and life reveals many things to the religious man that it is not ever going to reveal to the scientist. The scientist will always be gathering crumbs fallen from the table. The scientist is never going to be invited as a guest. Those who welcome life and accept it joyfully, with no question but with trust, are the ones who become the guests.

✳

How exactly does one treat the following ailments:
First, miserliness.
Second, nagging, worrying perfectionism.
Third, actor personality, that is, always behaving as if on show.

Fourth, pride. This includes pride about what I have lately begun to think is my peacefulness.

Is meditation sufficient to deal with these, or is anything additional needed, such as consciously indulging in them to the extreme, or trying to ignore them or perhaps consciously avoiding them?

Miserliness has almost become an inbuilt thing in you. The whole pattern of society creates it. It wants you to snatch things from people and not to give. It makes you ambitious, and an ambitious man becomes miserly. Whatsoever the ambition—worldly, non-worldly—an ambitious man becomes miserly. Because he is always preparing for the future, he cannot afford to live and share. He is never here now. If he has money, he has money for the future, not for now. And how can you share in the future? Sharing is possible only in the present. He has money for his old age. Or there are people who have their character, virtue, for the future life, for paradise. How can they share right now? They are accumulating, preparing for something great to happen somewhere in the future. Right now they are poor.

All ambitious people are poor, and because of their poverty, they become miserly. They go on holding everything, even useless things.

I used to live with a man. His whole house was just like a junkyard. It was difficult to live in that house; there was no space left. And he was continuously accumulating whatsoever. One day I had gone for a walk and I saw that man by the side of the road picking up a handle of a bicycle, just the handle. He looked all around and he saw that nobody was looking, and then took that handle to his home. When I came back, I went into the house and said, 'Where is that handle?'

He was a little embarrassed. He said, 'Have you seen it?'

'I was there.'

But he said, 'This is a good thing. And who knows? By and by I can collect the whole bicycle. And what is wrong in it? And I have not stolen it—somebody had thrown it.'

This way he went on accumulating things—useless things—but he is always thinking of the future. Someday these things will become useful; someday the need may arise. Who knows?

You may not be doing so in your house, but you all do so in your heart. If you go into your heart, into your mind, you will find it like a junkyard. You have accumulated many useless things there. You have never cleaned it. You go on putting in rubbish, and then you become heavy and then you feel burdened and then you feel disturbed. And then an inner ugliness arises.

But try to understand the base of miserliness. It is in the idea of living somewhere in the future. If you are to live here now, you are never miserly, because you can share. Why do you want to collect anything? Why do you want to accumulate? There is no necessity that the tomorrow is going to be; it may not be. Why not share? Why not enjoy? This very moment life is flowering in you. Enjoy it, share it.

Because by sharing, it becomes intense. By sharing, it becomes more vital. By sharing, it increases and grows.

So the whole point is to understand that the future is not. The future is created by the ambitious mind. The future is not part of time. It is part of ambition. Because ambition needs space to move, you cannot fulfil ambition now; you can fulfil life now, but not ambition. Ambition is against life, anti-life.

Just see yourself and others. People are preparing: someday they are going to live. That day never comes. They go on preparing until they die. It will never come because if you get into preparations too much that will become an obsession. You will simply prepare and prepare and prepare. It is as if somebody goes on accumulating foodstuff for some future use and goes on remaining hungry, starving and dying. That is what is happening to millions of people. They die, surrounded by much stuff which could have been used. They could have lived beautifully.

Nobody is hindering your path except your ambition. So miserliness is part of ambition.

This question is from Bodhidharma. He is very ambitious. Not in a worldly sense—he does not want a big house, he does not want a big car, he does not want a big bank account—no, he is simple that way, very simple, almost a mahatma. He has nothing much and does not bother about it. But he wants to be enlightened. That is his problem. And he is in such a hurry to become enlightened.

Drop all nonsense. Live right now. There is no need for any enlightenment in the future. If you live right now, you are enlightened. The day you will be able to find out that life has to be lived right now, you are enlightened. Then one never thinks of the past and never thinks of the future. This moment is enough, enough unto itself. All misery disappears.

Misery is because you are not capable of living. So you create some goals . . . enlightenment is a goal to give you a feeling that you are important, that you are doing something, your life is meaningful, you are not living a meaningless life, you are a great spiritual seeker. All these are ego trips.

Enlightenment is not a goal. It is a consequence. You cannot seek it. You cannot make a goal out of it. It cannot become an object of desire. When you start living without desire and in the present, suddenly it is there. It is a consequence. It is a consequence of a vital life, of an alive being—so alive and so intense, so aflame, that this moment he moves so deeply into time that he touches eternity.

There are two moments in time. One is from one moment to another, horizontal—from A to B, from B to C, from C to D. That is how you live; that is how desire moves—horizontal. A really alive man, sensitive, aware, does not move from A to B. He moves deeper and deeper into A; his movement is vertical.

This is the meaning of Jesus' cross. The cross is both vertical and horizontal. Jesus' hands are on the horizontal part of the cross. His whole body is on the vertical. Hands are symbolic of action. Action moves horizontally; being moves vertically.

So don't be absorbed in action too much; become more and more absorbed into being. That is what meditation is all about. It is to learn how to be without doing anything. *Wu-wei*—just to be. And you start falling into this moment, deeper and deeper. And this vertical movement of time is eternity.

Both time and eternity meet in you. Now it is for you to decide. If you move in ambition you will move in time, and death exists in time. If you move in desire you will move in time, and death exists in time. If you hanker for the ego you will move in time. Death, ego, desire, ambition, they all are part of the horizontal line.

If you start digging in the moment and move vertically, you become a non-ego. You lose your desires, you become non-ambitious; but suddenly you are aflame with life, you are an intense energy of life, existence has taken possession of you.

Move vertically, and all miserliness disappears.

'Nagging, worrying perfectionism.' That has also been forced upon you. You have been taught to be perfect. The real thing is to be whole, not perfect. Nobody can be perfect, because perfection is a static thing. Life is dynamic. Nothing can be perfect in life because further perfection is always possible. It goes on growing, endlessly. It is a continuous growth, a continuum. It is always evolution, it is always revolution. It is never at a point where you can say, 'Now, this is perfect.'

Perfection is a false ideal, but the ego wants it. The ego wants to be perfect, so it goes on nagging you: 'Become perfect.' Then it creates tensions, madness, insanities, and the ego goes on creating ego trips. Just the other day I was reading a definition. The definition says, 'The neurotic person is one who makes castles in the air, the psychotic person is one who lives in those castles, and the psychiatrist is the one who collects the rent.' If you want to become neurotic or psychotic, then try to become perfect.

And all the religions on the earth up to now—organized religions, the church—have been teaching people to become perfect. Jesus has not taught that, Christianity has. Buddha has not taught that, but Buddhism has. All the organized religions have been teaching people to become perfect.

Buddha, Jesus, Lao Tzu . . . they said something totally different. They say, 'Become whole.' What is the difference between 'whole' and becoming 'perfect'? Becoming perfect is the horizontal line; perfection is somewhere in the future. Becoming whole can be done this moment, it needs no time. Becoming whole is becoming authentic, becoming yourself—whosoever you are, whatsoever you are.

Ordinarily you live a very, very limited life. You don't allow your energy a full play . . . it becomes a fragmented life. You want to love somebody, but you don't love totally. Now I don't say make your love perfect love. It is not possible, because a perfect love would mean that there is no more growth possible. It will be a death. I say make your love total, whole. Love wholly. Whatsoever is in you, don't hold it. Give it totally, give in totally. Flow into the other totally; don't hold. This is the only thing that will make you whole.

If you are swimming, swim totally. If you are walking, walk totally. In the walking, just become the walking, nothing else. If you are eating, eat totally.

Somebody asked Chao-chou, a great Zen master, 'What did you do before you became enlightened?'

He said, 'I used to chop wood and fetch water from the well.'

The man asked, 'Now that you have become enlightened, what do you do?'

He said, 'The same. I chop wood and I fetch the water from the well.'

The man was a little puzzled; he said, 'But what is the difference then?'

Chao-chou said, 'The difference is much. Before, I used to do many more things side by side. Chopping wood, I would think of many things. Carrying water from the well, I would think of many things. But now I simply carry the water, I simply chop the wood. Even the chopper has disappeared. Just chopping; nobody's there.'

This will give you a feeling of wholeness. Make wholeness a constant concern. Remember it: drop the idea of perfection. It has been given to you by your parents, teachers, colleges, universities, churches . . . but they have all made you neurotic. The whole world is suffering from neurosis.

A mother took her little boy to a psychiatrist and asked, 'Doctor, can a boy of ten marry a film star like Elizabeth Taylor?'

The doctor said, 'Of course not, madam. It is quite impossible.'

The mother looked at her little boy and said, 'See, what did I tell you? Now go out and get a divorce.'

Not only is the boy neurotic, but also the mother—and the mother is even more so. Neurotic parents give birth to neurotic children.

Many times people ask me, 'Why don't you allow your sanyasins to have babies?' First I would like you to become non-neurotic; otherwise you will give birth to neurotic babies. The world is full of neurosis. At least don't increase it. I am not concerned about population; that is the politicians' concern. My concern is neurosis. You are neurotic; out of your neurosis you give birth to children.

They are also a distraction to you. Because you are fed up with yourself, you would like some distraction. Children are beautiful distractions. They create more troubles. Your troubles have become old; you are fed up with them. You would like some new troubles. The husband is fed up with the wife; the wife is fed up with the husband. They would like somebody to stand between them: a child. Many marriages are held together by children. Otherwise they would have fallen apart. Once the children are there, the mother starts thinking of the responsibility to the children, the father starts thinking of the duty to the children. Now there exists a bridge.

And the mother and the father both are loaded with their own madness, problems and anxieties. What are they going to give to these children? What have they to give? They talk about love, but they are violent. Their love is already poisoned, they don't know what love is, and then in the name of love they torture. In the name of love they try to kill the life in the children. They make their life structured. In the name of love they dominate, they possess. And of course the children are very helpless, so you do whatsoever you want to do: Beat them, mould them this way or that, force them to carry your unfulfilled desires and ambitions so that when you are dead they will be carrying your ambitions and they will be trying the same nonsense that you were trying to do.

I would like you to have children, but to become a father, to become a mother, is not so easy.

Once you are whole, then become a mother, become a father. Then you will give birth to a child who will be a freedom, who will be graceful, who will be health and wholeness—and that will be a gift to the world. And he will make the world a little better than it is. Otherwise don't—you are enough!

'Why did you put me in the same room with that fellow?'

asked the indignant patient in the asylum.

'The hospital is crowded,' explained the doctor. 'Is he being troublesome then?'

'Troublesome? He is nuts! He keeps looking around the room saying, "No lions, no tigers, no elephants", and all the time the room is full of them!'

Mad people think others are mad. Mad people never think they are mad. Once a madman recognizes that he is mad, he is already on the path of sanity. Try to see your madness, recognize it. That will help you to become sane.

Try to be whole; otherwise that perfectionism will nag you. Become whole. Do whatsoever you want to do, but do it totally. Dissolve into it, melt into it, and by and by you will have a flowering of your being. Then there is no idea of perfection in you.

But you are incomplete, divided, fragmentary. That is why continuously the question of 'how to be perfect' arises. Be whole, and the idea will drop on its own accord.

'Pride and actor personality'. Of course, people who are trying to be perfect will become 'actor personalities'. They will have personas; they will hide themselves behind masks. They will not allow their reality to be seen by others. They will always try to pretend; they will be hypocrites. They will always try to perform, to prove. They know who they are, and they will try to prove that they are somebody else.

And the difficulty is that they may not be able to convince others, but they can always convince themselves. That is how neurosis arises.

Just be yourself, at whatsoever cost. Whatsoever the cost, be yourself. Be sincere. In the beginning there will be much fear because you think that you are a great man and suddenly you reveal yourself to be an ordinary man. There will be fear, the ego will feel hurt; but let it feel hurt. In fact, let it starve and die. Help it to death.

Be ordinary, be simple, and you will become more whole and the tension will dissolve and there will be no need to continuously perform. It is such a great tension—continuously on performance, continuously in the show window, just watching what people are thinking and what you have to do to prove that you are something special. But just think about others also: they are all doing the same thing!

The whole world is worried too much because everybody is trying to prove something which they are not, and others are doing the same. And nobody wants to see that *you* are great. They know that you are not, because how can they believe in your greatness? They themselves are great. You also know that nobody is great other than you. You may not say so, but everybody deep down goes on believing it.

I have heard that in Arabian countries they have a joke that whenever God makes a new man he plays a trick. He whispers in his ear, 'You are the best I have yet made—the greatest.' But he has been doing that to everybody, so everybody is convinced of his own greatness.

Try to walk on earth. Be realistic. And if you are ordinary, you will suddenly see many doors opening, which were closed before because of your tense state. Relax.

And of course pride comes again and again in different ways, so watch out. And always remember, it will come in subtle ways, so make your watching more accurate, exact and alert.

Yes, meditation will do. Nothing else is needed. Just meditate more, so you can see things clearly.

✳

*Slowly I feel that you are me. But then who is
this guy in white sitting every morning on that
chair?*

G.O.K.

Now let me explain to you this code word 'G.O.K.'—
that will be my answer.

A doctor was shown around the London hospital by
several physicians. He looked at the filing system and noticed
the bright idea they had of abbreviations—'D' for diphtheria,
'M' for measles, 'TB' for tuberculosis and so on. All the
diseases seemed to be pretty well under control except one
indicated by 'G.O.K.'

'I see that you have a sweeping epidemic of G.O.K. on
your hands,' he said. 'But just what is G.O.K.?'

'Oh,' said one of them. 'When we can't diagnose we
put G.O.K.—God Only Knows.'

I don't know who is this guy sitting here on this chair
and talking to you. G.O.K.!

7

The Eternal Now

Performing samyama *on the present moment, the moment gone, and the moment to come, brings knowledge born of the awareness of the ultimate reality.*

From this comes the ability to distinguish between similar objects which cannot be identified by class, character or place.

The highest knowledge born of the awareness of reality is transcendent, includes the cognition of all objects simultaneously, pertains to all objects and processes whatsoever—in the past, the present and the future—and transcends the world process.

WHAT IS TIME? Patanjali asks the timeless question, the perennial question, and he comes to it at the very end of *Vibhuti Pada*, because to know time is the greatest miracle. To know what time is, is to know what life is. To know what time is, is to know what truth is. Before we enter into the sutras, many things have to be understood; they will become an introduction into the sutras.

Ordinarily what we call time is not real time. It is chronological time. So remember that time can be divided, classified, in three ways. One is 'chronological', another is 'psychological' and the third is 'real'.

The chronological time is clock time. It is utilitarian; it is not real. It is just a belief agreed upon by society. We have agreed to divide the day into twenty-four hours. It is very arbitrary—because the earth moves one complete circle on its axis in twenty-four hours, so we have decided to divide it into twenty-four. Then we have decided to divide each hour into sixty minutes.

There is no intrinsic necessity to divide it that way. Some other civilization may divide it in a different way. We can divide the hour into a hundred minutes and nobody is going to prevent us. Then each minute we have divided into sixty seconds. That too is arbitrary, just utilitarian. It is clock time. It is needed; otherwise society will fall apart.

Something as a common standard is a necessity for society—just like money. A hundred-rupee note, a ten-dollar bill or anything else—it is just a common belief that society has agreed to use. But it has nothing to do with existence. If man disappears from the earth, the pound sterling, the dollar, the rupee will all disappear immediately. Without man, the earth will be without money immediately. Rocks will be there, flowers will still flower, the spring will come and birds will sing and in the fall old leaves will fall; but there will be no money. Even if there are piles of money on the roads, it will not be money at all—because to call it money, man is needed. To respect it as money, man is needed.

The government goes on promising, and on each note the promise is written. The finance governor promises to pay you ten rupees worth of gold if you produce the note to the bank. It is just a promise. When there is nobody to promise, the currency disappears.

When man is not there on the earth, clocks may go on chiming time, but it will not be time at all. Nobody will bother, nobody will look at them. Clock time will stop immediately if man is not there; so it is man-created, a social by-product.

The higher a society moves—and when I say 'higher' I mean the more *complex* it becomes—the more it becomes obsessed with chronological time. A primitive man has no use for a watch. If you present him a watch, he will simply be puzzled—what is it for? What is he going to do with it? A civilized man cannot live without a watch. It is almost impossible to live in a civilized society without a watch because the whole society runs according to the clock, even sometimes to ridiculous states.

I will tell you an anecdote:

There was a loud knock at the door just as the doctor had settled down to sleep. He got up and asked the man at the door, 'What is it!'

'I have been bitten by a dog,' said the man.

'Well, don't you know that my hours of consultation are between 12 p.m. and 3 p.m.?'

'Yes,' groaned the patient. 'But the dog did not know and he bit me at 3.40 p.m. So what am I supposed to do?'

Dogs don't believe in clocks, and things can go to ridiculous ends.

Once you think in terms of the clock, you forget that this is just utilitarian. It is not real time.

At another doctor's:

The sign behind the desk at the reception of the hospital said: 'Emergency Casualty Registrations'. A man staggered in, bruised and muddy. He was plastered with blood and bandages, limping on both legs and clutching his arm to stem the flow of blood. He crawled to the desk and groaned, 'Doctor, doctor.'

The receptionist asked, 'Have you an appointment, sir?'

Once the chronological time is taken too seriously, one forgets everything else. The whole West is obsessed with time too much. Everything has to be done 'at the time'.

One of my friends travelled in England with one of his English friends, and he later told me that everything has become so routine that in England you hear expressions like 'teatime', 'dinnertime', and 'lunchtime'. What do they mean? How can time decide the time for lunch, unless you are feeling hungry? When you say 'lunchtime', it means 'hunger time'—now be hungry! And if you are not, then something is wrong with you. Teatime means now be ready for tea. If you are not feeling like it, then something is wrong with you; you have to take it. By and by people have forgotten their real hunger, their real thirst. Everything is taken on time. The clock decides. The clock has become the dominator; it dominates. This is a very unreal world, dominated by the clock.

Now there are educators, psychologists who go on telling mothers to give the child milk only at certain times, and after every three hours. The child is hungry; it's crying, but the mother looks at the clock. It is not time yet. The child is hungry, but that is not anything to be worried about. The clock has to be looked at. Because when the child is hungry, the child is not to be believed, but the doctor. It is none of the doctor's business to interfere. But once you become obsessed with the unreal, many unreal things enter into your life.

I have heard:

An Irishman called Pat fell from a ladder and lay apparently unconscious on the ground. A crowd gathered around him and a doctor was called, who said at once that the poor man was dead. Pat opened his eyes and promptly denied the charge.

'Shush, Pat!' said one of the bystanders. 'Don't be talking nonsense. Surely the doctor knows best.'

Even if you are alive and the doctor says you are dead, you have to behave like a dead man—because, of course, the expert knows best.

With the chronological time, the world of the expert has come into existence, because you have lost your roots into reality. For everything you have to ask somebody. People come to me and they say, 'Osho, tell us how we are feeling.' How you are feeling you have to know. But I understand. The touch, the contact, the connectedness with reality is lost. Even how you are feeling, you have to go to ask somebody who knows; you have to rely on somebody else. This is unfortunate, but it has happened in slow steps and humanity has not been aware.

Chronological time is not being used now. It is no longer a means; it has almost become an end. Remember, it is false time. It has nothing to do with reality.

Deep down from it, just underneath it, is another time which is not real, but more real than the chronological time: that is psychological time. There is a clock, a biological clock, within you. Women are more alert about it than men. Their body functions as an inner clock. After every twenty-eight days, the menstruation comes. The body functions like an inner clock, a biological clock.

If you observe, then you will see that hunger comes at a

certain time every day. If you are healthy, then needs fall into a certain pattern; that pattern is repeated. It is only broken when you are not well; otherwise the body moves on smoothly, runs in a smooth pattern. And if you are aware of that pattern, you will be more alive than the man who lives by the clock. You are closer to reality.

The chronological time is fixed, it has to be fixed, because it is a social necessity; but the psychological time is fluid, it is not so solid, because each person has his own psychology, his own mind. Have you noticed that when you are happy, time goes fast? Your clock will not go fast; the clock has nothing to do with you. It moves at its own pace—in sixty seconds it moves one minute, in sixty minutes it moves one hour. It will continue regardless of whether you are happy or unhappy. If you are unhappy, your mind will be in a different time; if you are happy, your mind will be in a different time. If your beloved unexpectedly comes and knocks at your door, you will lose track of time. Hours will pass—you may not be doing anything, just holding hands and sitting and looking at the moon—hours will pass, and it will seem as if only minutes have passed. Time goes very, very fast when you are happy. When you are unhappy— say, somebody you loved has died—then time goes very, very, very slowly.

Just the other night, Meera came here. Her husband died a few months earlier. She had come to see me after the death, and I had told her not to be worried, the wound will heal. It will take a little time, maybe three months. But those three months were just an average because it will depend on the person. Now she came last night again and said, 'Now five months have passed and the pain is still there. Of course it is less, but it is still there, it has not gone; and you had said that within three months it will go.' I know. Sometimes it will take one year, sometimes it will take six months, and sometimes it may not even take three months, three days will do. It is not chronological; it is psychological. It depends on you, on the relationship, what type of relationship existed between you and the person who died.

And I know the relationship was not good. That is why the wound will take a long time to heal. This will look paradoxical, but this is how it is. If you have loved a man and he dies, you will feel sad, but you will recover—soon. There will be no wound. You loved the man; nothing is incomplete. But between Meera and her husband the relationship was not good; for years they were almost separate. She wanted to love but could not love. She wanted to be with him but could not be. Now the husband is gone, and her whole hope to be with him is gone with him.

She hankered, she desired, she wanted, but it couldn't happen. Now the man is gone; now there is no possibility. Now her aloneness is sealed, now there is no way to love this man. When he was alive, she could not love; there were problems between them. Now the man is gone, so there is no possibility. Now this wound is going to heal very slowly—very, very slowly. And even when it is healed there will remain a certain sadness around it forever.

Anything incomplete is very difficult to drop. Complete things ripen and fall on their own accord. When a fruit is ripe, it falls. Of course, the tree feels for a few seconds that something is missing, and then it forgets, because ripe fruits have to fall. Everybody has to die. You loved while the man was alive—and you loved tremendously and totally. You are fulfilled; you cannot ask for more. As it was, it was already too much. You are grateful that existence gave you that much time. It could have taken the man a little earlier, but it gave you enough time, and you loved and you loved.

But that has not happened in Meera's case, so I can understand her misery.

But she has to face it and understand it. It is not only a question of the death of the husband. That is not such a big problem. Husbands die, wives die; that is not a big problem—that is natural. The problem is that love could not happen. It remained a dream, a desire, and now it is going to remain unfulfilled. You cannot find that man again, so that chapter cannot be completed. This incompletion will function as a wound. That is why it has taken a longer time. It will take a little longer still.

Psychological time is your inner time; and we live in the chronological time altogether—it is not personal. Psychological time is personal, and each person has their own psychological time. In fact, in the East we have been measuring states of mind through time. If time stops completely, then the state is of bliss. If time slows down very much, then the state is of misery.

In Christianity it is said that hell is eternal. Bertrand Russell has written a book, *Why I Am Not a Christian*, in which he gives many arguments to support why he is not a Christian. One of the arguments is this: 'I cannot believe that hell can be eternal because whatever the sins, they are limited. You cannot do unlimited sins. So for limited sins unlimited punishment is unjust.' The argument is simple. Nobody can argue against Bertrand Russell; he is saying a simple fact. He himself said, 'If I am punished for all the sins that I have committed in my whole life, then not more than four years' imprisonment. And even if those sins are included that I have not committed but only thought of, then at the most eight years, or a little margin more, ten years. But infinite, eternal hell?' Then God seems to be too revengeful; He does not look divine or godly, but seems like a very horrible, devilish force.

Because you loved a woman who was not your wife, you will suffer—eternally. This is too much. You have not committed such a great sin. It is human to fall in love, and when one falls in love it is difficult to decide whether to fall in love with a woman who is not somebody else's wife . . . love is almost blind; it possesses you.

Yes, Bertrand Russell seems to be right, his argument seems to be valid; but I say the argument is not valid. He has missed the whole point. And no Christian theologian has answered him on that point yet. They cannot answer because they have also forgotten. They go on talking about theories, but they have forgotten realities.

When Jesus said hell is eternal, he meant psychological time, not chronological time. Yes, if he meant chronological time, then it is absolutely absurd to throw a man in eternal hell. He meant psychological time. He meant that one moment in hell would seem like eternity. It will slow down so much, because you will be in such anguish and pain, that even a single moment will seem like eternity. You will feel it is not going to end.

It does not say anything about time; it says something about your feeling when you are in deep pain, anguish. And of course hell is the ultimate in pain. And Jesus was perfectly right, Bertrand Russell wrong, but Bertrand Russell misunderstood it because Jesus had not exactly said 'psychological' time. He said 'eternity', because in those days the language was understood. There was no need to make such qualifications.

The psychological time is personal. You have yours, your wife has hers, your children have theirs—and all are different. That is one of the causes of conflict in the world. You are honking; and your wife says from the window, 'I am coming', and she goes on standing before the mirror. You go on honking and saying, 'It is time and we will miss the train', and she gets angry and you get angry. What is happening? Every husband is annoyed when he is sitting in the driver's seat and honking the horn and the wife is still getting ready. She is still choosing the sari. Now, trains don't bother about which sari you are wearing: they leave on time. The husband is puzzled—what is going on? Two different psychological times are in conflict.

Man has moved to chronological time; the woman still lives in the psychological time. As far as I see, women use wristwatches, but they are ornamental. I don't see that they really use them, particularly not in India. I have come across a few women, who don't know how to tell time, but they have wristwatches, beautiful gold watches—they can afford them.

The child lives in a totally different world. The child has his own psychological time, completely unhurried, almost in a dream. He cannot understand you, you cannot understand him. You are far apart; there is no way to bridge. When an old man is talking to a child, he is talking from another planet; it never reaches the child. The child cannot see why there is so much hurry—for what?

Psychological time is absolutely personal. That is why chronological time has become important; otherwise where do we meet, how do we function, how do we be efficient? If everybody comes to the office at their own feeling, then it is impossible to run the office. If everybody comes to the station at their own time, then trains can never leave. Something arbitrary has to be fixed.

The chronological time is history, and the psychological time is myth. That is the difference between history and myth. In the West, history is written; in the East, myth. If you ask when Krishna was born, the exact date, no answer will be coming from anywhere. And it is easy for historians to prove that if you cannot prove on what date, at what time chronologically, Krishna was born, and at what place—if you cannot show the space and time when the event of Krishna's birth happened—then it is doubtful whether Krishna was ever born or not.

The East has never bothered. The East simply laughs at the whole absurdity of it. What has chronological time to do with Krishna's birth? We don't have any record. Or we have many records, contradicting each other.

But, see, I was born on 11 December. If it can be proved that I was not born on 11 December, will it be enough proof that I was never born?

In the East, nobody remembers their own birthday. Just the other day Vivek was worried about her father's birthday. Maybe it is the twenty-seventh, or maybe some other date, and she is worried that if she writes and asks, then they will feel offended. And I told her that I don't know my mother's birthday or my father's birthday and I don't even know if they know it or not. But that cannot prove that they have never existed or they are not there.

The East has written myth. Myth is totally different; it is with psychological time.

The chronological time moves linearly. That is why in the West they say that history never repeats itself. Time moves in a line, so how can history repeat in a line? Each event seems to be unique. In the East we say history is a wheel. It does not move linearly; the movement is circular. And in the East we say that history continuously repeats itself.

In the East we say that in each age Krishna is born again and again. It is a wheel. In each period between creation and destruction, Krishna is born again and again. His form may differ, his name may differ, but he is born again and again; so why bother? Just describe who he is and don't be worried too much about non-essential details. So it may be that the figure of Krishna may not belong to any Krishna in particular. It may be just a synthesis of all the Krishnas. That is how it is.

If you ask, 'Is Buddha's statue true to his image?'—it is not. Yet it is true because a Buddha has to be like that. It is not a question whether *this* Buddha—Gautam Siddhartha, son of Shuddhodhana, born in Kapilavastu on a particular date—was like this statue. No, that is not a point. But all the Buddhas are always synthesized in this statue. They represent. This statue is just a statue of Buddha-hood, not of any Buddha in particular. All Buddhas are included in it.

This is difficult for the West. You cannot make any difference between Buddha and Mahavira except for a small symbol just down near their feet. Jains have twenty-four *tirthankaras*, great masters, but you cannot make any distinction. Go to a Jain temple and just look; they all look alike. It is not possible that twenty-four persons were all alike. Impossible! Two persons are never alike. But those statues don't represent the outward; they represent the *inner* experience. Yes, two persons cannot be alike, but two experiences can be alike.

When you fall in love and somebody else falls in love, the love is alike. When you meditate and somebody else meditates, the meditation is alike. When you become enlightened and somebody else becomes enlightened, enlightenment is alike. These twenty-four statues of Jain masters are not of twenty-four persons but of one state reflected in twenty-four personalities. They are all representative.

If you see Jain *tirthankaras*, you will see very long ears, almost touching their shoulders. Now Jains say that all *tirthankaras* have very long ears. And there are foolish people who think that Mahavira really had such long ears.

I was invited by a Jain, Acharya Tulsi, to one of his conferences. He has very long ears, so one of his disciples came to me and he said, 'See how long Acharya Tulsiji Maharaj's ears are? That is symbolic of being a great master. Soon, in one of his lives, he is going to become a *tirthankara*.' Just by coincidence, or by synchronicity, a donkey passed by, so I told that disciple, 'Look at Acharya Donkeyji Maharaj. He is already a *tirthankara*!' That disciple has been angry since then; he has never come to me.

Long ears are just symbolic that these people were capable of hearing—that is all. They were capable of hearing the sound, the soundless sound, the sound of one hand clapping. They were capable of hearing the truth. These are just symbolic, not that they are actually representative of some real person. It is foolish, but that is how it goes on: myth is symbolic.

It is said Ram was born in Ayodhya. Now *ayodhya* is a state of inner peace; it has nothing to do with the town named Ayodhya. The town is named as a representative of the inner state of *ayodhya*—a very peaceful, silent, blissful state. Of course Ram has to be born out of that.

That is the meaning of Jesus' birth—out of a virgin soul. Not that actually he was born of a virgin Mary, no; but out of virginity, out of pureness, innocence, uncorrupted purity of being he was born. That was his real womb.

These are symbolic, these are mythological. They are not chronological.

Historians go on collecting rubbish, unnecessary details. Just look in any history book. You will be surprised. Why are there so many people doing such foolish work? Dates and dates and dates, and names and names and names, and they go on and on. Thousands of people waste their whole lives, and they call it research. Then there are journalists, editors, newspaper people; they are chronological. They just go on looking for unnecessary details in the world, for news.

The truth is never news, because it is always there. It does not happen; it has already happened. Untruth is news.

Somebody asked George Bernard Shaw, 'What is news?' He said, 'When a dog bites a man it is not news, but when a man bites a dog it is news.' News has to be something new. A dog biting a man is not news because it is not new. It has always been so and it will always be so. But when a man bites a dog, certainly it is news.

You will not find more futile and superficial people than journalists. They have a knack for finding out useless things. Journalists are impotent politicians. Politicians make news; journalists collect it. Journalists are like shadows to politicians. That is why newspapers are full of politicians; from this end to that, from the beginning to the end, just politics, politics, politics. A journalist is one who has failed in making news; now he collects it. His relationship to the politician is exactly the same as the relationship of a critic to the poet: he, who has failed to become a poet, becomes a critic.

I have heard about a famous actor. In a certain film he needed a horse, and a horse owner brought his horse. It was an ordinary horse, but the owner started praising the horse very highly, and he said, 'This is no ordinary horse. Don't go by the form; look at his spirit. He is a very great horse, and he has worked in so many movies that you can almost call him an actor.'

Exactly at that moment, the horse broke wind, long and loud.

The actor said, 'I can see. He is not only an actor but also a critic.'

The journalist, the critic, the historian, the politician, they all hang with the chronological time, with the very periphery of life, the most futile and useless effort that goes on in the world—and has become so important. We have made it so important because we have forgotten that the clock is not life.

The psychological time is dream time. Myth, poetry, love, art, painting, dancing, music, intuition—they all belong to psychological time. You have to move towards psychological time. The chronological time is for the extroverted mind, the psychological time is for the introvert, one who has started moving towards his inner soul.

There are dangers in psychological time also—that is why those who are obsessed with the chronological are against the psychological. There are dangers. There is a danger you may get trapped in it. Then you will become insane because you will be out of touch with the world, with people, with the society.

Let me tell you an anecdote:

An inoffensive-looking man was busy talking to an old friend of his and completely forgot the time. Suddenly he looked at his watch and said, 'Oh, dear, it is 3 p.m., and I have an appointment with my psychiatrist right now; but it will take me at least fifteen minutes to get there.'

His friend said, 'Now take it easy. You will only be a few minutes late.'

'You don't know him. If I am not there on time he will start without me.'

There is a danger of taking the dream to be the real. There is a danger of believing in your imagination too much. You can become so obsessed with your inner fantasy or dream world, that you can live in a fog. But even with the dangers it is very important to understand it and to pass through it. But remember, it is a bridge to be passed. When you have passed it, you will come across real time.

Chronological time corresponds to the body, psychological time to the mind, real time to your being. Chronological time is the extroverted mind, psychological time is the introverted mind and real time is no-mind.

But one has to pass through the psychological. That territory has to be passed fully alert. You should not make your abode there. It is a bridge to be passed. If you make your abode there, you will become mad. That is what has happened to many people who are in madhouses—they have forgotten chronological time, they have not reached real time, and they have started living on the bridge, the psychological time. That is why their reality has become personal and private.

A madman lives in a private world, and the man you call sane lives in a public world. The public world is with people, the private world is just confined to the self. But the real world is neither public nor private—it is universal, beyond both. And one has to go beyond both.

A man had a reputation as a road hog. He was lying in a hospital bed after an accident.

The doctor asked the nurse, 'How is he this morning?'
She said, 'Oh, he keeps putting his right hand out.'
'Ah,' said the doctor. 'He is turning the corner.'

A road hog, an automobile addict, even in his sleep goes on driving fast. Whatsoever you do in your dream reflects your desire, your goals, what you would like to have.

Primitive societies live in the psychological time. The East has lived in the psychological time; the West lives in the chronological time. If you move farther into the primitive societies hidden behind the hills and the forests, you will see they live absolutely in psychological time. There are a few primitive societies in which dreams are more important than reality, and the first thing a child has to do before breakfast is to relate his dream to his elders. The first thing is psychoanalysis. The dream has to be related to the elders before breakfast, and they all gather together and they analyze the dream. And then they tell the child to do something, because the dream is symbolic and it shows that something is needed to be done.

For example, a child dreams that he was fighting with a friend in the dream, and in the morning he says so to his elders. They will interpret it, and they will send the child with gifts and sweets and toys to the other's house, to the other child, to give him presents, and to tell him his dream . . . because he has committed a crime.

In the West you cannot conceive of it. What have you done? You have not done anything, you have simply dreamt, but that particular primitive society says that you dreamt it because you wanted to do something like that, otherwise why would you dream it? It must be a desire, hidden, repressed. As far as the mind is concerned, you have committed it. Go and tell the child so that no subtle anger goes on surrounding you. Tell the whole thing and ask his forgiveness and present these gifts to him.

Real gifts for a dream fight . . . but a miracle has happened to that society. By and by as the child grows, he stops dreaming. Dreams disappear. A grown-up man is one, according to that primitive society, who does not dream. This seems to be beautiful. Of course that society will not be very appreciated by psychoanalysts because their whole profession will be gone.

The young girl went to see her psychiatrist and he asked her what she had dreamt the previous night. She told him that she had not had any dreams at all that night, whereupon he got very angry and said, 'Look, if you don't do your homework, how can I help you?'

Dreaming is homework; and a psychoanalyst lives on your dreams. He goes on analyzing them. But this is something absurd—if you cannot analyze your own dreams, how can somebody else do it? Because psychological time is personal, nobody can understand your dreams more than you yourself can. How can somebody else understand them? His interpretations are going to be falsifications. His interpretations are going to be *his* interpretations. When Freud analyzes your dream, his interpretation will be different. When Jung analyzes the same dream, his interpretation is different. When Adler analyzes the same dream, his interpretation is different. So what has to be thought about it? You have dreamt one dream and three great psychoanalysts interpret it in three different ways.

Freud reduces everything to sex. Whatsoever you dream makes no difference. He will find a way and reduce it to sex. It seems he was obsessed with sex. He was a great pioneer, he has opened a great door, but he had phobias and was afraid of sex. And he was afraid of other things also. His fears were so great that he could not even cross the road; that was one of his great fears. Now you cannot think of Buddha being afraid of crossing a road. This man himself is ill. He was so afraid of talking with people, that he created psychoanalysis. In psychoanalysis the psychoanalyst sits behind a screen and the patient lies down on a couch and goes on talking and the psychoanalyst simply listens—no communication. He was afraid to communicate. In personal encounters, person to person, he was always awkward. Now his whole mind has entered into his interpretation—that is natural, that is how it should be.

Jung brings everything to religion, everything. Whatsoever you dream, he will interpret it in such a way that it becomes a religious dream. The same dream becomes sexual with Freud; with Jung it becomes religious. With Adler it becomes politics; everything is ambition, and everybody is suffering with an inferiority complex, and everybody is trying to gain more power—'will to power'. And now there are a thousand and one psychoanalysts all over the world, of different denominations. The denominations are as many as in Christianity. So many schools, and every psychoanalyst starts his own school—and nobody is bothered with the patient, that it is *his* dream.

The problems of the psychoanalysts enter into their analysis and interpretation. This is not a way to help. In fact, it is going to make things more complicated. A better society will teach you how to analyze your own dreams, how to psychoanalyze your own dreams—nobody can be more certain than you because nobody can be closer, only you.

The beautiful young lady went to see a psychiatrist. The doctor looked at her for a few seconds and then said, 'Come over here, please.' He then promptly put his arms around her and kissed her. As he finally released her, he commented casually, 'That takes care of my problem. Now what is yours?'

They have their problems. They have their minds, obsessions.

In the East there has never existed anything like a psychoanalyst. Not that we were not aware of the psychological world. We were aware more deeply than any society has ever been aware, but we had created a totally different type of person to help. We call that person the guru, the master. What is the difference between a guru and a psychoanalyst? The difference is that while the psychoanalyst still has his problems, unsolved, the guru has no problems. When you don't have any problems then your vision is clear, then you can put yourself in the other's situation. When you don't have any problems, any obsessions, any complexes, nothing—you are completely clean of the mind, the mind has disappeared and you have attained no-mind—then, then you can see. Then you will not interpret in a personal way. Your interpretation will be universal, will become existential.

And the third is real time, existential. The real time is no time at all, because the real time is eternity. Let me explain it to you.

The chronological time is arbitrary. In the West, Zeno proved it long ago. In the East, Nagarjuna proved it so deeply that he has never been refuted. In fact Zeno and Nagarjuna have remained irrefutable. Nobody can refute them; their arguments are so deep and absolute. Zeno and Nagarjuna say that the whole concept of time, chronological time, is absurd. Let me tell you a few things about these two persons and their analysis of chronological time.

They achieved the highest peak of time analysis. Nobody has ever been able to surpass them or improve upon them. They say, 'What is time?' You say, 'It is a process. One moment moves into the past, disappears; another moment moves from the future into the present, remains there on the threshold for a time, then again moves into the past, disappears.' This is the time process. You have only one moment at one time, never two moments together. The past, the future, and just between the two, the threshold, the present.

Now Nagarjuna and Zeno say, 'Where does the moment come from? Is the future already existent? If it is not existent, then how can the moment come out of the non-existential?' Now they create trouble. They say, 'Where does the present moment move to in the past? Does it still remain accumulated in the past?' If you say it still remains in the past, then it has not become past yet. If you say it was there in the future and just now it has been revealed to us—it has always been there in the future—then Nagarjuna and Zeno say that you cannot call it the future. It has always been present. If the future is, then the future is not; because the future means that which is not yet. If the past is, then the past is not; because the past means that which has gone out of existence.

If you say the future is not and suddenly out of the blue the present moment appears, they both laugh. They say, 'You are talking nonsense. How out of non-existence can existence come? And how can the existential move into non-existence again?' They say, 'If there is non-existence on both sides, then just in the middle how can existence be? It must also be non-existential. You got deceived.'

Then they say, 'You take time as a process? You say one moment is joined with another?' Nagarjuna and Zeno ask you: 'There are two moments; how are they related? Is there a third moment between the two which relates them?' Again they create a difficulty, because to relate, a link is needed.

To relate two things, to relate the past with the present and the present with the future, links are needed. Then where do those links exist? What are those links? They can only be of time. So between one moment and another there is another moment to join these two. So instead of two there are three, but again they will have to be joined. Infinite regress arises.

Look at my two fingers. These two are needed to be joined; they become three fingers. Now there are two holes instead of one, two blanks. They have to be joined; they become five. Now there are more gaps to be joined, and so on, so forth.

The chronological time, Nagarjuna and Zeno say, is utilitarian. It is not substantial. The real time is not a process because, Nagarjuna says, if time itself is a process then it will need another time. For example, you walk: you need time. You have come to me from your home. It took fifteen minutes for you to come here. If there is no time, how will you come here, because walking needs time? Walking is a process; you need time. All processes need time. Now Nagarjuna says, 'If you say time itself is a process, it will need another time, a supertime. And that too is a process. Then a super-supertime . . . ' Again infinite regress arises. Then you cannot solve it.

No, time—real time—is not a process. It is simultaneity. Future, past, present are not three separate things; so there is no need to join them. It is eternal *now*, it is eternity. It is not that time is passing by. Where will it go? It will need another medium to pass through, and where will it go and from where will it come? It is there; or rather it is here. Time *is*. It is not a process.

Because we cannot see the total time—our eyes are confined, limited; we are looking out of small slits—that is why it seems you can see only one moment at a time. It is your limitation, not a division of time. Because you cannot see the whole time as it is—because *you* are not whole yet—that is why.

Now, the sutras:

> *Performing* samyama *on the present moment,*
> *the moment gone and the moment to come, brings*
> *knowledge born of the awareness of the ultimate*
> *reality.*

If you bring your *samadhi* consciousness to the process of time—to the moment which is, to the moment that is gone, to the moment that is to come—if you bring your *samadhi*, suddenly you have the knowledge of ultimate reality. Because the moment you look with *samadhi*, the distinction between present, future and past disappears. The distinction is false. Suddenly you become aware of eternity. Then time is simultaneity. Nothing is passing, nothing is coming in; everything is, simply is.

This is-ness is known as godliness; this is-ness is the idea of godliness.

If you can see time through the eyes of satori, *samadhi*, time disappears. After that there is only *kaivalya*, liberation. When time disappears, everything disappears because the whole world of desire, ambition and motivation is there because of the wrong conception of time. Time is created; time as process—past, present, future—is created by desiring. This is one of the greatest insights of the Eastern sages: that time, the process, is really a projection of desire. Because you desire something, you create future. And because you cling, you create past. Because you cannot leave that which is no longer before you, and you want to cling to it, you create memory. And because something has not come yet, you expect it in your own way, you create future. Future and past are mental states, not part of time. Time is eternal. It is not divided. It is one, whole.

Kshana-tat-kramayoh samyamad vivekajam gyanam. One who has come to know what the moment is and the process of it becomes aware of the ultimate; becoming aware of time, one becomes aware of the ultimate. Why? Because the ultimate exists as *real* time.

If you live in the chronological, then you live in the newspaper world. Then you live in the world of the politicians—mad, ambitious people. Or if you live in the psychological time, you live in the world of the insane or in the world of fantasy, dreams and poetry.

A new doctor was looking around the asylum. He came across one inmate and said to him, 'Who are you?'

The man drew himself up to his full height and said, 'I, sir, am Napoleon.'

The doctor said, 'Really? Who told you that?'

The patient said, 'God told me, who else?'

A little man lying in the next bed looked up and said, 'I didn't.'

Go to the madhouses; they are worth visiting. Just see people. They are living in a fantasy world. They have completely moved out of the collective world but have not entered the universal world. They are hanging in between.

The psychiatrist was surprised to see his young woman patient standing outside his office looking very perplexed. It was not half an hour since he had been treating her. He said, 'What is the matter?'

She said, 'Oh dear, I don't know whether I am coming or going.'

The doctor said, 'Exactly, that is why you have come to see me.'

'Oh,' she said. 'Who are you then?'

'I am your lousy psychiatrist.'

A world of limbo arises. If you lose contact with the chronological world and you don't become connected with the world of the universal, the ultimate, suddenly you don't know whether you are coming in or going out. Everything becomes doubtful, everything becomes suspicious. You cannot trust yourself, you cannot trust your eyes—you cannot trust anybody. You are closed in, caved in. You become a windowless being, a monad. This is what hell is. You cannot move out of yourself; you are crippled.

Remember, a mediator passes consciously through the world of the madman—consciously. And it is good to pass consciously because if you don't pass consciously then there is every possibility you will become an unconscious victim of it. It is better to go through it alert and aware, rather than being forced into it. If life forces you into it, then you will not be able to come out of it. It will be very, very difficult.

And the psychoanalyst can only help to bring you back to the chronological world. That is the difference between a master and a psychoanalyst. The psychoanalyst brings the man who has got lost in the psychological back to the chronological. The master, if you are lost in the psychological, takes you further back in, takes you to the universal. You will never become part of the chronological world, but you will become part of the universal time.

From this comes the ability to distinguish
between similar objects which cannot be identified
by class, character or place.

Once you know the ultimate, a totally different kind of knowing arises in you. Right now you know things only from the outside. Somebody comes, you look at their clothes, and you think, 'Yes, she is a woman', or 'he is a man'. You look at the tree and you recognize it—'it is a pine tree'— because you know the description. You see a man and you know that he is a doctor because of his stethoscope. But these are outer indications of things. He may not be a doctor; he may be just a pretender. And the pine tree may not be a pine tree; it may just look like a pine tree. And the woman may not be a woman; she may be just acting. She may be a man; 'she' may be a 'he'. You cannot be absolutely certain about it, because you know only from the outside.

When time disappears and eternity surrounds you, when time is no longer a process but a pool of energy, eternal now, then you become capable of entering into things and of knowing without any definitions from the outside.

That is what happens between a master and a disciple. He need not ask you, really. He can see from your very being. He can stand in you—not only in your shoes but in your being. He can fit exactly in your innermost vacuum. He can be you, and look from there.

The highest knowledge born of the awareness of reality
is transcendent, includes the cognition of all objects
simultaneously, pertains to all objects and processes
whatsoever—in the past, the present and the future—
and transcends the world process.

*Tarakam sarvavishayam sarvathavishayam
akramam cheti vivekajam gyanam.*

Through the eyes we can see only a part of reality.
Because of that part, life looks like a process. For example,
say you are sitting under a tree and the road is empty, and
suddenly a man appears on the road from the left side; he
goes to the right side, and after walking a little distance he
disappears again. But suppose somebody is sitting in the
tree. Long before the man appeared to you, he appeared to
the person who is in the tree. When the man disappears to
you, he does not disappear for the person who is sitting in
the tree; but after a time the man disappears for that person
also. Now suppose there is also someone in a helicopter.
His vision goes farther; the man continues to walk—long
before you became aware that he was on the road and long
after he disappeared for you.

What is happening? This is exactly the case with things.
The higher you rise, the closer you reach the *sahasrar*. You
are climbing the tree of life. *Sahasrar* is the ultimate point
to look from. There is nothing higher than that. From
sahasrar you see things: everything goes on and on and on.
Nothing stops, nothing disappears.

It is very difficult; it is as difficult as the physicists'
explanation of the ultimate electron, quanta, that it is both
a wave and a particle, both a dot and a line.

You are flying in an airplane over the Ganges, and the
Ganges is flowing. If I ask you, 'Is the Ganges a process? Is
the Ganges flowing, or is it that the Ganges *is*?' What will
you say? You will say, 'Both.' You will say, 'the Ganges is',
because you can see it from one end to the other
simultaneously. You can simultaneously see the Ganges in
the Himalayas, on the plains and falling into the ocean—

past, present, future have disappeared. The whole Ganges is available to you from a certain altitude. It is, and yet you know it is flowing. It is both being and becoming; it is both wave and particle, dot and line; *is* and still a process.

It is paradoxical—it looks paradoxical, because we don't know how things appear from that height.

This sutra says: *The highest knowledge born of the awareness of reality is transcendent* . . . It transcends all dualities, polarities of *is* and process, of static and dynamic, of wave and particle, of life and death, of past and future— all dualities, all polarities. It is transcendent. *Tarakam sarvavishayam*—it transcends all the objects of knowledge. . . . *includes the cognition of all objects simultaneously* . . . And for this consciousness the word used is 'omniscient'. Everything exists for it simultaneously. It is very difficult to understand, almost impossible to comprehend. It means for a man of ultimate understanding, if he looks at you, he will see you in your mother's womb and your birth, simultaneously. And you are growing and you have become a child and you have become a young man and you have fallen in love and you are marrying and your children are born and you have become old and you are dying and people are going in a funeral procession—all simultaneously. The whole will appear as total.

Difficult to comprehend, because how is it possible? A child is being born. How can he die right at this moment? He is either young or old, either in the womb or in the coffin, either in the cradle or in the grave. But that is *our* division because we cannot see totally.

A certain scientist in Russia has photographed buds with sensitive photographic instruments and films that nobody has tried before; and the picture of the flower has emerged. The bud has been photographed, but in the photograph the flower has come. It is still a bud. Why has this happened? Because the bud is also a flower, simultaneously. You cannot see it because you see only in parts. First you see it as a bud; then a few petals open, then a few more, then a few more; then the whole flower opens. But with a very sensitive camera, Kirlian photography has given a tremendous insight into reality. You can photograph a bud, but the photograph is of a flower. Because when the bud is there, deep down, surrounding the bud, the energy flower has already opened. The visible petals will follow, but the energy field has already flowered. It is there. And later on, when the real flower had flowered, they were surprised to see that the photograph was absolutely exact. They could compare the real flower later on.

Some day it will be possible to photograph a seed, and not one but many photographs will come—of the seed, of the sprout, of the buds, of the flowers, of the tree, and the falling of the tree and the disappearing of the tree.

Ordinarily we see everything in karma, in a gradual process—a child becoming older, a young man becoming an old man—slowly, as if a film is being projected very slowly on the screen. That is how we see it. But the ultimate knowledge is total and absolute; in a single moment everything is revealed.

Ordinarily we move with a small torch in a dark night. When the torch shows us one tree, other trees are hidden in darkness. When the beam of light moves to other trees, the first tree has moved into darkness. You can see only a little patch of the path. But that ultimate knowledge is like lightning: suddenly you see the whole forest, in one vision.

These are all just symbolic. Don't extend and don't stretch these symbols too much. They are just to give you subtle indications of what happens. In fact, it cannot be said.

Chronological time is politics, history, economics, money, intellect, the stock market. Psychological time is dream, myth, poetry, love, art, intuition, painting, dance, drama. Real time is existence, science and religion.

Science is trying to penetrate existence through the objective approach, religion tries to penetrate the same reality through the subjective approach, and yoga is the synthesis of both.

The word 'science' is beautiful; it means the capacity to see. It exactly means what the Indian word 'darshan' means. The word 'darshan' should not be translated as 'philosophy'; it can be translated more accurately as 'science'—the capacity to see.

Science is trying to penetrate the ultimate through the objective, from the outside. Religion is trying to penetrate the same ultimate through the subjective. And yoga is the highest synthesis; yoga is both, science and religion together.

Yoga is the supra-science and supra-religion. Yoga is neither Hindu nor Mohammedan nor Christian—it is supra-religious. And of course it is a supra-science because it is the science of man—it is the science of the scientist himself. It touches the ultimate. That is why I call it the alpha and the omega, *unio mystica*, the ultimate synthesis.

8

Life Lives for Itself

*The days of life ahead, if any, are so unknown
and unpredictable. These days a deep feeling
is arising in me that one has to just live the
remaining years of life. How? Why? What for?
Nothing is clear. But this feeling goes on
deepening. Hence what I am eating, what I
am doing, what is happening all around—
nothing seems to bother me.*

*Since my very childhood, whenever I saw a
dead body, always the thought flashed to me
that if death is to come then what is the sense
in living.*

*Since those very days of my childhood, a sort
of non-interest has surrounded my whole
pattern of life, and probably that might be the
reason why I got interested in religion and
could reach you.*

Are such feelings going to be harmful to me?

CERTAINLY. THEY ARE going to be harmful because you have

misunderstood the whole point of religion. The first thing: life is unpredictable; that is why it is beautiful. If it were predictable, who would like to live it? If everything was charted beforehand and the day you were born you were given your whole life, like a railway timetable, so you can consult and see what is going to happen and when and how—who would like to live such a life? It will not have any poetry. It will not have any dangers. It will not have any risk. It will not have any opportunity to grow. It will be absolutely futile. Then you will be just a robot, a mechanical thing.

The life of a mechanism can be predicted, but not of man, trees, birds—because they are not machines. The more alive you are, the more unpredictable you become. The life of the tree is more predictable than the life of a bird. The life of a bird is less predictable than the life of a man. And the life of a Buddha is absolutely more unpredictable than your life.

Unpredictability means freedom. Predictability will mean determinism. If you can be predicted, then you are not a soul; then you are *not*. Predictability will mean that you are simply a biological mechanism.

But there are many people who think that life is not worth living because it is not predictable. These are the people who go to the astrologers. These are the people who go on finding fortune-tellers. These people are foolish; and the astrologer and the fortune-teller, they live on your foolishness.

In the first place, the very idea that tomorrow is fixed and can be known will destroy the very aliveness of it. Then you will be as if you are seeing a movie for the second time—you already know everything. Why do you get bored seeing a movie the second time and the third time and the fourth time? If you are forced to see the movie many times, the same movie, you will go mad. For the first time you are curious, alive. You are wondering what is going to happen, you don't know what is going to happen; that is why you are interested, the flame of interest remains burning.

Life is a mystery; it cannot be predicted. But there are many people who would like to have a predictable life, because then there will be no fear. Everything will be certain; there will be no doubt about anything.

But will there be any opportunity to grow? Without risk has anybody ever grown? Without danger has anybody ever sharpened his consciousness? Without the possibility of going astray, is there any point in being on the right path? Without the alternative of the devil, is there any possibility of achieving godliness?

The alternative is needed; the opposite has to attract and distract you. Choice arises. You have to become more sensitive, more alive, more aware. But if everything is determined and everything can be known beforehand, then what is the point of being aware? Whether you are aware or not will not make any difference. Right now it makes tremendous difference.

Let me tell you, the more aware you become, the less predictable you get, because you move higher and higher and farther and farther from matter, which is predictable. We know if you heat water to a certain degree of heat, the water evaporates. It is predictable. But it is not the same with a person: you cannot fix a degree of insult where a person becomes angry. Each person is so unique. A Buddha may not become angry at all, whatsoever the degree of your insult.

And you know this: sometimes you may become angry by a slight provocation—or even without provocation, and you may start evaporating in anger, without any heat—and sometimes even a great provocation may not disturb you. It depends how good you are feeling at that moment, how alert you are feeling at that moment.

Beggars come in the morning to beg, not in the evening, because they have understood a simple fact of psychology—in the morning people are more in the mood of sharing; they are more alive, alert, rested. By the evening they are tired and exhausted and fed up with the world; to hope to get something from them is impossible. When people are feeling good themselves, then they share. It depends on their inner feeling.

Remember that life is beautiful because you are capable of becoming more and more alive. No need to be bothered by tomorrow. Live today and don't allow tomorrow to destroy your today. And move so freely today that tomorrow brings more freedom to you.

Never ask for predictions. Remain open. Whatsoever happens let it happen, allow it to happen; pass through it. It is a gift of existence. It must have some deep significance.

'The days of life ahead, if any, are so unknown and unpredictable. These days a deep feeling is arising in me that one has to just live the remaining years of life.' 'Just live?' Then your life will become boredom. And you may interpret that this is a religious life; this is not. A bored man is not a religious man. A blissful man is a religious man.

But I know many bored people have pretended to be religious. Many people who were impotent in life—uncreative, were not capable of any happiness—have turned against life, have become life-negative. And they have created a long tradition of condemning life, of saying that it is worthless, that there is no meaning in it, that it is just accidental, that it is a chaos: 'Drop out of it, destroy it.'

These people you have called mahatmas; you have called them great saints. They were simply neurotic. They needed medical care. They needed to be hospitalized. 99 per cent of your so-called saints are perverted, but they are hiding their perversion in such terms that you cannot see the point.

In Aesop, there is a fable:

A fox is trying to jump to get grapes. They are ripe and alluring, and their smell is making the fox crazy, but the bunch of grapes is too far away. The fox tries and tries, but fails and cannot reach them. Then she looks around—has somebody seen the failure?

A small hare is hiding under a bush, and he says, 'Auntie, what has happened? You couldn't reach them?'

She says, 'No, that is not the point. The grapes are not ripe yet; they are sour.'

This is what you have known as religion up to now—'the grapes are sour'—because these people could not get to them, could not reach. These people were failures.

Religion has nothing to do with failure. It is a fulfilment, a fruition, a flowering, a matrix, a climax, a peak. Abraham Maslow is right when he says that religion is concerned with 'peak experiences'.

But look at your religious people in the churches, in the monasteries, in the temples: fed up, bored, long faces, just waiting for death to come and 'deliver' them. Anti-life, against life, *fanatically* against life, and wherever they see any sign of life, they jump upon it to kill and destroy it. They will not allow you to laugh in the church, they will not allow you to dance in the church, because any sign of life troubles them—because any sign of life makes them aware that *they* have missed it, they could not reach it.

Religion is not for the failures. It is for those who have succeeded in life, who have lived life to its deepest core, to its depth and height, in all dimensions, and who have become so enriched by the experience that they are ready to transcend it. These people will never be anti-life; they will be life-affirmative. They will say life is divine. In fact they will say, 'Forget all about God. Life is divine.' They will not be against love, because love is the very juice of life. They will say, 'Love is like blood circulating in the body of the divine.' Love is to life exactly as blood is to your body. How can they be against it?

If you become anti-love, you start shrinking. A really religious person is expanding. It is an expansion of consciousness, not a shrinking.

In India we have called the ultimate truth 'Brahman'. The word 'Brahman' means 'who goes on expanding'—on and on and on, and knows no end. The very word is beautiful, has a tremendous significance. This ongoing expansion, this endless expansion of life, love, consciousness—this is what godliness is.

Beware, because the life-negative religion is very cheap; you can get it by just being bored. It is very cheap because you can get it just by being a failure, just by being uncreative, lazy, desperate or sad. It is really cheap. But real religion, authentic religion, is at a great cost: you have to lose yourself in life. You have to pay the cost. It is earned, and it is earned the hard way. One has to move through life: to know its sadness, its happiness, to know its failures, its successes, to know sunny days and cloudy ones, to know poverty and richness, to know love and to know hate—to touch the very rock bottom of life, the hell, and to soar high and touch the highest peak, heaven. One has to move in all the directions, in all the dimensions; nothing should remain covered. Religion is a discovery; it is to unveil life.

And of course pain is part of it. Never think only in terms of pleasure; otherwise soon you will get out of life, out of touch. Life is both pain and pleasure. In fact it will be better to call it 'pain-pleasure'; even 'and' is not good, because that divides. Pain-pleasure, hell-heaven, night-day, summer-winter, good-evil—life is this tremendous opportunity of polar opposites. Live it, be courageous, risk it, move in danger; and then you will attain a totally different kind of religious understanding, which comes out of bitter and sweet experiences.

A person who has known only sweet experiences and has never known bitter experiences is still poor, not rich. One who has not known love—its beauty and its terror, its ecstasy and its agony, one who has not known the meeting and also the divorce, the arrival and also the departure, has not known much. He has lived on goodies and will become ill sooner or later, and will be fed up and bored.

Life is a tremendous challenge. So if you say that 'one has to just live the remaining years of life', then these remaining years will not be of life. You will have died before your death.

I have heard:

A beautiful woman reached the Pearly Gates. St. Peter felt a tremor. The woman was really beautiful, even St. Peter could not see her eye to eye. He started looking in his files, and he said, 'Where have you been? What have you been doing? Have you done any sin on earth?'

The woman said, 'No, never.'

St. Peter could not believe it. 'Were you married?'

She said, 'No, I have never been interested in sex.'

'Have you been with any man?'

She said, 'No, I am a virgin.'

And so on and so forth. St. Peter looked into the records; they were all empty. She has not committed any sin, but how can you do something virtuous if you have not committed any sin? He became worried.

The woman asked, 'What is the matter? I am a virtuous woman.'

St. Peter said, 'You have lived under a wrong notion. To become a saint, one has to become a sinner. The record is completely empty. Now I have only one question to ask: Where have you been for these thirty years?'

She said, 'What do you mean?'

St. Peter said, 'You have been dead for thirty years—you should have reported earlier! You have not lived.'

Your so-called saints will have to face the same thing. They have not lived—and that I call irreligious. To refuse the opportunity that existence has given you is to be irreligious. Not to live it in its totality is to be irreligious. If existence has made you in such a way that the sin arises in you, don't be worried too much. There must be some significance in it; it must be part of your growth.

God said to Adam, 'Don't eat the fruit of the tree of knowledge.' He played a trick on Adam. That was a way to provoke him, certainly—you cannot find a better way of provoking. The garden of God was very big. Left to himself, Adam would not yet have discovered the tree. Just think. God's garden was so infinite, that Adam, left to his own wits, would not have been able to discover it. God must have known it. Christians don't interpret it that way, but I know God played a trick. He befooled Adam. He said, 'Remember, never eat the fruit of this tree.' Now this tree became a constant obsession. Adam was not able to sleep well. In the night he dreamt of the tree. And when God has said so, there must be something in it. And God Himself eats from that tree! This is impossible. This is like a father who smokes and goes on telling the child, 'Never smoke. This is very bad, and you will suffer.'

Of course Adam had to eat it, but God is the culprit. He has to be because He is the foundation of all. So if sin happens He has to be the criminal; if virtue happens He has to be the cause of it.

Adam could not understand; a little psychology was needed. It is not a religious question; it is a psychological question. And even then God was not sitting silently and waiting, because maybe Adam may be very obedient and may not eat; so He had to make other arrangements—the snake. God must have felt that Adam seems to be too docile, obedient, a good boy; so He had to bring in a girl, Eve, and a snake. The snake provokes Eve and Eve provokes Adam. Now the thing becomes simple. Adam can throw the responsibility on Eve, and Eve can throw the responsibility on the snake. And of course snakes don't speak so they cannot write bibles and they cannot throw the responsibility on God—but the responsibility *is* His.

There is only one irreligion and that is to refuse life, to refuse love. And there is only one religion: to accept it in its totality and to move in it unafraid.

So this attitude is harmful.

'How? Why? What for? Nothing is clear.' But why should it be clear? Why in the first place do you want it to be clear? And if it is absolutely clear, the whole point will be lost, the whole game will be lost. If everything is absolutely clear, then there is no alternative. Then you cannot go astray. If everything is absolutely clear, then you will always do the right thing. Then you cannot stumble; then you cannot move in the darkness and go far away from existence.

But you need to go far away because only when you have gone very, very far away does a thirst arises to come back home.

In fact, now modern psychology says exactly this: every child has to go away from the mother. First the child is in the womb, then one day he has to come out of the womb. That is the beginning of going far away from the mother. Now he is no longer part of the mother. The cord is cut; he starts functioning independently. But still he will cling to the mother, to the breast, because she is still his whole being—out of the womb, but he will still go on clinging to the mother, he will remain in the motherly atmosphere. But then that too has to go: The child is growing. One day the milk is stopped, the breast is taken away, and the mother forces the child to become more independent. Now he has to choose his own food and he has to chew his own food. Then still more—he has to go to school or boarding house. Then he moves far away. Then one day he falls in love with a woman; that is the last step.

That is why mothers can never forgive their daughters-in-law. Impossible, because they are the last straw—they have taken their son completely. Now the son has become completely independent. He has his own family; he has started his own unit. Now he is no longer attached to the mother.

Exactly the same thing is happening in the world of consciousness. Man has to go away from the mother. And existence is more a mother than a father, remember. Man is born out of the womb of existence, and then it takes care.

Just watch. It is taking more care of the trees, the animals and the birds—that is the womb. They are still inside the womb. It is not so careful about man; man has to become independent. Have you not observed that man is born the most helpless animal in the world? Because existence is taking its help away, withdrawing itself. The trees, the animals and the birds exist in its womb. They are pre-human.

That is the whole theory of rebirth, of evolution. In the East we say that every man has passed through all these stages. Once you were a lion, once you were a dog, once you were a tree, and once you were a rock as well. Then you became man. *Man* means you came out of the womb. The Garden of Eden is the womb of existence.

Adam was 'expelled'. The word 'expulsion' is not good. If we in the East had written the story of the Bible, we would have said, 'God *sent* man farther away from Himself—to grow'—because it is difficult to grow if you continuously go on hanging around your mother. If you continuously go on living on her milk, it will be impossible to grow. You will remain childish.

And you have to fall in love with some woman, so much so that if the woman says, 'Kill your mother', you will start thinking of killing your mother. That is how Eve persuaded Adam to eat the fruit. What is the significance of the story? The significance is that Adam chose Eve's advice against God's commandment. He thought, 'Okay, forget that old fellow. Don't be worried.' He chose foolish Eve's advice.

And of course women are not very rational; they live by hunches. She has been advised—by a snake. Just look at the absurdity of it. But when a wife insists, the husband has to follow.

Adam is sent forth into the world, not expelled. How can God expel anybody? It is impossible; compassion will not allow it. This is part of your growth that you should go away and you should commit mistakes, because only then by and by will you become aware, alert. And with your own awareness, mistakes will start dropping. You will come back home. And you will always find God ready to welcome you.

Existence is your source, and is the source of all that happens to you.

Don't ask 'How? Why? What for? Nothing is clear'. It has to be that way. If everything is clear, there is no need to grow. Because nothing is clear, you have to grow in awareness, so things become clear.

Mulla Nasruddin was in the hospital; he had some eye trouble. After a week the doctor asked him, 'Are the medicines helping you, Nasruddin?'

He said, 'Certainly. I can see clearly, more clearly. For example, the nurse becomes plainer and plainer every day.'

When you can see clearly, of course the nurse becomes plainer and plainer. When you cannot see clearly, every woman is beautiful.

If everything is clear, then there will be no need to make your eyes clear. The whole thing is this, the whole game is this: things are *not* clear. So you have to bring more clarity to your mind so that you can choose your path. Things are in a chaos. You have to bring awareness within you so that you can choose and move rightly into the chaos. Chaos is meant to be there. It is not because of the Devil the chaos is there; it is because of God.

It is like a jigsaw puzzle. If everything is clear then what is the point of the puzzle? You give a jigsaw puzzle to a small child, you mix all the parts, you confuse the child and then you tell him, 'Now you work it out.' Working it out, he is really becoming more alert, absorbed, contemplative and meditative. If you give him a solved puzzle, what is the point of giving the puzzle to him?

The world is a jigsaw puzzle and existence goes on mixing and confusing it.

That is what I am doing here with you. Somehow you try to fix your jigsaw puzzle, I again do something and mix you and confuse you. Because the more you have to work on the puzzle, the more aware you will become. You would like me to give you a certain catechism, like Christians give to their followers. A few people come to me—foolish people they are—they say, 'It is very difficult, Osho, to find out from your books what you want. Just make a small book like Mao Zedong's *Red Book*: just small, handy, which can be kept in a pocket—and say exactly what you want, in short.'

I am not going to give you a *Red Book*, because then what is the point? Then there is no need for any awareness— you just look into the *Red Book* and everything is clear. All copies of the *Red Book* are worthy of being burned. Anything that solves your life's puzzle is your enemy because once the puzzle is solved, you will plop into unconsciousness. The puzzle has to be made more complicated. That is why if Lao Tzu cannot do, I bring Patanjali. If Patanjali cannot do, I bring Buddha. If he fails, then I bring Jesus or Mahavira. And then I find people—Tilopa, Naropa— nobody has bothered much about them. And I will go on puzzling you.

Amidst this confusion *you* become clear, not the things around you. The clarity has to be inner. There are two types of clarities. One is just in the arrangement of things around you—the furniture arranged by an interior decorator, everything in its place—but then you are not clear. Things are systematic and they take the very opportunity to be clear from your hands. In the other type, things remain as they are, but you attain an intensity of awareness. You become more and more alert. You look at things deeply, you start seeing more clearly. Things are the same, but you are different. The change has happened to you, not in the world.

And that is the difference between the communist, the socialist, the politician and the religious man. They all are sorting out *in* the world—Marx, Mao, Stalin. They are all trying to fix the world, the puzzle, so you need not be worried. They are chewing food for you and they are trying to make you small babies so you can live on the breasts of the state—and everything is made clear by the government, everything nationalized, and everything is put in its right place. So you simply move without any worry on your part.

I am not in favour of any of that type of systematization in the outer world. The outer world has to remain a beautiful chaos so that you have to struggle for inner awareness. I hope you can see the point. If you are moving in a dark night alone, you move more alert, more cautious. If you are moving on a superhighway in full daylight, of course there is no need for awareness and alertness.

Have you ever been in a haunted house at night, alone? You will not be able to sleep. Just a small noise—a dead leaf falls from the tree in the courtyard—and you will jump. A cat jumps on a rat and you will jump. Just a breeze passes and you will be standing with the torch in hand.

I have heard about a man who took a challenge and stayed in a haunted house. Just at the time when he was going to retire for the night, he asked the butler who had brought his milk, 'Tell me one thing. Has anything exceptional happened here in the past few years?'

The butler said, 'Not for twenty years.'

The man felt relieved. As the butler was leaving, he said, 'Wait. Just tell me what had happened twenty years ago.'

The butler said, 'Twenty years ago, a very exceptional thing happened. A man stayed in the same bed you are staying in—and the next morning he came down for breakfast. Never again has it happened, and never before. We were not even waiting for him, but he came down the stairs.'

Now can you think of this man not remaining alert? Can you think of this man falling asleep? Even tranquilizers won't help. Even if you give him morphine it may not work. His awareness will become a very crystallized thing.

Buddha used to send his disciples to the cemetery to stay there overnight—just to become more aware. Because when you are alone in a cemetery, you cannot fall asleep. In fact, there is no need to make any effort to be aware. Awareness comes easy. It is really beautiful; you should try it sometimes.

The clarity has to come to you in your inner quality of consciousness. 'How? Why? What for? Nothing is clear.' Absolutely beautiful—that is how it should be.

And let me tell you one more thing—life exists for itself. It has no extrinsic value to it; it is intrinsic. Never ask the purpose of life, because you ask a wrong question, you ask an irrelevant question. Life is the ultimate; beyond it there is nothing. Life lives for itself. A rose is a rose is a rose—life lives for more life, more life lives for still more life. But there is no extrinsic value; you cannot answer why.

You can see the point: if you can answer the 'why' then again the question will arise. If you say, 'Life exists for God', but then why does 'God' exist? What is the purpose of His being? And when the query has to stop somewhere, why start it in the first place? You say, 'God created life'? Then who created God? No, I don't say that. I say, 'Godliness is life.' It has not created life; it *is* life.

So if you are an atheist there is no problem with me. You can drop the word 'God'. It is only a linguistic question. If you like the word 'God', good. If you don't like, very good. 'Life' will do. I am not worried about words. I don't argue about words. Who bothers about what you call that ultimate truth? Life, God, Allah, Ram, Krishna—or whatsoever catches your fancy—Jehovah, Tao; all these are words, indicating something so subtle that it is impossible to express it.

But if you ask me, 'life' seems to be very, very beautiful. With 'God' somehow you feel the smell of the church—and it is a bad odour; it is not good. With 'life', the flowers, the trees and the birds come to mind. Have you ever watched the reaction, the response in your mind? I say 'God'—cathedrals arise, man-made things—priests, popes. Of course, it is very dramatic, but a little ridiculous too—in their long, pretentious robes, crowns, hypocrisies. I say 'life'—no cathedral arises in your consciousness, no temple—instead, rivers flowing, flowers flowering, birds singing, the sun shining, children laughing and running, people making love, the sky and the earth. The word 'life' is really more beautiful, less corrupted. It has not fallen in the hands of priests; they have not been able to corrupt and destroy its beauty. They have not been able to cut it into a shape—it has not yet been tailored. 'Life' remains wild.

But I tell you, that is what godliness is: absolutely wild.

Never ask why life is, because who is going to answer? There is nobody else other than life.

And don't think that you have to live only when there is a purpose, otherwise how can you live. I don't see the point. Flowers flower; they don't know any 'why'. And they flower beautifully. And I cannot conceive that if they are taught, 'There is a purpose in your flowering', then they will flower better; I can't see it. They will just flower the same way. They have been doing their uttermost. Do you think cuckoos will be singing better if they are told what the purpose of singing is?

I always think that animals must be laughing at man. There must be many jokes about man prevalent among animals. Man must be a very odd, ridiculous phenomenon on the earth.

A flower goes on flowering—it needs no purpose to flower. But you need a purpose. You can love somebody, but what is the purpose? If love needs a purpose, then you will miss the whole thing. There are people who also love purposefully.

Life is not economics. It is intrinsically valuable. And once you understand this, a great, immense mutation happens to you. Then you simply breathe and breathing is so beautiful, so peaceful, so graceful. Then each moment becomes its own meaning; the meaning is not outgoing. Then you live this moment for itself. You sing because you love singing. You dance because it is so beautiful to dance. You love because there is nothing like love. If you ask the purpose, then you have a prostitute's mind. The prostitute can love, but there is a purpose in it.

People who are always asking, 'What is the purpose of life?' have a prostitute's mind. They cannot accept life as it is. They need something else to make it meaningful.

Just try to understand: each moment is enough unto itself, each act is total unto itself, and, whatsoever you do, the doing itself has grandeur. Nothing else is needed.

Then suddenly you become free. Because a man who is

purpose-oriented can never be free. Purpose is always in the future. You live today for something which is going to happen tomorrow. Who knows? You may die. Then you will live an unfulfilled life; and tomorrow again you will live for a 'future tomorrow' because each tomorrow comes as a today and you have learned the wrong way—of sacrificing today for tomorrow.

If you have become addicted to the question of purpose you will go on asking. Whatsoever happens, you will ask, 'What is the purpose of it?' People come to me and they say, 'You tell us to meditate, but what is the purpose of it?' What purpose is needed to meditate? Meditation is so silent, so overflowing with bliss, that no other purpose is needed. It is not a means to something else. It is an end unto itself.

'Hence what I am eating, what I am doing, what is happening all around—nothing seems to bother me.' You are becoming insensitive and dull. Don't think this is religion. This is just slow suicide. You are poisoning your being. Become more alert, become more aware, become more sensitive. Because if you are not sensitive, life will go on passing you by and you will not be able to live it. You will remain untouched. Life will go on showering on you, and you will remain closed, you will not be open for it. Existence will go on giving to you, but you will not receive. Become more sensitive, more responsive. Be like a string of a veena— if somebody just touches it, what a response! The string is alive. Don't be loose; otherwise there will be no response. Of course don't be too tight, otherwise you will be broken.

This is the whole art of religion: how to be balanced, how not to become lopsided. The strings of a veena have to remain in a perfect poise, in a perfect equanimity, in perfect balance—neither this way nor that—just in the middle, exactly in the middle. You touch it and it responds.

They say that if a veena has been fixed correctly by a master and you put that veena in the corner of the room and you play on another veena, the veena in the corner will start responding to the other veena's music. It responds because the throbbing, the vibration, the pulsation reaches it. When one veena starts a tremendously beautiful vibration, it fills the whole room. And the other veena is waiting there, perfectly ready—neither loose, nor too tight, just in the middle; immediately those subtle vibrations hit it. Without even being touched by a human hand it starts responding, it becomes alive. *That* is the way to live.

Meditation is just to make you balanced, in the middle, tranquil, silent and happy. Life is coming to you every moment. Millions are its gifts; you go on missing them because you are not ready. You are like a deaf person who is sitting and somebody is playing on the veena. You go on missing it.

I have heard about a great musician who had heard that when Tansen, another great musician, used to play on his veena, animals would gather together to listen to him. He wanted to know if it was true. He went to the forest and started playing on his veena; by and by, animals started coming. A great crowd gathered—the elephant, the zebra, the tiger, the leopard, the foxes, the wolves—all sorts of animals, small and big, and they were enchanted, hypnotized. And then suddenly a crocodile came and jumped on the musician and gulped him in one bite. All the animals were very angry. They said, 'What is this nonsense?' The crocodile cupped his ear and said, 'What? What are you saying?'

The crocodile was deaf. Don't be deaf, don't be blind. Be alive, responsive.

Truth is knocking on your door every moment. If you become insensitive you will not hear the knock. Jesus says, 'Knock, and the door shall be opened unto you.' I say to you there is no need for you to knock—truth is knocking on the door. Listen! In fact, truth is seeking you from everywhere. The search is not one-sided—it is not that only you are searching, but it is also seeking you. But you have to become available.

And this is no way to become available.

'Since my very childhood, whenever I saw a dead body, always the thought flashed to me that if death is to come then what is the sense in living.' That is why there is sense in living—because death *is* to come. If there was going to be no death and you were going to be here forever, just think what will happen. You will be bored. You will start praying for death.

There is a beautiful story about Alexander the Great. When he came to India, he came for many reasons—to conquer India, to meet the wise men there, and also to find a certain well, about which he had heard, whose water, if drunk, makes one immortal.

I do not know how far the story is true. I cannot vouch for it, but it is beautiful. And a story has to be beautiful to be true; there is no other truth except beauty.

And he travelled and he asked many wise men, and finally he found the well. But he was surprised because the people who guided him were not much interested in it . . . that was something unbelievable! And the man who took him to the well was not even interested to wait there.

Alexander asked, 'Are you not interested in eternal life? Don't you want to be immortal?'

The man laughed. He said, 'I have learned much about

life. The desire arises in childish minds. But fulfil it.'

There was a staircase going into the well. He went inside. He was just going to drink the water when a crow who was sitting there said, 'Wait! Listen a minute. Don't do that foolishness. I have done it. Now I am suffering because I cannot die. I have lived for many thousands of years. Now the only prayer in my heart is: "God, help me to die." And I have been seeking wise men and asking them, "Is there some well which can function as an antidote to this foolishness?" I am a foolish crow, so I committed this mistake. Please, think again: you will never be able to die then.'

It is said Alexander thought it over and left the well immediately because there was every possibility that he may get tempted. He didn't drink.

Just think—if there was no death, life will lose much. Without the polarity, everything becomes dull, hopeless. It is as if there is just the day and there is no night to rest—only day . . . scorching heat, and nowhere to hide, nowhere to dissolve into the darkness, nowhere to forget oneself into oblivion. It will be difficult. It will be very arduous and pointless. Rest is needed; death is rest.

So if you have seen dead bodies being taken to the cemetery or to the funeral ground, you have not seen much. And if you thought that now life is meaningless, then you have missed the point. Seeing a dead body, remember death is coming. Use this opportunity to be alive as intensely as possible, and then there is rest. Earn the rest!

This is one of the things I would like to tell you: if you don't live well, you will not die well. Your death will also be just dull. It will not have any flame in it, it will not be beautiful. If you live intensely, you die intensely. If you live happily, you die happily. The taste of your life is carried to the peak by your death. Death is a culmination, a crescendo. If you have been singing a beautiful song, then death is the crescendo, the highest peak.

Death is not against life. Death is a background. It makes life richer. It makes life more alive. It gives contrast.

'Since those very days of my childhood, a sort of non-interest has surrounded my whole pattern of life, and probably that might be the reason why I got interested in religion and could reach you.' Maybe. That may be the reason why you could reach me, but now that will be the reason you will not be able to understand me. It has brought you to my door, but it will not bring you to my heart.

Now please drop that, because here I am teaching life. Of course, I am teaching death also, but my death is a beautiful truth and your life is an ugly fact. I am teaching you an alchemical magic: how to transform even death into a beautiful experience. Of course, life will become more beautiful when even death has become beautiful. How to transmute baser metals into gold—that is what I am teaching here.

Maybe you have come here because of these ideas of yours, but now drop them—otherwise they will be barriers between me and you.

✳

Are you really just a man who got enlightened?

Just the other way round: a god who got lost and has found himself again, a god who rested and slept deeply and dreamt of being a man and is now awake. And the same is true about you. You are not just men. You are gods—dreaming that you are men. It is not that men have to become God, only that gods have to become a little awake—then the dream of 'man' disappears.

This is the difference between the Eastern and the Western attitudes. The West tries to explain the highest by the lowest. If you attain *samadhi*—for example Ramakrishna attains *samadhi*, is lost in the infinite—ask Freud, and he will say this is a sort of repressed sex: *samadhi* is to be explained by sex. Ask me about sex, and I will say this is a first glimpse of *samadhi*.

The highest is not to be reduced to the lowest. The lowest has to be raised to the highest.

Ask Marx and he will say consciousness is nothing but a by-product of matter. Ask me: I will say matter is nothing but an illusion of consciousness.

In the East we have tried to explain the mud, the dirty mud, by the lotus. In the West you have tried to explain the lotus by the dirty mud it comes out of. And it makes a great difference. When you try to explain the lotus by the dirty mud it comes out of, the lotus disappears: only dirty mud in your hands. All beauty, all greatness, all truth disappear: only dirtiness remains in your hands. Everything can be reduced to the lowest because the highest and the lowest are joined together. The highest rung of the ladder is joined to the lowest rung of the ladder, so nothing seems to be wrong in it, but there is much which is important to be understood.

If you explain the dirty mud by the lotus—'When the lotus has arisen out of this dirty mud, even this dirty mud is not really dirty. Otherwise how can the lotus arise out of it? The lotus is hiding in it. We may not have been able to see the lotus in it—that is our limitation'—the dirty mud disappears: your hands are full of lotuses.

Now it is for you to choose. The East makes you rich, superb and divine. The West makes you very ordinary, material, it reduces you to things, and all that is grand in human beings becomes suspicious, suspected.

Remember, you are an evolution from godliness to godliness. In between is the world; a dream we call it. That is why we call it *maya*, a dream—godliness dreaming to be lost. Enjoy it! There is nothing wrong in it. Sooner or later you will wake up and you will laugh; it was a dream.

If you ask psychoanalysts about the divine, they say it is something in your imagination. You ask Shankara, you ask Eastern sages, and they say you are something in the divine's imagination. It is tremendously beautiful. You are something in the divine's imagination; the divine is imagining you, dreaming you. Ask Freud; he says, 'Divine? You are dreaming; you are imagining something.'

Both are true! And it is for you to choose. If you want to be in despair, anguish and agony forever and ever, choose the Western attitude. If you want to flower and be happy—unconditionally—choose the Eastern attitude.

✳

You are the best killer. One year with you and slowly your poison is working in my mind. Whatever I pretended to be looks ugly and dirty; everything is in turmoil.

But now, in such great confusion, how do I find a small door for the divine to enter?

Let that be the divine's worry. Why should you be worried? You just be yourself. He will find the way.

And you are right: I am a killer—almost a murderer.

One man was dying in a hospital, and he said to the doctor, 'Doctor, I am very worried. It seems I am dying.'

The doctor said, 'Don't worry, leave it to me.'

That is what I say to you—'Don't worry, leave it to me. I will kill you'—because that is the only way to give you a new release, a new lease of life. I will give you the cross so that you can be reborn.

✳

You have been talking a lot about sex, which is good, because it has been kept in the dark for such a long time. However, I have personally never heard you talk about homosexuality; only very, very briefly, and actually always to put it down.

Please talk about it, because no matter what the cause of 'this perverted act', as you describe it, homosexuality did and does exist in the world. Can't the moon side meet the sun side in whatever body? Is Tantra only for heterosexual people? Should people repress their homosexual tendencies?

The first thing: the questioner has not signed his question. That shows that he is also feeling guilty about it. He does not want his name to be known. In not signing the question, he has already condemned homosexuality.

I am not against anything, but I am for many things. Let me repeat: I am not against anything, but I am for many things. I am not against the mud, but I am for the lotus: sex has to be transformed. If it is not transformed, you remain at the lowest rung of your being. So the first thing to be understood: I talk about sex so that you can understand it and transcend it.

Homosexuality is even lower than heterosexuality. Nothing wrong in it—you still have a lower rung in your ladder. That has to be transcended. So the first thing: sex has to be transcended. The second thing to be remembered: homosexuality is a lower rung.

Every child is born auto-sexual, every child is masturbatory. That is a stage—the child has to go beyond it. Every child likes to play with his genital organs, and it is pleasurable, nothing wrong in it. But it is childish. It is the first learning of sex, a rehearsal, a getting ready, preparation. But if you are thirty-five, forty, sixty, and still masturbatory, then something is wrong.

When I say something is wrong, I only mean you have not been able to grow; your mental age has remained retarded.

After the masturbatory period I call 'auto-sexual', the child becomes homosexual. Near the age of ten, the child becomes homosexual. He becomes more interested in bodies similar to his. This is natural growth. First he is interested in his own body; then he becomes interested in others' bodies which are like his—a boy is interested in boys, a girl is interested in girls. That is a natural stage. But the boy is going away from himself, moving his sexual energy, his libido, to other boys. And this seems natural because other boys look more similar to him than girls. But he has taken a step: he has become homosexual. Good, nothing wrong in it, but at the age of sixty if you are still homosexual, then you are retarded—you are 'boyish'. That is why homosexuals retain the boyish attitude and they look 'gay'. They look happier than the heterosexual; that is certain. Even in their faces they retain the boyishness. It is very difficult to hide your homosexuality: your face, your eyes, everything shows it. You remain boyish. It is good to pass through it, but it is bad to cling to it.

Then comes the third stage, heterosexual: A boy becomes interested in a girl, and a girl becomes interested in a boy. That is the highest stage as far as sex goes, but that too up to a point. If you are still interested in sex after forty-two, something is missing. Then you have not lived it rightly. At the age of fourteen, you become really sexual, ready to give birth to a child, to become a mother or a father. It takes fourteen years to prepare you. Another fourteen years, by the age of twenty-eight, you are at the peak of your sexuality. After another fourteen years, at the age of forty-two, you are moving back. The circle is complete. Jung has said, 'After the age of forty, whosoever comes to me has a religious problem.' If after the age of forty-two you are still sexually puzzled and in a problem, something in your life has been missing.

After another fourteen years, by the age of fifty-six, one is simply freed of sex. Another fourteen years, from fifty-six to seventy, is the next childhood. Before death you have to reach the same point as when you were born. The circle is complete. That is what Jesus means when he says, 'Unless you become like children, you will not enter into my kingdom of God.'

This is the seventy-year cycle, more or less. It will differ if you live eighty years or a hundred years; then you can divide.

I am not against anything, but I will not help you to cling to any place. Go on, go on and never cling to any place. I am not condemning anything. Use that opportunity, but go on.

A few anecdotes:

An obviously distressed gent staggered into a psychiatrist's office and said, 'Doctor, you have got to help me. Every night I dream I am marooned on a desert island with a dozen blondes, a dozen brunettes and a dozen redheads, each more beautiful than all the rest.'

'You must be the luckiest man alive,' said the doctor. 'What do you need my help for?'

'My problem,' said the patient. 'Is that in my dreams I am a man.'

You get it? Otherwise let me tell you another joke:

Two retired army colonels were talking in their club.

'Did you hear about old Carstairs?' asked one.

'No, what about him?' said the other.

'Got posted to India as military adviser to one of these maharajah chappies. One day, he went off his chump, ran off into the jungle and turned native. Now he is living up a tree with a monkey!'

'Good Lord!' exclaimed the second colonel. 'Is it a male monkey or a female monkey?'

'Oh, female monkey, of course, old chap. Nothing bent about old Carstairs.'

Homosexuality is a retarded state, but in the West it is becoming more and more prevalent. There are reasons. I would like to tell you a few.

In their wild states animals are never homosexual, but in zoos, where they are not free and don't have enough space and are crowded too much, they become homosexual. The world is getting too crowded. It is becoming more like a zoo. All natural growths are disappearing and people are becoming too tense. That is one of the causes of homosexuality growing.

The second thing: in the West sex is thought to be more as fun than as a commitment. One wants to have casual affairs. To get involved with a woman is to get into troubled waters. To get involved with a woman means a great involvement: children, family, job, house, ca, and a thousand and one things. Once the woman enters, the whole world enters. The Western mind is becoming more and more afraid of getting involved; people would like to remain uninvolved. It is easier to be uninvolved in a homosexual relationship than in a heterosexual relationship. No children, and immediately the commitment becomes almost none.

The third reason: women are becoming lesbians in the West because of the lib movement, the idea that man has oppressed women up to now. And man *has* oppressed—it has been one of the greatest slaveries ever. No other class has been oppressed as much as women. Now the revolt, the reaction, is happening. There are organizations of Western women which promote lesbianism, homosexuality—'Get out of all relationships with men. Forget loving the enemy. Man is the enemy; get out of all relationships with men. It is better to love a woman; a woman loves a woman.'

Women are getting more and more aggressive; man is also getting more and more afraid of getting into relationships.

These situations are creating homosexuality, but it is a perversion. If you are in it, I don't condemn you. I simply say get deeper into your feelings, meditate more, and by and by you will see that your homosexuality is turning into heterosexuality. If you are masturbatory, I would like you to become homosexuals—that is better. If you are homosexuals, I would like you to become heterosexuals—that is better. If you are already heterosexual, I would like you to become celibates—that is better. But go on.

I don't condemn anything.

The questioner says, '. . . homosexuality did and does exist in the world.' That is right. Tuberculosis also did exist and still exists, cancer also, but that does not mean they are good. A really better world will become more and more heterosexual. Why? Because men and women—or yin and yang—when they meet, the circle becomes complete, as negative electricity and positive electricity meet. When a man meets man, it is negative electricity meeting negative, or positive electricity meeting positive. It will not create the inner energy circle. It will leave you incomplete. It will never be fulfilling. It can be convenient, but it can never be fulfilling, and fulfilment is the goal, not convenience.

Remember that if inside you are going to become asexual one day, the *brahmacharya* has to arise, the purest celibacy has to arise—then it is better to move on the natural way. It is my understanding that it is simpler for a heterosexual to go beyond sex than for a homosexual. Because one rung is missing, it will take more effort for a homosexual.

But still I am not against anything. If you feel good, you have to decide it. I don't call it a sin and I am not saying that if you are homosexuals you are going to be thrown into hell. All nonsense! If you are homosexual you will miss something—the feeling when yin meets yang, the feeling where negative meets positive, night meets day. You will miss something—not that you will be thrown in hell, but you will miss something of heaven in your life.

But still you have to decide. I am not giving you a commandment.

In fact, the religious commandments have created a situation in which homosexuality was born for the first time. You will be surprised to know that religions are the cause of homosexuality in the world, because they insisted that monks should live in one monastery, nuns should live in another monastery, and they should not meet. Buddhists, Jains, Christians all forced thousands of men into one herd and thousands of women into another herd, and broke all the bridges between the two. They were the first breeding grounds of homosexuality. They have created the situation, because love is such a deep desire that if you don't allow the natural outlet it becomes perverted. It finds ways and means somehow to express itself.

In the army, people become homosexual easily. In boys' boarding houses and girls' boarding houses people turn homosexual easily. If homosexuality is to disappear from the world, then all segregation between man and woman should disappear. Hostels should be for both the sexes together. And the army should not comprise only men; women should be allowed there. And clubs should not be only for boys; that is dangerous. And monasteries should allow both sexes; otherwise homosexuality is natural.

But it is a perversion—a disease. When I say 'disease' I don't condemn it. I call it 'disease' with compassion. When somebody is suffering from tuberculosis, we don't condemn him. We help him to get out of it. So when people come to me and confess that they are homosexuals, I say 'Don't be worried. I am here. I will bring you out of it.'

Sex continues to be important till the very end of life— *if* you are not alert, *if* you are not transforming it. And to die sexual is an ugly death. One should come to a point when sex has been dropped far back.

Three very ancient members of the Army and Navy Club were discussing the subject of embarrassing moments over brandy and cigars.

The first two related incidents in their lives which they looked back on with shame. When it came to the turn of the third old codger, he told of how he had been caught peeping through the keyhole of the maid's bedroom.

'Ah yes,' said one of the others with a chuckle. 'We certainly got up to some pranks in our younger days.'

'Younger days, nothing!' said the third old boy. 'This was last night.'

But it is ugly if an old man should become like a small child again. When sex disappears, all desires disappear. When sex disappears, the interest in the other disappears. Sex is the link with the society, with the world, with matter. When sex disappears, suddenly you start floating like a cloud. You are uprooted; your roots are no longer here in this world.

And when your energy is not moving lower, downwards, then it starts rising higher and reaches *sahasrar*, where the ultimate lotus is waiting for the energy to come and to help it flower.

9

Absolute Aloneness, Absolute Liberation

Liberation is obtained when there is
equality of purity between the purusha *and*
satva.

The *Chhandogya Upanishad* has a beautiful story. Let us begin with it:

Satyakam asked his mother, Jabala, 'Mother, I want to live the life of a student of supreme knowledge. What is my family name? Who is my father?'

'My son,' replied the mother. 'I don't know. In my youth, when I went about a great deal as a maidservant, I conceived you. I do not know who your father is. I am Jabala and you are Satyakam, so call yourself Satyakam Jabal.'

Then the boy went to Gautama, a great seer of those days, and asked to be accepted as a student. 'Of what family are you, my dear?' inquired the sage.

Satyakam replied, 'I asked my mother what my family name was, and she answered, "I don't know. In my youth, when I went about a great deal as a maidservant, I conceived you. I do not know who your father is. I am Jabala and you are Satyakam, so call yourself Satyakam Jabal." Sir, I am therefore Satyakam Jabal.'

The sage then said to him, 'None but a true Brahmin, a true seeker of truth, would have spoken thus. You have not swerved from the truth, my dear. I will teach you that supreme knowledge.'

The first quality of the seeker is to be authentic. Not to swerve from truth, not to deceive in any way, because if you deceive others, eventually you are deceived by your own deceptions. If you tell a lie too many times, it almost starts looking like a truth to you. When others start believing in your lies, you also start believing in them. Belief is infectious.

That is how we have got into the mess we are in.

The first lie that we have accepted as truth is that 'I am a body'. Everybody believes in it. You are born in a society which believes that we are bodies. Everybody reacts as a body; nobody responds as a soul.

And remember the difference between reaction and response: reaction is mechanical; response is alert, aware and conscious. When you push a button and the fan starts moving, it is a reaction. When you push a button, the fan does not start thinking, 'Am I to move or not?' When you switch the light on, the electricity does not respond; it reacts. It is mechanical. There is no gap between your pushing the button and the electricity's functioning. There is no little gap of thought, of awareness, of consciousness.

If you go on reacting in your life—somebody insults you and you become angry, somebody says something and you become sad, somebody says something else and you become very happy—if it is a reaction, a push-button reaction, then by and by you will start believing that you are the body.

The body is the mechanism. It is not you. You live in it, it is your abode, but you are not it. You are totally different.

This is the first lie that cripples life. Then there is another lie: I am the mind. And this is deeper than the first, obviously, because the mind is closer to you than the body. You go on thinking thoughts, dreaming dreams, and they move so close to you, almost touching your being, just surrounding you; you start believing in them also. Then you become the mind. The mind also reacts.

You become a soul the moment you start responding. Response means now you are not reacting mechanically. You contemplate, you meditate and you give a gap for your consciousness to decide. *You* are the deciding factor. If somebody insults you, in reaction, he is the deciding factor. You simply react, he manipulates you. In response, you are the deciding factor: if somebody insults you, that is not primary, that is secondary. You think over it. You decide whether to do this or that. You are not overwhelmed by it. You remain untouched, you remain aloof—you remain a watcher.

These two lies have to be broken. These are fundamental lies. I am not counting the millions of lies that are not fundamental. You go on identifying yourself with a name. A name is just a label, utilitarian. You don't come with a name, and you don't go with a name. A name is just used by society; it will be difficult to exist in society without a name. Otherwise, you are nameless. Then you think you belong to a certain religion, to a certain caste. You think that you belong to a certain man who is your father, a certain woman who is your mother. Yes, you come through them, but you don't belong to them. They have been passages, you have travelled through them, but you are different.

In Kahlil Gibran's masterpiece, *The Prophet*, a woman

asks the prophet Almustafa, 'Tell us something about our children,' and Almustafa says, 'They come through you, but they don't belong to you. Love them, but don't give your thoughts to them. Love them, because love gives freedom, but don't possess them.'

Your body can be possessed; your mind can also be possessed. But your innermost core belongs to nobody; it is not anybody's possession. It is not a thing. It cannot be possessed.

When you become a Mohammedan, your mind is possessed by people who call themselves Mohammedans. When you become a Hindu, your mind is possessed by people who call themselves Hindus. When you become a communist, you are possessed by *Das Kapital*. When you become a Christian, you are possessed by the Bible. When you think yourself as the body, you think yourself in terms of white, of black.

Your innermost core is neither Christian nor Hindu, white nor black, communist nor anti-communist. Your innermost core remains absolutely aloof from the body and the mind. It is higher than the body and higher than the mind. The mind cannot touch it; the body cannot reach it.

Why did the great sage Gautama accept Satyakam Jabal? He was true. He could have deceived; the temptation is easy. To move in the world, saying to people, 'I don't know who my father is', is very humiliating. But the mother was also true. It is easy to deceive the child because the child has no means to discover whether you are deceiving or not. When a child asks his mother, 'Who created the world?' there is every temptation for the mother to say 'God created the world' without knowing at all what she is saying.

This is the basic reason why, when children grow up, they become almost antagonistic towards their parents. They can never forgive them because they lie too much. They lose all respect for them. Parents go on saying, 'Why? We loved you. We brought you up. The best we could do we have done. Why don't children respect us?' You have lost the opportunity because of your lies. Once the child discovers that his mother and father have been lying, the whole respect disappears. Deceiving a small helpless child? Saying things they did not know anything about?

That Jabala was a rare mother. She said, 'I don't know who your father is.' She accepted that when she was young she was moving with many men. She loved many men and was being loved by many men, so she does not know who the father is. A true mother—and the child was also brave. He told the master; he repeated exactly those words that the mother had said.

This truth appealed to Gautama and he said, 'You are a true Brahmin.' This is the definition of being a Brahmin; a true man is a Brahmin. A Brahmin has nothing to do with any caste. The very word comes from *Brahman*; it means 'a seeker of truth', a true authentic seeker.

Remember, the more you get involved in lies, howsoever paying they appear in the beginning, in the end you will find that they have poisoned your whole being.

Be authentic. If you are authentic, sooner or later you will discover that you are not the body—because authenticity cannot go on believing in a lie. The clarity dawns, the eyes become more perceptive and you can see: you are in the body, certainly, but you are not the body. When a hand is broken, you are not broken. When you have a fractured leg, you are not fractured. When there is a headache, you know the headache; you are not the headache itself. When you feel hungry, you know the hunger, but you are not hunger. By and by the basic lie is sabotaged. Then you can enter deeper and can start seeing your thoughts and dreams floating in the consciousness. Then you can distinguish, discriminate—what Patanjali calls *vivek*—then you can discriminate between the cloud and the sky.

Thoughts are like clouds moving in empty space. That empty space is the real sky, not the clouds—they come and go. Not the thoughts, but the empty space in which those thoughts appear and disappear.

Now let me tell you one very basic yoga structure of your being.

Just as physicists think that the whole consists of nothing but electrons, electric energy, yoga thinks that the whole consists of nothing but sound electrons. The basic element of existence for yoga is sound because life is nothing but a vibration. Life is nothing but an expression of silence. Out of silence we come, and into silence we dissolve again. Silence, space, nothingness, non-being, is your innermost core, the hub of the wheel. Unless you come to that silence, to that space where nothing else remains except your pure being, liberation is not attained. This is the yoga framework.

They divide your being into four layers. I am speaking to you; this is the last layer. Yoga calls it *vaikhari*; the word means 'fruition', flowering. But before I speak to you, before I utter something, it becomes manifest to me as a feeling, as an experience; that is the third stage. Yoga calls it *madhyama*, 'the middle'. But before something is experienced inside, it moves in a seed form. You cannot experience this ordinarily unless you are very meditative, unless you have become so totally calm that even a stirring in the seed which has not sprouted yet can be perceived; it is very subtle. Yoga calls that *pashyanti*; the word *pashyanti* means 'looking back', looking to the source. And beyond that is your fundamental being out of which everything arises. That is called *para*; *para* means 'the transcendental'.

Now try to understand these four layers. *Para* is something beyond all manifestation. *Pashyanti* is like a seed. *Madhyama* is like a tree. *Vaikhari* is like fruition, flowering.

Let me tell you another story, again from the *Chhandogya Upanishad*:

'Fetch me from thence a fruit of the nyagrodh tree,' said the father, the great sage Uddalak, to his son.

'Here is one, sir,' said Svetketu.

'Break it.'

'It is broken, sir.'

'What do you see there?'

'These seeds, almost infinitesimal.'

'Break one of them.'

'It is broken, sir.'

'What do you see?'

'Nothing, sir. Absolutely nothing.'

The father said, 'My son, that subtle essence which you do not perceive there—of that *very* essence this great nyagrodh tree exists. Believe it, my son, that there is the subtle essence. In that all things have existence. That is the truth. That is the self. And that, Svetketu, that art thou— *tatvamasi*, Svetketu.'

The nyagrodh tree is a big tree. The father asks for a fruit; Svetketu brings it. Fruit is *vaikhari*—the thing has flowered, fruition has happened. Fruit is the most peripheral thing, absolutely manifested. The father says, 'Break it.' Svetketu breaks it and finds millions of seeds. The father says, 'Choose one seed. Break it as well.' He breaks that seed also. Now there is nothing in hand—inside the seed there is nothing. Uddalak says, 'Out of this nothingness comes the seed. Out of the seed comes the tree. Out of the tree comes the fruit. But the basic is nothingness, the silence, the space, the formless, the non-manifest, the beyond, the transcendental.'

At the point of *vaikhari*, you are very confused because you are farthest from your being. If you move deeper into your being, when you come closer to *madhyama*, the third point, you will be a little closer to your being. That is why it is called the middle, the bridge. That is how a mediator enters into his being. That is how mantra is used.

When you use a mantra and you repeat rhythmically 'aum, aum, aum . . . ', first it is to be repeated loudly: *vaikhari*. Then you have to close your lips and you have to repeat it inside—nothing comes out: *madhyama*. Then you have to drop even repeating inside. It repeats itself. You get in such tune with it that you drop the repeating and it goes on, by its own accord. Now you have become a listener rather than repeating it. You can listen and watch and see: it has become *pashyanti*. *Pashyanti* means looking back to the source; now your eyes are turned towards the source. Then by and by that 'aum' also disappears into the formless. Suddenly there is emptiness and nothing else. You don't hear 'aum, aum, aum . . . '—you don't hear anything. Neither is there anything heard nor the hearer. Everything has disappeared.

'*Tatvamasi*, Svetketu,' Uddalak said to his son. 'That art thou'—that nothingness, when the chanter and the chanting have disappeared.

Now if you are attached to things too much, you will remain at the point of *vaikhari*. If you are attached to your body too much, you will remain at the point of *madhyama*. If you are attached to your mind too much, you will remain at the point of *pashyanti*. And if you are not attached at all, suddenly you dissolve into *para*—the transcendental, the beyond. That is liberation.

Being liberated means coming back home. We have gone far away. Just see: out of nothingness comes the seed, then out of the seed the sprout, then a big tree, then fruits and flowers. How far things have gone. But the fruit falls back into the earth; the circle is complete. Silence is the beginning, silence is the end. Out of pure space we come and into pure space we go. If the circle is not complete, then you will be stuck at some point where you have become almost frozen and you cannot move; you have lost the dynamism, the energy, the life.

Yoga wants to make you so alive that you can complete the whole circle, the wheel of life, and you can come to the very beginning again. The end is nothing but the very beginning. The goal is nothing but the source. It is not that we are going to achieve truth for the first time. We had it in the first place. We lost it. We will be regaining it, reclaiming it. Truth is never a discovery; it is always a rediscovery. We have been in it, in that womb of peace and silence and bliss, but we have gone farther away.

It was also part of growth to go far away because if you have never gone out of your home, you will never know what home is. If you have never gone farther away from home, you will never know the beauty, the peace, the comfort, the rest of your home. To come to one's own home one has to knock at many doors. To come back to oneself one has to stumble upon many things. To come to the right path one has to go astray.

This is necessary, absolutely necessary for growth, but don't get stuck somewhere. People are stuck. A few people are stuck with their bodies, with their bodily habits. A few people are stuck with their minds, ideologies, thoughts and patterns of dreams.

The *Katha Upanishad* says, 'Beyond the objects are the

senses.' Beyond the senses is the mind. Beyond the mind is the intelligence. Beyond the intelligence is the soul. Beyond the soul is the non-manifest. Beyond the non-manifest is the Brahman. And beyond Brahman himself, there is nothing.' This is the end, the pure consciousness.

And this pure consciousness can be achieved through many paths. The real thing is not a path. The real thing is the authenticity of the seeker. Let me emphasize this.

You can travel on any path. If you are sincere and authentic, you will reach the goal. Some paths may be hard, some may be easier, some may have greenery on both sides, some may be moving through deserts, some may have beautiful scenery around them, some may not have any scenery around them—that is another thing; but if you are sincere and honest and authentic and true, then each path leads to the goal. Krishna has said in Shrimad Bhagavad-Gita, 'Whatever path people travel is my path. No matter where they walk, it leads to me.'

So it can be simply reduced to one thing: authenticity is the path. No matter what path you follow, if you are authentic, every path leads to Him. And the opposite is also true: no matter what path you follow, if you are not authentic, you will not reach anywhere. Your authenticity brings you back home, nothing else. All paths are just secondary. The basic is to be authentic, to be true.

There is a Sufi story:

A man heard that if he went to a certain place in the desert at dawn and stood facing a distant mountain, his shadow would point to a great buried treasure. The man left his cabin before the first light of day and at dawn was standing in the designated place. His shadow shot out long and thin over the surface of the sand. 'How fortunate,' he thought as he envisioned himself with great wealth.

He began digging for the treasure. He was so involved with his work that he did not notice the sun climbing the sky and shortening his shadow, and then he noticed it. It was now almost half of the previous size. He became worried and started digging again in the new spot.

Hours later, at noon, the man again stood in the designated spot. He cast no shadow. He became very much worried. He started crying and weeping—the whole effort was lost. Now where is the place?

And then there passed a Sufi master, who started laughing at him and he said, 'Now the shadow is pointing exactly to the treasure. It is within you.'

All paths can lead to it because in a way it is already achieved. It is within you. You are not seeking something new. You are seeking something which you have forgotten. And how can you really forget it? That is why we go on searching for bliss—because we cannot forget it. It goes on resounding inside us. The search for bliss, the search for joy, the search for happiness is nothing but the search for godliness. You may not have used the word 'godliness', that doesn't matter, but all searching for bliss is the search for godliness—is the search for something that you knew, that once was yours and you lost it.

That is why all the great saints have said, 'Remember.' Buddha calls it *samyak smriti*, 'right remembrance'. Nanak calls it *nam smaran*, 'remembering the name'—remembering the address. Have you not observed that many times it happens, when you know something and you say, 'It is on the tip of my tongue, but still I can't say it.' Godliness is at the tip of your tongue.

In a small school, the chemistry teacher wrote a formula on the blackboard and he asked a small boy to stand up and tell him what this formula represents. The boy said, 'Sir, it is just on the tip of my tongue, but I cannot remember.'

The teacher said, 'Spit it out! Spit it out! It is potassium cyanide!'

Godliness is also on the tip of the tongue, and I will tell you, 'Swallow it! Swallow it! Don't spit it out! It is godliness!' Let it circulate in your blood. Let it become part of your innermost vibrations. Let it become a song inside your being, a dance.

The identification with the body is nothing but a habit. A child is born, he does not know who he is, and the parents have to create some identity; otherwise he will be lost in the world. They have to tell him who he is. They also don't know. They have to create a false label. They give him a name, they give him a mirror, and they tell him, 'Look. This is your face. Look. This is your name. Look. This is your home. Look. This is your caste, your religion, your country.' These identifications help him to feel who he is— without knowing who he is. These are habits.

Then by and by his mind starts developing. If he is born in a Hindu home, he reads the Gita, listens to the Gita. If in a Christian home, he is brought to the church. A new identity starts, an innermost identity—he becomes a Christian, a Hindu or a Mohammedan. If he is born in India, he becomes an Indian. In China, he becomes Chinese and he starts identifying himself with the tradition of the country. A Chinese person identifies himself with Chinese tradition and history, the past of China. Then one feels at home, one has roots—the whole tradition. If one is Indian, one has roots, one is not a vagabond. One has created a certain home: in the tradition, in the country, in the history, in the heroes—Ram, Krishna—now one feels at home. One has found his place, but that is not a real place. This identity is utilitarian.

And then this habit becomes so solid that when one day you come to know what nonsense it is to think that you are Indian, Hindu, Mohammedan, Christian or Chinese, even then the old habit will persist.

Bertrand Russell has written that he knows that he is no longer a Christian, but somehow he goes on forgetting it again and again. The whole conditioning is such that even if you go against the tradition, you will still cling to it. Even people who become revolutionaries remain attached to their traditions; maybe in a negative way. If a Hindu goes against Hinduism, he will still talk about Krishna—against him; he will still talk about Ram—against him. If a Mohammedan goes against his tradition, he will be criticizing the Koran, criticizing Mohammed—but he remains attached to the tradition.

A real rebel is one who drops the tradition so deeply, so utterly, that he is not even against it. He is neither for nor against; then he is free. If you are against, you are still not free. If you are against anything, you will find you are bound with that thing; there is a connection.

And habits become unconscious. I knew a very, very learned man, very scholarly, very famous, and really a great intellectual. He had been a follower of J. Krishnamurti for long, almost forty years. And whenever he would come to see me, he would say, 'There is no meditation. What are you teaching to people? Krishnamurti says there is no meditation; all mantras are just repetitive, and all meditations, all methods, condition the mind. I don't meditate.'

I waited for a right moment to hammer the truth home. Then he had a heart attack. I rushed to see him, and heard him repeating, 'Ram, Ram, Ram . . . ' I could not believe it. I shook his head and I said, 'What are you doing? You are a follower of Krishnamurti. Have you forgotten?'

He said, 'Forget all about that. I am dying. And who knows? Maybe Krishnamurti is wrong. There is no loss by just repeating "Ram, Ram, Ram . . ." and it is very consoling.'

What happened to this man? Forty years of listening to Krishnamurti, but his Hinduism is there. At the last moment, the mind will start reacting. No, he was not a rebel. He thought he was a rebel. He had been fighting everything, had been against all that Hindus say, but in the last moment the whole edifice falls.

Life ordinarily is nothing but a habit, a mechanical habit. Unless you become aware, unless you become *really* aware, it will be difficult to get out of it.

I have heard about a gambler:

An inveterate gambler died, and his ghost wandered around disconsolately for several weeks. Although he was entitled to be admitted to heaven, he found himself bored by the place. No gambling, no gamblers—what is the use of going to paradise or heaven?

Eventually he asked St. Peter if he could go and take a look at the other place.

'I'm afraid that is impossible,' said St. Peter. 'If you go down there, you won't be allowed back.'

'But I only want to have a look round,' said the gambler's ghost.

So St. Peter agreed to issue him with a special pass allowing him to stay for just twenty hours.

Off went the gambler to have a look round hell, and the first thing he saw when he arrived was a group of old acquaintances playing poker. However, they refused to admit him into the game because he had no money.

'I will soon fix that,' he said, and off he went down one of the corridors. Ten minutes later he was back, flourishing a big roll of ten-pound notes.

'Where did you get all that money?' asked one of the others.

'I sold my pass,' replied the gambler.

Habits can be too much; you can even refuse heaven. In a fit of habit you are almost unconscious and helpless. That is why the insistence of yoga is to bring more awareness to your ties. Remember as much as you can that you are not the body. And remember one thing more, that it is difficult to break a habit, but not difficult if you create another to substitute it. And that is how it happens; people go on substituting habits. If you tell them, 'You are not the body', they will start thinking they are the mind—then nothing but the name of the habit changes.

This I see. If I tell somebody, 'Stop smoking', he starts chewing pan. If I tell him to stop chewing pan, he starts chewing gum. Or if you stop him from that too, he starts talking too much; that too is the same thing. In the beginning he was just smoking; at least he was harming only himself. Now he cannot smoke, so he talks too much; now he is destroying others' peace and silence also. A smoker is good in a way; he remains confined to himself. Women talk too much; once they start smoking, their talking becomes less.

In fact, you must have observed: whenever you feel nervous, you start smoking. That smoking is just to escape from nervousness. And the same happens whenever you start talking. You are feeling nervous; you want to distract yourself with something.

I have heard an anecdote:

The patient, who was only eighteen, caused a lot of worry to his parents because he would spend hours in his room dressing himself very meticulously in his smart clothes. He would take ages brushing his hair, polishing his shoes, and then he would go into the kitchen, stick a carrot in his left ear and go dancing at a disco.

Naturally his parents were worried about all this and they persuaded him to see a psychiatrist. He arrived at the psychiatrist's office, beautifully groomed and wearing a stick of celery in his left ear. The doctor gently mentioned that his parents were a little worried about him and then he asked, 'By the way, is there any reason for you to have a stick of celery protruding from your left ear?'

The boy looked surprised and said, 'Of course there is. Mum did not have any carrots.'

If a carrot is dropped, then celery . . . people go on changing habits.

Sometimes it happens that you can change a bad habit into a good habit, and everybody will be happy and satisfied. But yoga will not be satisfied. You can stop smoking and you can start repeating a mantra. Now if you don't repeat your mantra one day, you feel uneasiness in the same way as you used to feel before, when you were smoking and if you had not smoked for one day—the same desire to follow the routine, to do whatsoever you have been doing, mechanically. You can change a bad habit into a good habit, but the habit is still a habit. It may be good in the eyes of society, but for your inner growth it has no meaning.

All habits have to be dropped. I am not saying become a chaos. I am not saying live a life absolutely hectic and haphazard, zigzag, no. But let your life be decided by your awareness.

It is possible you can get up at 5 a.m., out of habit; and it is also possible to get up early, at 5 a.m., not out of habit but out of awareness. And both are so different, their quality is absolutely different. When a person rises at 5 a.m. just out of habit, then he is almost as mechanical as the other person who gets up at 9 a.m. out of habit. Both are in the same boat. And the person who rises at 5 a.m. will be as dull as the person who rises at 9 a.m. because the dullness is not a question of when you get up. The dullness is a question of whether you get up through habit or awareness.

If you get up through awareness, you will be alert. It may be 9 a.m., but if you get up aware, you will be sensitive, you will see things with clarity, and everything will be beautiful. After a long rest all the senses have rested, have become alive again, more alive; the dust has disappeared, everything is more clear. Rested, deep down into your *para*, your beyond, you had fallen in your sleep—all thoughts, body, forgotten, left far away. You had moved to your home. You come back from there rejuvenated, fresh; but if it is just a habit, then it is as useless as any other habit.

Religion is not a question of habit. If you go to the church or to the temple just as a habit, a formality, a routine in which you have got into, you have been trained into, then it is useless. If you go to the temple alert, then the temple bells will have a totally different meaning for you, a different significance. Those temple bells will ring something within your heart. Then the silence of the church will surround you in a totally new way.

So remember, it is not a question of habit. Religion is not a question of practice. You have to understand, and this is how Patanjali has brought you, by and by, giving you more and more understanding, revealing to you more and more of the path.

The more you become clear, the more you can read the message written everywhere, on every leaf, on every flower. The message is from existence. Its signatures are everywhere. You need not go into the Bhagavad-Gita; you need not go into the Bible and the Koran. The Koran and the Bhagavad-Gita and the Bible are written all over existence. You only need penetrating eyes.

I have heard:

A young married woman in London believed she was pregnant and went to the doctor to verify it. The doctor gave her a cursory examination and assured her that her suspicions were correct. Then, to her astonishment, he simply took a rubber stamp, printed something with it on her abdomen, and said, 'That is all.'

The wife related this strange event to her husband, and he asked, 'What does it say?'

'Well, read it,' she replied.

He found that the print was too small for him to read, but a magnifying glass made everything clear. It read: 'When you can read this without a magnifying glass, rush your wife to the hospital.'

Right now you need a magnifying glass—of a Buddha, of a Jesus, of a Krishna, of a Patanjali. And then too you cannot read because your eyes are almost blind. Once your eyes are clear, his message is everywhere. And so clear is the message that you will simply be astonished that you missed it for so long, that you couldn't see it.

But if you live in the body, you will not hear it. If you live in the mind, you will hear it a little, but you will theorize about it and you will miss it. If you go deeper than the mind into *pashyanti*, where meditations lead you, you will be able to read the message and you will not become a victim of theorization—you will not philosophize. And once you don't philosophize about it, once you don't think *about* truth but you *see* it and you don't go round and round, about and about, and you penetrate directly—you disappear from *pashyanti*, the seed is broken. You fall into the abyss of *para*, the beyond.

The circle is complete: from silence to silence, from space to space, from truth to truth. The beginning is truth, the end is truth. The alpha and omega—it is both.

Now the sutra:

Sattva-purushayoh shuddhi-samye kaivalyam.

Liberation is obtained when there is equality of purity between the purusha *and* satva.

Yoga divides existence in two. The non-manifest is one, but the manifest is two, because in the very process of manifestation things become two. For example, you look at a rosebush and you see the beautiful flowers. You just look. You don't say a word. You simply see the rose, not even uttering a word inside. The experience is one. Now if you want to say to somebody, 'The flowers are beautiful', the moment you say 'The flowers are beautiful', you have said something about ugliness also. The flowers are 'not ugly'. With beauty, ugliness enters. If somebody asks, 'What is beauty?', you will have to use ugliness to explain it.

If you look at a woman and no word arises in you, then the experience is one—non-dual. The moment you say 'I love you', now you have brought hate in, because love cannot be explained without hate. The day cannot be explained without night and life cannot be explained without death. The opposite has to be brought in.

At the point of *vaikhari*, everything is clear-cut duality; night is separate from day, death is separate from life, beauty is separate from ugliness, light is separate from darkness— everything divided in an Aristotelian way . . . clear-cut, no bridge. Move a little deeper: At the point of *madhyama*, division starts but is not so clear; night and day meet, mix, as in the evening or in the morning. Go still deeper: at the point of *pashyanti*, they are in the seed, the duality has not arisen yet; you cannot say what is what, everything is undifferentiated. Move still deeper: at the point of *para*, there is no division, whether visible or invisible.

At the point of expression, yoga divides reality in two: *purusha* and *prakriti*. *Prakriti* means 'matter'; *purusha* means 'consciousness'. When you are identified with the body-mind, with *prakriti*, with nature, with matter, both are polluted. Pollution is always double.

For example, if you mix water and milk, you say, 'The milk is no longer pure', but you have not observed anything: the water is also no longer pure. Because water is free, nobody is worried—that is one thing. But when you mix water and milk, both become impure—this is something, because both were pure; water was water, milk was milk, both were pure. This is a miracle: two purities meeting and both becoming impure.

Impurity has nothing condemnatory in it. It simply says that a foreign element has entered. It simply says something which is not of its innermost nature has entered—that is all.

This sutra is very beautiful. *Vibhuti Pada* ends with this sutra; it is a culmination. This sutra says that when you are identified with the body, you are impure, your body is impure. When you are identified with the mind, you are impure, your mind is impure. When you are not identified, both become pure.

Now this will look like a paradox. A *siddha*, or a Buddha—one who has achieved—his mind functions in purity, his genius functions in purity; all his talents become pure. And his consciousness functions in purity. Both are separated—milk is milk, water is water. Both have become pure again.

The sutra says: *Liberation is obtained when there is equality of purity between the* purusha *and* satva.

Satva is the highest point of *prakriti*—nature, matter. *Satva* means the 'intelligence' and *purusha* means the 'awareness'. That is the most subtle tie inside you because they are so similar. Intelligence and awareness are so similar that many times you may start thinking that an intelligent man is an aware man. It is not so.

Einstein is intelligent, tremendously intelligent, but he is not a Buddha. He is not aware. He may even be more unaware than ordinary people because he will be inside his intelligence so much.

It happened that Einstein was going somewhere in a bus, and the conductor came and asked for the fare. He gave him the money. The conductor gave Einstein his change. Einstein counted it but counted it incorrectly—the greatest mathematician of the world—and he said, 'You have not given me the right change.'

The conductor counted again. He said, 'Don't you know figures?'

He was not aware that this is Albert Einstein. There has never been such a great mathematical genius ever, and the conductor said, 'Don't you know figures?' Nobody has known anything more than this man about figures, but what happened?

People who are very intelligent almost always become absentminded. They are moved by, and attached to, their intelligence so much that they become oblivious to many things in the outside world.

I have heard about a great psychoanalyst, a very intelligent man. He was absorbed so much in his experiments that for two or three days he didn't turn up home. His wife was worried. The third day she could not wait anymore, so she phoned and said, 'What are you doing? Come back; I am waiting for you. And supper is ready.'

He said, 'Okay, I will come. What is the address?'

He had forgotten completely—his wife and the home and the address also.

Intelligence is not necessarily awareness. Awareness is necessarily intelligence! A man who is aware is intelligent, but a man who is intelligent need not be aware, there is no necessity in it. But both are very close. Intelligence is part of body-mind, and awareness is part of *purusha*—the ultimate, the beyond.

The sky meets the earth. That point, that horizon where the sky meets the earth, is the point to become perfectly unidentified—there, where intelligence meets awareness. Both are very similar. Intelligence is purified matter, so pure that one can get into it and think, 'I have become aware.' That is how many philosophers waste their lives: they think their intelligence is their awareness. Religion is the search of awareness; philosophy the search of intelligence.

Liberation is obtained when there is equality of purity between the purusha *and* satva. But how does one attain liberation? First you have to attain to the purity of *satva*— intelligence. So move deeper: *vaikhari* is intelligence manifest;

madhyama is intelligence manifest only to you, not to the world; *pashyanti* is intelligence in seed form; and *para* is awareness. By and by detach yourself, discriminate yourself, start looking at the body as an instrument, a medium, an abode; remember this as much as you can. By and by the remembrance settles. Then start working on the mind. Remember you are *not* the mind; this remembrance will help you to become separate.

Once you are separate from the body-mind, your *satva* will be pure. Your *purusha* has always been pure; just the identity with matter has helped it to appear impure. Once both mirrors are pure, nothing is mirrored. Two mirrors facing each other: nothing is mirrored, they remain empty.

This point of absolute emptiness is liberation. Liberation is not from the world. Liberation is from identification. Don't be identified, never be identified with anything. Always remember that you are the witness, never lose that point of witnessing; then one day the inner awareness rises like thousands of suns rising together.

This is what Patanjali calls *kaivalya*, liberation.

The word *kaivalya* has to be understood.

In India different prophets have used different words for that ultimate thing. Mahavira calls it *moksha*. *Moksha* can be rightly translated as 'absolute freedom', no bondage; all imprisonment has fallen. Buddha has used the word *nirvana*; *nirvana* means 'cessation of the ego'. As you put a light off and the flame simply disappears, just the same way the light of the ego disappears: you are no longer an entity. The drop has dissolved into the ocean; or the ocean has dissolved into the drop. It is dissolution, annihilation.

Patanjali uses *kaivalya*; the word means 'absolute aloneness'. It is neither *moksha* nor *nirvana*. It means absolute aloneness: you have come to a point where nobody else exists for you. Nothing else exists; only you, only you, only you. In fact it is not possible to call yourself 'I', because 'I' has reference with 'thou', and 'thou' has disappeared. It is no longer possible to say you are in *moksha*—freedom, because when all bondage has disappeared, what is the meaning of freedom? Freedom is possible if imprisonment is possible. You are free because the prison exists near the neighbourhood. You are not inside the prison, there are other people inside the prison, but potentially, theoretically, you can be put into the prison any day. That is why you are free. But if the prison has disappeared absolutely, utterly, then what is the point of calling oneself free?

Kaivalya means just aloneness. But remember, this aloneness has nothing to do with your loneliness. In loneliness 'the other' exists, is felt; the absence of the other is felt. That is why loneliness is a sad thing. You are 'lonely': that means you are feeling the need for the other. 'Alone' is when the need for the other has disappeared . . . you are enough unto yourself, absolute unto yourself, no needs, no desires, nowhere to go. This is what Patanjali means when he says 'you have come home'. This is liberation in his description; this is his *nirvana* or *moksha*.

Glimpses can come to you if you sit silently and detach yourself. First detach yourself from the objects: Close your eyes and forget the world; even if it exists, just take it as a dream. Then look at the ideas and remember that you are not them, they are floating clouds. Detach yourself from them; they have disappeared. Then one idea arises: that you are detached. That is *pashyanti*. Now drop that too because otherwise you will hang there. Simply be a witness to this idea also. Suddenly you explode into nothingness. It may be only for a single split moment, but you will have the taste of Tao, the taste of yoga and Tantra; you will have the taste of truth. And once you have had it, it becomes easier to approach. Allow it. Become vulnerable to it. Become available to it. Every day it becomes easier. The more you travel the path, the more the path becomes clear.

One day you go in and never come out: *kaivalya*. This is what Patanjali calls the absolute liberation. This is the goal in the East.

Eastern goals reach much higher than Western goals. In the West, heaven seems to be the last thing; not so in the East. Christians, Mohammedans, Jews—for them heaven is the last thing, nothing beyond it. But in the East we have worked more, we have drilled into reality deeper. We have drilled to the very end, when suddenly the drill comes to face the emptiness and nothing can be drilled any more.

Heaven is a desire, desire of being happy. Hell is a fear, fear of being unhappy. Hell is pain accumulated; heaven is pleasure accumulated. But they are not freedom. Freedom is when you are neither in pain nor in pleasure. Freedom is when the duality has been dropped. Freedom is when there is no hell and no heaven: *kaivalya*. Then one attains the uttermost purity.

This has been the goal in the East, and I think this *has* to be the goal of all humanity.

Silence Is the Answer

> *I was doing* sadhana *under the guidance of some other teacher. At that time I had no problem of sex. But tensions existed in my mind. After coming to your shelter, tensions have disappeared, but a new problem of sex has arisen. Due to sex, a new tension has started. What do I do in this state? Please guide me.*

ONCE YOU TAKE anything as a problem, it becomes impossible to solve it. No problem as such can be solved. If you look deeply into any problem, without accepting it as a problem, the solution surfaces itself. So the first thing to be learned is: drop the old habit of looking at things as if they are problems. You make them problems.

For example: sex. It is not a problem at all. If *it* is a problem, then you can turn anything into a problem. You can turn breathing into a problem. Once you look at breathing as a problem, you will start asking how to get rid of it. You will become afraid of breathing. Sex is not a problem—sex is a simple, pure energy. But living with some teacher you have been conditioned because almost 99 per cent of teachers take sex as a problem. They are not teachers, in fact. They have not solved anything in their own life. They are as much in trouble as you are; they have as much neurosis as you have.

A man of insight has no problems, and a man of insight never helps anybody else to have a problem.

I cannot solve your problem if you have the mechanism to create it. But I can give you my insight to see through and through, to see more transparently, with more clarity and perception.

So the first thing to be considered: why you call sex a problem. What is problematic in it? If sex is a problem, then why isn't food a problem? If sex is a problem, then why isn't breathing a problem? If sex is a problem, then why, anything can be converted into a problem. You just need to look that way and it becomes a problem.

In different cultures and societies, different things are thought to be problematic. If you have been brought up under the influence of Freud, then sex is not a problem at all. Then *not* to be sexual will become a problem. That has become a problem to many Westerners.

One woman came to me, must be about sixty-five, and she said, 'Osho, my sex desire is disappearing. Help me.' If you have been influenced by Freud too much, then sex is almost equivalent to life. If the sex desire is disappearing, you are dying; death is very close by. So till the very end, on the death bed also, you have to remain sexual beings. You have to force yourself to be sexual beings.

This is altogether a new problem, particularly for Indians, who cannot think of it as a problem. If it happens to them, they will go to the temple and thank God. Even when they are young, if the sex desire disappears, they will be very, very happy—tremendously happy: 'God has been very helpful: the problem is solved.' But the problem may not be solved; they may be simply getting impotent.

The problem arises because of a certain outlook. The problem is not a problem in itself; it depends on your outlook. If you are a Westerner, then drinking alcoholic beverages is not a problem. It is just like any other drink—Coca-Cola or Fanta. If you are a German, beer is simply water—no problem in it. But if you are an Indian, then the difficulty arises . . . even Coca-Cola is a problem. Gandhi will not allow you to drink Coca-Cola. He had prohibited tea in his ashram. Tea! It became a problem to him because it has some quantity of caffeine in it. For Buddhists, tea has never been a problem. It is almost a religious ritual in Japan and China.

A Buddhist monk starts his life with tea. In the early morning, before he goes to meditate, he drinks tea. After he has meditated, he drinks tea, and drinks it in a religious way, with grace and dignity. It has never been thought of as a problem. In fact, Buddhists discovered it. Legendarily, it is connected with Bodhidharma.

Bodhidharma is thought to have discovered tea. He used to live on a hillside. The mountain's name was Ta, and because the tea was first discovered there, it is called ta, tea, cha, chai—they are all derivations from Ta. Why did Bodhidharma discover it, and how did he discover it?

He was trying to attain a point of absolute awareness . . . it is difficult. You can live without food for many days, but without sleep? And he was trying not to allow any sleep. After a period of seven or eight days, suddenly he felt sleep coming. He tore away his eyelids and threw them, so there would be no problem any more. It is said those eyelids fell into the ground and sprouted as tea. That is why tea helps awareness. If you drink too much tea in the night you will not be able to sleep. And because the whole Buddhist mind is about attaining a point where sleep does not interfere and you can remain perfectly aware, of course tea became almost a sacred thing.

In Japan, they have small houses in the monasteries—teahouses. When they go to a tea-house, they go as if somebody is going to church or to the temple. They take a bath; they wear new fresh clothes; they leave their shoes outside; they move in silence, in grace; they sit . . . it is a long ritual. It is not just that you go and take a cup of tea and drink and you are gone—not in such a hurry. Gods have to be treated well, and tea is a god—god of awareness. So they will sit silently while the kettle sings its song; first they will listen to it, and then prepare the tea. They will meditate on the singing kettle.

Then the cups and saucers will be given to them. They will touch the cups and saucers and look at them because they are pieces of art. And nobody likes to use cups and saucers purchased from the market. Every monastery makes its own. Rich people make their own. Poor people, if they cannot afford to make their own, purchase them from the market, then break them and glue the pieces back together; they become perfectly unique then.

Then the tea is poured. Everybody is in a deep, receptive, meditative mood, breathing slow and deep. And then the tea is drunk, as if something divine is descending in you.

Mahatma Gandhi cannot think of this. In his ashram tea was not allowed; tea was on the blacklist. It depends on your attitude.

What I would like to tell you is that it is up to you how many problems you want to create. Drop as many as possible. The fewer problems you have, the better, because then, if you cannot drop those few, if they are not really because of your attitude but are intrinsic to life; then they can be solved.

I have heard:

One man went to his psychiatrist. The poor man had big bags under his eyes. He looked very tired. 'I dream every single night, doctor,' he told his physician. 'Last night it was terrible! I was in a big plane, I had my parachute on, and we were climbing up to 40,000 feet from where I was going to jump to establish a new altitude record. We reached 40,000 feet. I opened the door, I took one step forward—I pulled the rip cord—what do you think happened?'

The doctor said, 'I have no idea.'

The man said, 'My pyjamas fell down!'

Now is this a problem? When you are 40,000 above the earth, is this a problem? And that too in a dream!

Another story:

Two beggars were sitting and talking on a park bench. I was just passing by. One beggar said, 'I dreamt that I got a good job.'

The other said, 'Yes, you look tired.'

Drop nonsense. Sex is not a problem. Sex is your life energy. Accept it. If you accept, it can be transformed. If you reject it, you will be in a mess. If you fight with it, with whom are you fighting? Just think: with yourself—half-half, divided. And if you are fighting with yourself, of course you will be more and more crippled. Never fight with yourself.

Sadhana is not a conflict, it is not a struggle. *Sadhana* is a deep understanding, a transformation, an awareness in which you start loving, accepting yourself, and getting higher and higher through understanding. Nothing is to be excluded from your being. Everything is as it should be. It has to be used for a higher harmony—that is all. The veena is not to be thrown. If you cannot play it, learn how to play. Nothing is wrong with the veena. If you cannot play and you do play on the veena, of course you create mad noise. The neighbours will go and report you to the police station. Your wife will immediately give you a divorce. Your children will become nervous. And you will get more and more discordant in yourself.

But nothing is wrong with the veena, remember. You just don't know how to play it.

Sex energy is a tremendous energy. You don't know how to play with it. And you have been taught for centuries to be against it. Just look what your religious people have done to the world. They have been teaching against sex, and sex becomes more and more important because of their teachings. The whole world is almost neurotically sexual. A few are indulging in it as if there is nothing else in life, and a few are escaping from it as if there is nothing else in life. A few are just escaping and a few are just fighting—both are wasting their lives.

This is some great energy, a gift of existence. Many treasures are hidden in it. It has to be learned. The book has to be opened; one has to go into it. It has to be studied deeply, understood deeply—the key of infinite life is there.

Now that you have come to me, I go on insisting for understanding. A certain intellectual understanding arises. But the old conditioning goes on and on. It is not that only in this life you have been conditioned; for centuries, for many lives, you have been conditioned. That conditioning has become almost second nature to you. The mention of the word 'sex' causes something to become restless within you. The very word creates a reaction inside you. It is difficult to talk about it without any passion—objectively and scientifically. Either this way or that you become passionately involved in it.

Drop all ideas and prejudices. Just look at the truth of ɩ. You are born of sex energy. Your mother and father were not praying when you were born. They were making love. And they were not in a church or in a temple. You never think about it; people avoid such things. It will be difficult for you to conceive that your father and mother were making love. Impossible; it is other people—dirty people—who make love. Your father and mother? Never. That is why so many stories have been prevalent all over the world. A child is born, and other children ask, 'From where has it come?' You have to give them false answers—the stork, the bush, or that the gods have dropped it from the kitchen chimney.

I have heard:

The mother was pregnant and the grandmother was worried about the other little child, because sooner or later he will ask. So she wanted to prepare him.

She took him aside and told him, 'Do you know, your mother is going to be presented again with a great gift from God. It will come in a bundle and it will be dropped from the chimney hole in the night when everybody will be asleep.'

The boy said, 'It's okay, but let me tell you one thing. Don't let God drop the bundle too loudly because my mother is pregnant. She may be disturbed in the night. Let it be with the least noise possible.'

Stories have been invented to avoid sex. It is difficult to talk to children about how a child is born, and this is the beginning of falsity, beginning of hypocrisy. Sooner or later the child will find out, and then he will also discover that the mother and the father have been telling lies. Why have they been hiding such a vital fact? And if they are untrue about such a vital fact, what about other things? Once the doubt arises in the mind of a small child that he has been deceived, he loses the capacity to trust.

And then you go on telling him to trust in God the Father who has made us all, who is there in heaven. But he cannot believe the real father who is in the house, who is a deceiver. How can he believe the Father, God the Father? Impossible!

No, listening to me, you will have to come to an understanding of life as it is. I am not theorizing about it. I am not interested in any speculative business. I am simply giving you facts. And those are simple because you can listen to them.

If you are a great poet, it is sex energy transformed in poetry—nothing else—because that is the only energy available to you. If you are a great painter, it is sex energy moving into colours, to the canvas. If you are a great sculptor, then it is sex energy creating beautiful pieces out of marble and stone. If you are a singer, it is sex energy becoming a song. If you are a dancer, it is sex energy going into the dance. Whatsoever you are, it is in some way or other a transformation, transmutation of sex energy—your prayerfulness also, your meditation also.

Sex is the beginning; *samadhi* is the end—but the energy is the same. *Samadhi* is sex at its highest peak, and sex is *samadhi* at its lowest. Once you understand that, then you know how one has to evolve higher.

Nothing is to be rejected; everything has to be used. Every rung of the ladder, even the lowest, has to be used, because the ladder will not exist without it. The whole ladder is based on it. If you cut anything out of your life, you will never be whole—and you will never be holy. That part which has been denied will always remain there to be reaccepted, and that part will go on rebelling against you and fighting against you.

I have heard:

Comrade Cohen was a member of a Russian trade mission to an English industrial town. One evening, the Russians were guests at the local workingmen's club. One of the club members was Joe Chubb, an earnest young socialist, who eventually manoeuvred Comrade Cohen into a corner by himself.

'Comrade Cohen,' said young Chubb. 'I understand you are a good Jew; I understand you are a man of integrity; I understand you possess considerable political acumen. Now because you have all these fine qualities, it would be of great interest to me to have your opinion of the Soviet attitude to the Arab-Israeli conflict—and why the Russians support the Egyptian fascists against the democratic Israelis.'

Comrade Cohen was silent. He gave a slight shrug.

'But, come, Comrade Cohen,' the young man persisted. 'After all, you are a Jew. Despite the official attitude of your country, of your party, you must have your own view as to where justice lies—of whose cause is the right one.'

But Comrade Cohen would say nothing, not a word.

Joe Chubb leant nearer. In a tone almost of pleading he urged, 'But surely, Comrade Cohen, you must have an opinion.'

Comrade Cohen stirred in his chair and regarded the young man with a steady gaze, and he broke his silence. 'Comrade Chubb,' he said. 'I have an opinion.' He paused, and then said, 'But I do not agree with it.'

Now this is the situation of most of the people. You know the fact but you don't agree with it because you have been prepared not to agree with it. You know the truth as it is, but you have been conditioned to have a prejudice about it.

Just put aside all prejudices. Simply watch life. Let life reveal itself to you as if you have never been conditioned, as if you have just come from another planet to this earth. Simply watch, with no ideology behind it—Hindu, Christian or Mohammedan. With no past, look at the present. Don't allow the past to interfere with the present. That which is, let it reveal itself to you.

Then where is the problem? Why is sex the problem? There is nothing more lovely than it. You go on praising the flowers, but you never have thought that they are sexual efforts of the tree. They are carrying sexual germs, sexual cells. The tree uses the flowers to deceive butterflies and bees into taking their sperms to the feminine plant. You praise them, not knowing that you are praising sex energy. All flowers are so beautiful, but they all are sexual energy. You praise the songs of the birds, but do you know that they are nothing but seductions? The male bird goes on calling the female, tries in every way to allure her, through sound, through song. You must have seen a peacock dancing. Nothing like it—but it is just a magical trick to seduce the other sex. If you look around, you will be surprised. All that is beautiful is sexual.

Your saints go on praising the flowers; they are just against the flowering of human sex. They may not have observed well what they are doing. You go with many flowers to the temple and you put them at your god's feet without knowing what you are doing—it is a sexual gift!

All that is beautiful—flowers, singing, dancing—is sexual. Wherever you have any experience of beauty, it is sexual. All beauty is sexual; it has to be that way.

But only in human beings has a dichotomy been created.

Drop that dichotomy. I am not going to solve your problem. I am simply saying your problem is foolish, stupid. And don't think that you are bringing a very great spiritual problem to me. You are simply bringing a foolish thing which has nothing to do with spirituality. Drop that.

I am not saying remain satisfied with your sex. I am saying accept it. There are greater possibilities hidden in it, but the first door opens with acceptance, then another door becomes available. It is sex energy which moves into other wheels of energy—goes higher and higher and higher.

Sex can become a problem if you are stuck somewhere, but then too the problem is not sex but being stuck. Let this emphasis be absolutely clear to you. Sex is never a problem, but your being stuck somewhere is a problem. That is a totally different thing. So don't get stuck anywhere, don't freeze. Remain fluid and go on moving.

Intellectually you understand this but your past interferes. Now you will have to make a great choice, a great decision: whether to listen to the past or to listen to your present fresh understanding. With whom are you going to be? With your past, dull and dead, or with your fresh understanding which has happened to you just now?

There were once two friends, one of whom was very fond of playing practical jokes on the other. One evening the joker hid behind a gravestone in a dark cemetery, knowing that his friend would be taking a shortcut through the churchyard. After a short while, he heard his friend approaching; and as he drew near, the joker let out a bloodcurdling shriek. The first man started and froze in his tracks.

'Is that you, John?' he said. There was no reply. 'I know that is you, John,' said his friend. 'But I am going to run anyway.'

If you know, then why are you going to run anyway? Live with the fresh understanding. Live with this moment. Don't be distracted by the past. Always be with the fresh and the new and that which is just dawning on the horizon of your consciousness; then you will grow. If you are always with the old, the withered away, you will wither away; you will never grow.

Growth is in the present, growth is of the fresh and the young, growth is of the new. So every day, drop the dust that ordinarily collects on the mirror of your consciousness. Keep your mirror clean so that whatsoever comes in front of you is mirrored perfectly and live out of that mirroring— live out of that fresh reflection.

'I was doing *sadhana* under the guidance of some other teacher. At that time I had no problem of sex.' You will not have problems if you are being taught how to suppress it. It can be suppressed so deeply that you will start feeling as if it is not there.

'But tensions existed there in my mind.' Tensions will come up because no suppression can be without tensions. In fact, the tense state of your mind is nothing but a reflection of subtle suppressions. You can relax only if you have no suppressions whatsoever. A man who has no repressions is relaxed. A man who has repressions cannot relax, because relaxation will go against his repressions. Try to understand the mechanism.

When you repress something, you have to be constantly alert, constantly repressing it. Repressing is not something that you have done once and for all. It has to be done every moment of your life. If you don't do it, those things that you have repressed down will surface. You have to be constantly sitting on their chest, holding them there. If you leave them even for a single moment, the enemy will be up and again there will be the same struggle and the same fight.

That is why your saints cannot take any holiday. How can you take a holiday, because the holiday will disturb everything? Your saint has to be constantly on guard. That is the tension—they have to remain constantly alert. A woman is coming: shrink your energy continuously, hold it there, and let the woman pass. But they are passing continuously. Or if they are not passing, then it is something else. The whole of life is sexual.

If you somehow avoid women and escape to the Himalayas, birds will be there making love to each other. What will you do? Animals will come and disturb you. The whole life is sexual; you cannot escape anywhere. The whole ocean is of sexual energy.

There is nothing wrong in it. It is beautifully so.

Godliness has manifested in the world as sex. If you go to the old scriptures you will find it so, particularly in Hindu scriptures. Why did God create the world? Hindu scriptures say, 'Because desire arose in him, sex arose in him, he created the world.' All creation is out of sexual energy, desire—*kama*. But Hindus have been, in a way, very courageous. They say God created the world; then he started creating animals, trees. How did he create so many trees? How did he create so many animals? What was his plan, his blueprint? How did he start working on such a complex world? Hindus say it is very simple. First he created a cow. Hindus love the cows, so of course God has to create the cow first. And the cow looks also so divine, so silent and graceful. He created the cow, and then he fell in love with the cow. No other religion is so daring . . . the father falling in love with the daughter— because the cow is his daughter; he has created it. He fell in love; what could he do? He was in a mess himself. So he became a bull, because that is the only way to love a cow.

Female energy escapes. That is the game. Not really that a woman wants to escape; she plays the game of escaping. If a man approaches the woman and she simply is ready to go to bed with him, the man will start feeling a little worried. What is wrong with the woman? This is because the game was not played. The whole beauty of love is not so much in the love as in the foreplay. You make so many efforts—the courtship—but the courtship is possible only if the woman is receding. Just see: whenever you are talking to a woman, if you are interested in her, she will be moving back and you will be moving forward. But there is always a wall, so the woman goes against the wall; then she is caught. She always moves towards the wall—that too is intentional! It is all intentional. It is the whole game, and a beautiful game.

So the cow started running to escape from the bull. She became a tigress. Then God had to become a tiger. She became a lioness—just to escape. God had to become a lion. And that is how the whole world was created: the woman escaping; the man chasing. A beautiful story, and very true.

That is how the whole world has been created: one energy escaping, another chasing. Hide-and-seek . . . the beauty of it . . . and she hides, and God finds her again—in new forms, in new flowers, in new birds, in new animals. And the game goes on . . . infinite is the *leela*. Hindus say God's play is infinite.

But all play is sexual. Play as such is sexual because it is not work. You play it for its own sake. That is why the Hindu conception of 'God' is far superior to the Christian and Mohammedan and Jewish conceptions of 'God'. The Jewish God looks like a worker, almost proletarian. The Hindu God is not worried about work; he does not belong to any union of workers. He is a player, an actor. The whole world is his play—he enjoys it and there is no end to it. In itself, it is the end; it is not a means.

That is the difference between work and play: work is always end-oriented. In itself, it is useless—you would not like to do it. You go to the office, to the factory, to the shop, and you work the whole day because something that you want—a car, a good house, a beautiful woman—is possible only if you earn money. You are not working in the factory because you love to; you are not in the office because you love it. You love certain other things, but they are not available without the work, so you have to fulfil the condition somehow. So you carry the work; the goal is somewhere else.

A play is totally different. You are playing; there is no goal to it. In itself, it is the goal. You are enjoying the very activity in itself.

I have heard:

Lords Carnforth, Yewley and Donnington were having tea on the lawn one Sunday afternoon. The conversation turned to the subject of making love. Lord Carnforth maintained that it was 90 per cent pleasure and 10 per cent work; Lord Yewley said it was 50 per cent pleasure and 50 per cent work; Lord Donnington, the eldest of the three, said it was 10 per cent pleasure and 90 per cent work.

To settle the argument, they called over an old gardener who was working on the flower beds. When they put the question to him, he said, 'Why, it is 100 per cent pleasure, of course, your Lordships. If there was any work involved, you would have us servants doing it for you.'

Play is 100 per cent pleasure. The Hindu concept of God is that of a player, and the whole creation is out of play. And sex is the energy involved in the play.

Don't get stuck there, because there are higher games, subtler games to be played with. First you play with a woman outside; that is the lowest possibility. Then you start playing with the woman inside. That is what yoga calls meeting of sun and moon, of *pingala* and *ida*. You start playing with the inner woman if you are a man, or if you are a woman, with the inner man.

And you have both in you: no man is just a man, he has a woman inside him; no woman is just a woman, she has a man inside her. It has to be so, because you come out of the meeting of both. Your father gives something to you; your mother also gives something to you. Whether you are a man or a woman makes no difference. You are a meeting of two—male, female—energies. Each contributes 50 per cent to you.

So what is the difference between a man and a woman? The difference is like two coins, both exactly the same, but one coin is heads up, another coin is tails up: both are exactly the same. The difference is of emphasis. The difference is not of quality, the difference is not of energy, the difference is only of emphasis. A man is consciously man, unconsciously woman; a woman is consciously woman, unconsciously man.

Once you know how to play the game with the outer woman—and that is what my insistence is, that you have to learn the game outside first—then you can start playing the game with the subtle inner woman and man. First you have to seduce the outer woman and man, and play the game there because it is very gross—can be learned easily. It is just a preparation for some greater play. Then you move within. Then you start seeking the other who is hiding somewhere in your being, find it and then a deep orgasm happens within you.

That orgasm goes on becoming higher and higher and bigger and bigger. And the ultimate orgasm happens at *sahasrar*, at the crown, in your last centre of being—where the ultimate awareness meets the ultimate nature, where two ultimates meet and mingle and merge into each other, where consciousness meets matter, *purusha* meets *prakriti*, where the visible meets the invisible, and the ultimate ecstasy happens.

This is a game. You have to go on playing it, and as beautifully as possible. And you have to learn the art of it.

So if you repress, you have to repress continuously. If you repress, you have to be continuously on guard and you cannot relax. Relaxation is possible only when you don't have any enemy within; only then can you relax. How can you relax otherwise? Relaxation is a state of mind where no repression is there, not even a trace.

A small child relaxes. The older you grow, the more difficult it becomes to let go. The small child relaxes so deeply. Just see. A small child, he may fall asleep while eating, on the dining table. He may fall asleep while playing with his toys. He can fall asleep anywhere. And it becomes more and more difficult for grown-up people to sleep, to relax, to love, to merge—so many repressions. You are all carrying the load; you are very loaded.

This load is very complex. If you suppress sex, you will have to suppress many other things side by side, because everything is interrelated. Inside, it is a very complicated thing. If you suppress sex, you will have to suppress your breathing as well. You cannot breathe well, deep, because deep breathing goes on and massages the inner centre of sex. If you really breathe well, you will feel sexual. You will have to suppress breathing; you cannot breathe deeply. If you suppress sex, you will have to suppress many things in your food because there are a few foods which give you more sexual energy than others. Then you will have to change your foods. If you suppress sex, you cannot sleep well because if you sleep well and you relax perfectly, you will have sexual dreams. You can have ejaculations in your sleep. The fear will be there. You will not be able to sleep well. Now your whole life will become an entangled thing, a complexity, a knot.

You can repress sex, but then you will have to become very, very tense, almost maddeningly tense. That is what must have happened: 'But tensions existed there in my mind.'

'After coming to your shelter, tensions have disappeared . . .' That is very good. Of course when tensions disappear, then the sex that you have been repressing through those tensions will come up, bubble up again.

'. . . but a new problem of sex has arisen.' Don't call it a 'problem'. Just put it like this: 'now sexual energy is flowing again'. Now again your sexual energy is no longer a solid thing. It has become liquid and flowing. Now your sex is again alive, not crippled and dead. You have become young again.

My whole effort is how to de-condition you from the teachers you have been with and the scriptures you have been reading and all the nonsense that you have gone through. 90 per cent of my work is because you have learned something wrong and you have to unlearn it. Now, if you again call it a problem, then it is not you; your so-called teacher's voice is again working through you. He is sitting there on the throne of your heart and saying, 'Look. The problem is arising again. Stop it! Repress it!' You will have to be indifferent to this voice.

If you want to be with me, you have to be alive—so totally alive that nothing is excluded from it, everything is included. That is the beginning of the work.

If you can relax, you can reach godliness. It is not an effort to reach it. It is effortless relaxation; it is a let-go.

✳

> *How can one be passively alert? How can one*
> *be neither extroverted nor introverted? And*
> *how does one be and yet not be? Please reply*
> *not through words but through void.*

Then you will have to ask through void. If you want my silent answer, you will have to ask silently. If you cannot ask silently, I can answer silently still, but you will not understand it. First you have to learn the language of silence. So if you want to receive something from me in silence, then prepare for yourself—and ask the question in silence. No need to write it—because I can give you only as much as you are capable of receiving.

And don't ask crazy questions, because I can answer in a very crazy way.

Let me tell you an anecdote:

A mother thought her little girl should be examined for any possible abnormal tendencies, so she took the tot along to the psychologist. Among other questions the doctor asked were: 'Are you a boy or a girl?'

The little girl answered, 'A boy.'

Somewhat taken aback, the doctor asked, 'When you grow up are you going to be a man or a woman?'

'A man,' she answered.

Afterwards as they were returning home the mother said, 'Why did you give those strange answers to the questions that man asked you?'

The little girl drew herself up with dignity and said, 'If he was going to ask me crazy questions, I was going to give him crazy answers—he could not kid me.'

Remember this. If you want to receive an answer in total silence, then learn how to be silent. Then you need not ask. You need not even formulate the question inside you; you need not even come to me because then physical closeness is not needed. Wherever you are you will be able to receive my answer. And that answer is not going to be mine or anybody else's; it will be your own heart's answer.

I have to give you answers because you don't know how to ask. I have to give you answers because you have not yet become capable of receiving the answer from your own being. Once you learn silence, you become tremendously capable. Just be silent and all questions disappear. Not that you receive an answer: simply, questions disappear—you don't have any questions to ask.

Buddha used to say to his disciples, 'For one year, just keep quiet and be silent. After one year, whatsoever you want to ask, you can ask.' But after one year, they will not ask, because questions wither away.

The more silent you become, the less questions arise, because questions are part of a noisy mind. Questions are not coming out of your life, out of your existence and being—they are coming out of a mad mind. When the maddening drops a little, noise stops a little, and the traffic disappears in the mind—along with the traffic and the noise, questions also disappear. Suddenly there is silence.

Silence is the answer.

❋

I dream a lot, but you rarely appear in my dreams. Nehru, Jaiprakash and Dinkar still frequent the scene; and that mischievous train which each time goes away with my luggage but leaves me behind. Once you drove me in your jeep along a bumpy riverside. And last night I saw you marrying a number of women, good ones, together, and I said to myself that you would manage them with ease and grace. Osho, would you please say what it all means for the dreamer himself?

It is from Maitreya. A beautiful question, and a beautiful and significant dream. It shows much about him.

First thing: in his past he was a politician, and he had much promise. He had been a colleague of Pandit Jawaharlal Nehru, Jaiprakash Narayan and Ramdhari Singh Dinkar. For many years he was a Member of Parliament. Somehow he got hooked with me, and all his dreams of becoming a great politician, a great political force, disappeared. But the past still clings.

These dreams, in which Nehru, Jaiprakash and Dinkar appear, are very indicative. They show that the political ambition is still lurking somewhere inside the unconscious. He has not been yet been able to get rid of it totally. He is sincerely with me, he is authentically with me, but the past still clings. He wants to get rid of it; that is why the past does not come in the day. It comes in the night when he is fast asleep and helpless. Then the mind starts playing old tricks again and again and again.

I don't come much in his dreams, because I am already here. In reality I am here, so what is the point of creating a dream about me? Remember, dreams are only about things which are not present; either they were in the past or you would like them to be in the future. Whosoever is part of your reality in the present will never come in your dreams. Your own wife will never come in your dreams; neighbourhood wives, they will appear. Your own husband will not come in your dreams. There is no point. But other people will appear.

A dream is a substitute for reality. It is complementary. If you have eaten well, enjoyed your food, loved it, and you are satisfied, you will not think and dream of eating again in the night; the dream will not come. Fast one day, and then you will have dreams of food, beautiful, delicious food—you are being invited by the royal family to the palace, and you are eating and eating and eating.

A dream simply indicates that which is missing in your life; that which is already there is never part of a dream. That is why an enlightened person never dreams, because he is not missing anything. Whatsoever he wanted has happened and there is no more to it. He has no past, no future to interfere with the present. His present is total. Whatsoever he is doing, he is enjoying it *utterly*. He is so contented that there is no need for any complementary dream.

Your dreams are your dissatisfactions. They are your discontents and your unfulfilled desires.

Maitreya was a politician, and the mind still carries. And that is why: '. . . and that mischievous train which each time goes away with my luggage but leaves me behind.' That too comes in his dreams many times; that is part of many people's dreams. A train: somehow you reach the train—willy-nilly, running, anyhow you manage to reach the platform—and the train leaves. And his difficulty is more: his luggage is also in the train, and he is left alone standing on the platform without any luggage. That is what has happened to him. Nehru has gotten on the train, Dinkar has gotten on the train, J.P. has gotten on the train; and they have taken his luggage also and he is standing on the platform, empty-handed. Those ambitions, political ambitions, are still lurking in the unconscious.

That is why I am not coming in his dreams. I am already here. I am not an ambition. I may come into his dreams when I am gone—when he has missed another train. One he has missed, and he has missed it absolutely. There is no way of going back, because a certain understanding has arisen in him. He cannot go back. He cannot become a politician again. There is no going back, but the past can cling; and the more it clings . . . he may miss another train.

And of course, 'Once you drove me in your jeep along a bumpy riverside.' It is a jeep, and along a bumpy riverside—it is very bumpy. To be with me is to be always in danger, in insecurity. I don't give you any security; in fact, I take all your securities away from you. I make you almost empty—nothing to hold, nothing to cling to. I leave you alone. Fear arises.

Now Maitreya is completely left alone—no money, no power, no prestige, no political status. Everything gone, he is just a *bhikhu*. I have made a beggar of him; and he was rising high. He was rising higher and higher. He would have been a chief minister somewhere by now, or he may have been in the central cabinet. He was very promising. All those dreams disappeared. Now they go on being created and haunting him; they are ghosts.

He will have to recognize the fact that going back is not possible. He has reached the point of no return. So now it is unnecessary to carry that load. Out of habit the mind goes on carrying it. Drop it. Recognize, see deeply into it. Don't be deceived by it.

I have heard:

Mulla Nasruddin's wife was very worried about her husband's heavy drinking. One night, she decided to give him a fright. She draped herself in a white sheet and went down to the local cemetery, knowing that her husband was in the habit of taking a shortcut through it on his way home from the pub. It was not long before he came staggering along, and out she jumped from behind a headstone.

'Ooooooo!' she screamed. 'I am the Devil!'

Mulla Nasruddin stuck out his hand, 'Put it there, pal,' he said. 'I am married to your sister.'

Recognize! These ghosts of Nehru and Dinkar and J.P., recognize them. Your past has been married to their sister: politics. Don't be deceived by these ghosts. They have left a mark; it has to be washed clean.

And I know it is very difficult. It is very difficult when you were just at the point of succeeding and suddenly you turned and changed your path. When he met me, he was an MP, but that accident changed his life. By and by he drifted away, became more and more interested in me and less and less interested in his political career. And he was just at the point of success. If he had succeeded—and suffered the pains of success and the *failure* of success—then it would have been easier for him to drop the old ghosts. He was just at the point of succeeding—just at the gate, when he was entering the palace, he met me. Now the dream of the palace and living there continues.

It would have been easier if he had lived in the palace a little while and had known that there is nothing in it; then it would have been much easier. That is why I say that if you are in some career, it is better to succeed in it and then renounce it. If you want to become wealthy, become wealthy—be finished with this. Once wealth is there, you will come to know it is frustrating, it is nothing. But if you leave it before you have succeeded, then there will be a problem. Many times the idea will repeatedly arise: 'Maybe there was something. Otherwise why is the whole world interested in wealth and politics and power? There may be something. Maybe I missed the train. I should have continued. I should have seen and experienced the whole thing.'

If you have succeeded to fulfil a certain desire, the desire itself leaves you without desire. The success kills the desire automatically. Then even with less awareness one can renounce it. But if you renounce something when you were just about to touch it, and everything was possible and you turn away, more intense awareness will be needed. So Maitreya will need a more intense awareness.

But that too was to happen, because you come in contact with certain influences which take you out of the world.

I was a guest at another politician's house and he had invited Maitreya as well. Because a senior politician had invited him, he must have come just to see what the matter was. But if you come in contact with some influence that can take you out of the world of ambition—and if you are a little sensitive and understanding (and he is)—then you understand the point immediately. That old politician with whom I was staying remained with me for many years but never understood me. Now he is gone and dead, but he died a politician and he died a member of Parliament. He was one of the longest-standing members in the whole world. He remained a member of Parliament for fifty years. But he never could understand me. He liked me very much, almost to the point of loving me, but understanding was not possible. He was very dull—a dullard.

Maitreya came to me through him, but he is a very sensitive soul. And I say to him that he was not only promising in his political career, he is very promising as a candidate for the ultimate also. You have missed one train; don't miss another. If you miss it this time, not only your luggage, your clothes are also going with it. You will be left naked.

Once a great politician died and his ghost decided to go to his own funeral. During the interment he met the ghost of another politician he had known years ago.

'Hello, old chap,' said the second ghost. 'Quite an audience, what?'

'Yes,' said the first ghost. 'If I had known I would pull this big a crowd, I would have died a long time ago.'

The politician's desire is a very childish desire: to look big and great in the eyes of others. This is easy to achieve because the masses are simply mad. You just have to know how to manipulate their madness. You just have to know how to provoke their appreciation. You just have to be a little cunning. That is all; nothing else is needed. The masses are foolish.

But to become really great is a totally different thing. To become really great, one has to go within; one has to become crystallized, conscious, without desire, unattached. One has to reach to the point of *para*—the beyond, the transcendental. It has nothing to do with others. Others are almost as mad as you are. You can manipulate them, you can provoke their clapping for you and their appreciation, but what is the point?

Just think about it in this way, be a little arithmetical. If one fool claps his hands in appreciation for you, will you be very gratified? You will not be. But what is the difference if one fool or one thousand fools or one million fools clap?

If one wise man looks at you with love and blessing, that is enough.

Two lions escaped from the zoo on the same day. After three weeks of liberty, they ran into one another. One of the lions was thin and emaciated, while the other was sleek and obviously well-fed.

'I am thinking of going back to the zoo,' said the thin lion. 'I have not had a bite to eat in nearly a fortnight.'

'Heavens,' said the fat one. 'You had better come with me. I am living in the gentlemen's washroom in the house of Parliament. I eat a politician every day of the week—and the beauty of it is this: they are never missed.'

All your so-called important people, who misses them? They think without them the whole world is going to collapse. Nothing collapses; everything continues as it used to.

Don't be worried that you have missed the train of ambition. It was not worth taking. If you had caught the train, you would have felt very frustrated and you would have repented. But this is how the mind functions. If you succeed, you repent; if you fail, you repent. Look, the mind creates misery somehow or other. Whatsoever happens, the mind creates misery out of it. That train was not worth it. Be happy that only your luggage has gone and you are left.

One day I was walking around a garden and I saw a beggar with only one shoe on. So I asked him, 'Poor man, have you lost your other shoe?' He said, 'No, I have found one.' Be positive.

A man undertook to stay the night in a haunted cottage for

a bet. In order to ensure that he did not leave the cottage during the night, the front and back doors were locked and the windows sealed. The next morning when the cottage was opened up, there was no sign of the man, but there was a large hole in the roof and it was obvious that he had made a speedy exit during that night. It was not until two days later that he arrived back in the village.

'Where on earth have you been for the past forty-eight hours?' his friends asked.

'Coming back,' he said. 'Coming back!'

In fear he must have run so fast that it took forty-eight hours to come back to the same village.

It is good, Maitreya, that you missed the train; otherwise it would have taken forty-eight lives to come back.

And the other part of the question: 'And last night I saw you marrying a number of women, good ones, together, and I said to myself that you would manage them with ease and grace.' Can't you see that I am managing them with ease and grace? Each disciple is a woman—man or woman, that doesn't matter—because a disciple has to be feminine; only then can he learn. There is no other way, because a disciple has to be receptive like a womb. He has to receive me totally. He has to be a passive receptor.

In India we have the myth that Krishna had 16,000 wives or girlfriends. It is not right to say 'wives', because he was really a revolutionary. He didn't believe in being a husband or a wife. He created the whole idea of the boyfriend or the girlfriend—*gopis*, girlfriends. 16,000 girlfriends? Seems to be a little too much to manage. But the myth is symbolic; it simply says '16,000 disciples'. They may have been men, they may have been women—that is not the point—but a disciple is feminine. A disciple is a *gopi*, is a girlfriend; otherwise he is not a disciple.

I have also got 16,000 sanyasins, the number has reached that exactly—and good ones, too. And you can see that I am managing well. In fact, it is not that I am managing it well; it is love that manages well. Love always manages well—with grace and ease. Love knows no tension.

You cannot manage even a single woman because you don't know love yet. You cannot manage a single love affair because love is missing. Only the affair is there and the love is missing, so of course it creates much trouble.

On my side, love is there, and there is no affair. Love manages.

> *In several personal interviews with you, you used to say several things to me. At the time, I used to think that it was only psychological encouragement by you, but in the course of time all your sayings were 100 per cent correct in my experience.*
>
> *In spite of these experiences, now when you tell me anything, I do not believe it at that time. I feel that your saying will again be 100 per cent correct, yet I do not obey you the time when you tell me. How do I get rid of this helplessness?*

Let me tell you an anecdote, and that is my answer:

A man lost all his savings at a race meeting, and he was so heartbroken that he went to Waterloo Bridge and prepared to throw himself off. Suddenly a ghostly voice whispered in his ear, 'Don't jump. Go to the racecourse again tomorrow and I will tell you what to bet on.'

The man went home and the next day he managed to borrow a few pounds and proceeded to the racecourse. Sure enough, as he queued at the window the ghostly voice said, 'Put everything you have on Blue Peter in the first race.' He did so and Blue Peter won. As he waited to bet on the second race, the voice said, 'Liberty Belle is the horse to bet on.' Sure enough, Liberty Belle won and the man made a packet.

This went on through the meeting, and by the time the last race came around, the man had won one million pounds. As he queued for the last time, the voice whispered, 'Don't bet at all on the last race.' However, the man was feeling lucky, so he put all his money on the favourite in the last race. It lost.

'Oh, no!' he said as the result was announced. 'What do I do now?'

'Now you can jump off Waterloo Bridge,' said the voice.

That is my answer. Now you decide.

Osho Commune International

An Invitation To Experience

OSHO COMMUNE INTERNATIONAL is a unique experiment: an opportunity for individuals to experience a radical approach to meditation and silence. This is the place for the evolution of Zorba the Buddha, someone whose feet can dance on the ground and whose hands can touch the stars. An environment beyond nations, races and religions—where the international language is laughter and silence. A place to be alone together, where each can learn from the other while respecting everyone's unique individuality.

As Osho describes it, 'The very air has a different vibe: even when you go away, your song, your dance, your joy go on vibrating here.'

Now Osho Commune International has evolved into the world's largest centre for meditation and spiritual growth, and offers hundreds of different methods for exploring and experiencing the inner world.

Every year, thousands of seekers from all over the world come to celebrate and meditate together in Osho's Buddhafield. The commune grounds are full of lush green gardens, pools and waterfalls, elegant snow-white swans and colourful peacocks, as well as beautiful buildings and pyramids. Such a peaceful and harmonious atmosphere makes it very easy to experience the inner silence in a joyful way.

(i) For detailed information to participate in this Buddhafield contact:

Osho Commune International
17 Koregaon Park, Pune-411001, MS, India
Ph: 020 4019999 Fax: 020 4019990
Email: visitor@osho.net Website: www.osho.com

(ii) Further Information
Many of Osho's books have been translated and published in a variety of languages worldwide.

For information about Osho, his meditations, and the address of an Osho meditation/information centre near you, contact:

Osho Commune International
17 Koregaon Park, Pune-411001, MS, India
Ph: 020 4019999 Fax: 020 4019990
Email: visitor@osho.net Website: www.osho.com

For information about Osho's books and tapes contact:

Sadhana Foundation
17 Koregaon Park, Pune-411001, MS, India
Ph: 020 4019999 Fax: 020 4019990
Email: distrib@osho.net Website: www.osho.com

www.osho.com
A comprehensive website in different languages featuring Osho's meditations, books and tapes, an outline tour of Osho Commune International, a list of Osho Information Centres worldwide, and a selection of Osho's talks.